MARRIAGE FOR LOVE

A 19th Century Lithuanian Woman's Fight for Justice

by Žemaitė

MARRIAGE FOR LOVE

A 19th Century Lithuanian Woman's Fight for Justice

Selected works by Žemaitė

Translated by

VIOLETA KELERTAS
and *MARYTE RACYS*

With an introduction by

VIOLETA KELERTAS

Birchwood Press
Los Angeles

Marriage for Love
Copyright © 2020 by Violeta Kelertas and Maryte Racys
The translation of this book was supported by the Bernice Kellogg Fund
for Baltic Studies at the University of Washington, Seattle.

Cover Art: Marta Frejutė
Formatting: Jurga Morkūnienė
Editing: Lois Smith

Published in the USA by:
Birchwood Press
Los Angeles, California
Send inquiries to birchwoodpress@gmail.com
www.birchwoodpress.com

BIRCHWOOD
PRESS

ISBN: 978-0-9965153-6-8 hard cover
ISBN 978-0-9965153-7-5 paperback
ISBN 975-0-9965153-8-2 eBook

Library of Congress Control Number: 2019949987

TABLE OF CONTENTS

SELECTED WORKS BY ŽEMAITĖ

Introduction
by Violeta Kelertas

How did a penniless nineteenth-century farm woman with an alcoholic husband, seven children, and little education, living in a rural backwater of the tsarist Russian empire far from any centers of culture, manage to become the initiator of literary prose fiction in the Lithuanian language and write six volumes of stories, plays, and letters? Not only that, but she also distinguished herself as a feminist activist against patriarchy, especially the centuries-long tradition of arranged marriages. During World War I while based in Chicago, she traveled the United States for five years, giving speeches from Illinois to New Hampshire to advocate for relief for the famine and suffering in her war-torn country. She raised $30,000 in today's currency to take back to her countrymen.

Writer Julija Žymantienė, popularly known by her pseudonym, Žemaitė (meaning a woman from the Lowlands of Lithuania), lived from 1845 to 1921. Her works became classics of Lithuanian literature not only because she was the first writer of prose fiction whose prime motives for writing were secular and social rather than religious or didactic, but also because she committed herself to fighting for human rights throughout her lifetime. Although she is primarily associated with feminism, she had an innate and persistent opposition to all kinds of injustice. Beyond her concerns of making life better for women, she felt compassion for the serfs (men, women, and children) in her surroundings as well. As she describes in her *Autobiography*, she was involved first hand in supplying and supporting the troops in the 1863 uprising against Russian control of her homeland,[1] thus demonstrating her commiseration for the wounded men battling the Russians who had occupied their land. Her stories also illustrate other kinds of injustice, such as the misery young men experienced when their religiously zealous parents would finance only schooling for the priesthood and medicine and no other professions. No doubt it was partly empathy for those living under the feudal system that led her to marry a handsome former serf, Laurynas Žymantas, causing her to leave her noble origins and background behind and to be condemned to the life of a subsistence-level farm wife. Žemaitė never lost her solidarity with the poor and downtrodden. Even in later years, when she became well known as an activist, writer, and speaker living in the capital, Vilnius, and traveling the world, she still refused to don a city hat and continued to wear the headscarf typically worn by rural women of the time to show that she identified with the lower classes.

Žemaitė, somewhat naively, took on a life of poverty and hardship when she married Laurynas, with whom she had seven children. She did not begin writing until the age of 49 because

---

[1] Ieva Šenavičienė, "Lithuania and the 1863–1864 Uprising" in ed. Gediminas Vitkus, *Wars of Lithuania* (Vilnius: Eugrimas, 2014), pp. 91–148, discusses the reasons for the uprising and stresses its political character in the desire of the populace to restore the Grand Duchy of Lithuania. Although serfdom was abolished in Žemaitė's region in 1861, much misery remained, since land reform was not carried out at that time.

her husband disapproved of her new occupation. Thus she had to write at night by oil lamp when her alcohol-loving husband was safely asleep. In the late nineteenth century, education was a luxury restricted to boys, and although Žemaitė had been taught to read by her father and, with her cousins, took part in two years of Polish home-schooling in her wealthy aunt's family, she was mainly self-educated. She read any great books she could borrow from neighbors, by authors such as Shakespeare, Ibsen, Molière, and Goethe, and the works of Henryk Sienkiewicz and contemporary Polish women writers including Eliza Orzeszkova and Maria Konopnicka. These were her literary models, since Lithuanian literature of the time, consisting mostly of didactic fiction written by priests and doctors, had no writers she could emulate.

Moreover, in the late nineteenth century, Lithuania was reawakening to a sense of itself as a nation. A ban on Lithuanian books in Latin script (1864–1904) had been implemented by the tsar as punishment for participating in the 1863 uprising. The rebels were exterminated after Russia sent the brutal Governor Muravjov, known as the Hangman, whose infamous goal was to give the tsar a Lithuania with nothing Lithuanian in it. The strategy was intended to lure the people away from Catholic Poland and bring them closer to Russia. To circumvent the ban, books and newspapers written in Lithuanian were printed in Prussia and secretly and dangerously brought into Lithuania by men, women, and children, who were known as the "book smugglers." Those writing, reading, and disseminating the publications risked being sent to Siberia, where death awaited them.

Thus, while Žemaitė knew Polish literary language, it was remarkable that she wrote in Lithuanian, given that it was necessary to hide behind a pseudonym. These were the conscious and daring choices of a Lithuanian identity, putting her at risk by publishing in the underground press. In addition, her knowledge of Lithuanian was limited to the Lowland dialect that was spoken in her vicinity. The Lithuanian language was not standardized until after her death in the 1920s; therefore, encouraged to write by a neighboring student, Povilas Višinskis, Žemaitė initially wrote as she spoke, continuously feeling her way, insecure as to spelling, narrative technique, and literary discourse requirements.[2]

Throughout her life and until recent times, Žemaitė's works met with much editing and sometimes direct censorship. Originally, as was not uncommon at the time, her writing was edited by the linguist Jonas Jablonskis, who erased her dialect usage, changed word order, and synchronized her orthography. At times, however, he put his own spin on the contents, as can be seen when comparing her early manuscripts with the written texts published during the course of the century that has passed since their writing. For example, often the feminine qualities of her metaphors were transformed and polished. They were provided with a neutral (thus, by convention, male) narrator, which subtly but importantly changed the effect on her readers, removing the oral qualities of her text and subverting the intent of some of her observations. Ramunė Bleizgienė has also remarked that, when edited, the stories lose their gentleness and empathy, making the relations between husband and wife appear coarse.[3]

---

[2] I have discussed the language, discourse manipulation, and oral qualities of Žemaitė's work in a chapter of my dissertation, "Oral and Written Narrative: Discourse Types and Functions," PhD Diss. University of Wisconsin-Madison, 1984.

[3] Ramunė Bleizgienė, *Privati tyla, vieši balsai. Moterų tapatybės kaita xix a. pabaigoje – xx a. pradžioje* (Vilnius: Lietuvių literatūros institutas, 2012), p. 180 *passim.*

During the interwar years, Žemaitė alienated the Catholic church's hierarchy with her anticlerical stories. In addition, the church did not approve of her feminist ideas, much less of what was perceived to be her socialist agenda. Even when her writing was reluctantly allowed to be published, her innocent eroticism, "radical" views, and realistic descriptions were tailored to meet some unspecified rules. The clergy liked to present her as a primitive villager who did not "create" her stories but who only "wrote what she saw," as if her realism were just a photograph that did not require artistry.[4]

After the communist takeover of Lithuania in 1940, Žemaitė's works were again categorized by those in power to fit their self-serving, hypocritical, and equally puritanical impetuses. This time it was from the opposite ideological camp; it was convenient to portray Žemaitė as a precursor to communism and use her work for propaganda purposes. At this time, her stories of social injustice, and especially the anticlerical ones, met with official approval, as reflected in the 1956-57 publication of her complete works in six volumes. Nevertheless, Žemaitė's *Autobiography* had all the anti-Russian elements censored and removed, distorting her keen understanding of politics, especially the influence of Russification.

Although Žemaitė's works have often been republished during the new period of Lithuanian independence since 1990, some publishers have not always been aware of the damage done to the writer and continue to propagate mutilated versions of

---

[4] Op. cit. Bleizgienė even claims that the prominent priest and writer Juozas Tumas-Vaižgantas described her as "an illiterate peasant." p. 150

her work. In this collection, the translators have chosen to be authentic to the original manuscripts as much as feasible and reinstated the censored fragments from other works.

In regard to the peculiarities of Žemaitė's style, one has to remember that she wrote in the *žemaitiškai* dialect, sometimes known as Samogitian or Lowland Lithuanian. The translators chose not to avoid a lower register English at times, to give readers the flavor of the original and to show Žemaitė's desire to characterize her protagonists by means of their speech. An attempt was made throughout the work to keep the overall language slightly archaic, steering clear of current American English vocabulary, focusing on retaining Žemaitė's colorful oral qualities and her repetition of characters' expletives to bring them to life. The translators also have aimed to retain, wherever possible, idiomatic expressions and gems of folk wisdom. What is lost in translation is one aspect of her now dated language, the abundance of Slavic loan words. Nevertheless, there is no way to demonstrate this in English, which is secure and very accepting of foreign words, while Lithuanian, which suffered under long years of Polish and then Russian influence, hurried to establish native vocabulary and rid itself of a lexis that it perceived as a reminder of colonialist subjugation. Our hope as translators is that touches of archaic language and the old-fashioned content will succeed in transferring Žemaitė's sometimes rough, yet always vigorous and vivid, expression to the reader.

Attention still needs to be drawn to one significant feature of her writing: her magnificent and elaborate descriptions of nature, which have brought delight to her many readers over the decades and been analyzed and deconstructed by literary critics.[5] For Žemaitė, nature is certainly as important as the human characters in her created world. She is highly aware of all its nuances, the many forms it can take, be it during the course of a day or a season. Focusing on the passage of the sun across the beautiful Lithuanian lowland sky, with its ever-changing cloud formations, the author sensitively employs various poetic devices for the enrichment of her stories. "Petras Kurmelis" is especially noted for its onomatopoeia in imitating the calls of the many birds in the forest.

To better understand Žemaitė's work, it might be helpful to know some of its historical context, especially feudalism. Bonded serfdom, instituted in the fifteenth century in Lithuania, was in effect during the author's early years. Serfs, little better than slaves, lived in huts and had few rights, being victims of the master's whims. They had to labor for their keep six days a week on the master's land (called the *corvée*), while maintaining their own meager plots to live on, and had to farm to support themselves. The manor's needs always took precedence. The serfs could not change owners without the master's permission.

Serfdom was abolished in the territory where Žemaitė lived in 1861, yet its aftermath lingered because it was not followed by land reform until many years later (1924), after Lithuania had regained its first independence (1918). Until then manors and land continued to be owned by the nobility, leaving the majority of people impoverished peasants. Since Žemaitė belonged to the

---

[5] Albertas Zalatorius, "Aprašymo funkcija ir struktūra Žemaitės prozoje" in ed. Kostas Doveika, *Žemaitė* (Vilnius: LTSR MA, 1972) pp. 407–27. See also Donatas Sauka, *Žemaitės stebuklas* (Vilnius: Vaga, 1988). Prominent feminist critic Viktorija Daujotytė even finds that Žemaitė's nature descriptions contribute to a sense of "the [world's] great cosmic order" in *Parašyta moterų* (Vilnius: Alma littera, 2001) p. 89.

landless gentry, she received nothing from her parents. Moreover, newly escaped from serfdom, her husband also owned no land, and thus the large family suffered great hardship and had to move from place to place, renting plots to live on and farm to support themselves.

Having once been the most powerful state in Europe in the Middle Ages, the Grand Duchy of Lithuania united with Poland and became the Polish-Lithuanian Commonwealth from 1386 to 1795. After several partitions, the territory came under the sway of Russia and was known as the Northwest territories of Russia, regaining its freedom only in 1918. The inhabitants in Žemaitė's day consisted of a Polish-speaking nobility (who often, like Tadeusz Kosciuszko and Adam Mickiewicz, considered themselves to have been born in Lithuania and even called themselves Lithuanian, but wrote in Polish), and Lithuanian-speaking gentry, villagers, and peasants. Nationalism with strict identity came about only in the late nineteenth century. The 1863 uprising, which was not class warfare so much as a revolt against Russian occupation, was fought by gentry and villagers (sometimes with pitchforks) but led by the Polish-speaking nobility; thus, Žemaitė calls the participants Lithuanians and Poles without distinguishing between them. As in most of Europe, the Jews among the population at the time were regarded as strangers, the Other, and lived side by side with the native population with mainly mercantile interaction, though they had lived in Lithuania since the fourteenth century.

Although Žemaitė's nominal upper-class roots shielded her from the exploitation and violence of serfdom, she was so taken with her husband's experiences that in her *Autobiography*, already unique for its time, she devoted about a third of her text about herself to retelling her husband's life in his voice and in what we are to presume is Laurynas's manner of speaking. There are very few Russian-era serf narratives in existence,[6] in part because few serfs were literate or had the opportunity to describe their lot other than orally. Thus Žemaitė's account, though second hand, is a valuable historical document that is rich in detailed description, easily flowing and full of narrated events and action. The narration of her own life is also very engaging, bursting with profuse, rather dramatic, and at times humorous renditions of a girl's upbringing in the countryside, her participation in the political events of her time, and then veering over to her adult life of poverty.

Since she was writing in her old age, Žemaitė was hurrying to wrap up her story; what is unfinished in the *Autobiography* are the years after her husband's death. These would have covered her activism in feminist and political affairs, her collegial and even collaborative relations with other women writers, the writing and editing of her works, and her exploits during her five-year journey to America. This is unfortunate for posterity, because one needs to read more of her many stories, her volume of journalistic articles and correspondence[7], and the accounts by numerous scholars over the years in order to fill in the blanks of her multifaceted undertakings and gain a proper appreciation of just how much she was able to accomplish with the limited resources at her disposal, especially considering that she only got freedom of movement after her husband died. She started her

---

[6] See the excellent collection by John McKay, *Four Russian Serf Narratives* (Madison: University of Wisconsin Press), 2009.
[7] Collected mainly in volumes 5 and 6 of her works, see Žemaitė, *Raštai* (Vilnius: Vaga, 1956).

Autobiography while in the United States and appears to have continued working on it up to the moment she fell ill with pneumonia and died at the age of 76 in 1921.

Another aspect of Žemaitė's writings that merits comment is her focus on combating the system of arranged marriages, with its elaborate customs and rituals. Her six initial stories, begun in 1894, dealt with women's issues. She had the idea to publish them together under the title *Laimės nutekėjimas* (Marriage for Happiness),[8] which in my estimation would have constituted a manual for young women to examine this barbaric custom and cause them to fight for their rights. More than likely, that is the reason the stories in the form she envisaged them were prevented from being published by the Catholic clergy and a conservative society and why they only saw the light of day in a small book in 1992. The practice of arranged marriage–with its matchmakers, dowries, parental authoritarianism, prevalent unhappiness, and suffering, if not worse–died out in the course of the 1920s. To demonstrate Žemaitė's originality, lucidity, and subtle understanding, I make use of the insights of contemporary philosopher Luc Ferry, who, among other things, was the French minister of education under French President Nicolas Sarkozy. In his book *On Love* (2012 French, 2013 English translation),[9] Ferry delineates the changeover in Europe from arranged marriages, which had lasted in all strata of society for centuries and were based on the economic interests of the families of the two

---

[8] The title could have an ironic meaning as well–The Flowing Away of Happiness. Since the author did use irony and humor at times, this cannot be ruled out.

[9] Luc Ferry, *On Love. A Philosophy for the Twenty-First Century*, Trans. Andrew Brown, (Cambridge and Malden: Polity Press, 2013). His entire book is devoted to "the revolution of love" and some of its consequences.

parties involved, to marriages based on love. Ferry designates this as one of the major paradigm shifts in the modern world.

Žemaitė had worked ardently on precisely this topic between 1893 and 1898 in the cycle of stories that she had hoped to collect and publish as a book. Thus, we have what appears to be an ordinary woman proving to be extraordinary because Žemaitė participated in an enormous social revolution and advanced society's thinking. Using only her feelings and experiences, relying on her acute observational powers, she captured the zeitgeist and verbalized the solution that she intuited on her own far from any centers of culture and influence. In a sense, it took a French philosopher to catch up to her in 2012 and only in hindsight brought to light the importance of the revolution in the value system of Western society that Žemaitė perceived on her own much earlier and spent her life working toward: the question of love's dominance over economics. Even today, this amazing feat has not gotten her the broad recognition she deserves.

Included in this book are two impassioned speeches that Žemaitė delivered at the Women's Congress in Kaunas in 1907, during the first wave of feminism on Lithuanian territory. These speeches powerfully describe the miserable conditions that women were subjected to under patriarchy and form a good introduction to the world of her stories. On this momentous occasion, Žemaitė wore her symbolic white scarf even though she was one of the organizers. The hall was packed with women from all strata of life, mostly farm women who were articulating the misery of their lives and demanding that something be done to improve their lot. Russian rule was still in effect, and typically its oppression led to attempts by men to escape through alcohol, consequently leaving no money for the wives and children, not even for children's medicine. The women attending the congress spoke with passion and tears. Although Žemaitė's first speech aimed to expose the injustice and misery of the tradition of arranged marriage, her second, written overnight after hearing her sisters' complaints, dealt with a way for women to tackle the widespread drinking problem and also to promote the need for women's education. In this book, Žemaitė's speeches seamlessly lead into and illuminate two of her most famous stories, "Petras Kurmelis" and "The Daughter-in-Law," intended for her cycle on marriage.

Like the speeches, the stories reveal the role of women as it was understood in the social context of the time. After a grueling courtship, during which the daughter's duty was to obey and yield to the father's wishes and marry the proposed suitor whether she liked him or not, the girl then went to live on the husband's farm. There a life of hard work awaited her. Women were expected to do the indoor and outdoor labor, to take charge of the kitchen, the household, the gardens, the children, and often the animals. The ability to save goods and money as well as to maintain a niggardly frugality were always great virtues. Because there was a constant shortage of food, it was kept under lock and key, away from the hired hands. The women had to weave all the clothes and linens and do much of the fieldwork at busy times, such as haying and harvesting. Women were forced to be industrious, or things would fall apart.

The contrast in "Petras Kurmelis" between Petras's mother and the wife he finally chooses, Marcė, can be seen in the women's attitudes toward work. Although the mother is mistress of the household, she is scrupulously hardworking, cares for the good of family and farm, but nothing misses her keen observation. Marcė comes from different stock. Her parents live in a filthy house; they are thieves and swindlers, cheating Petras out of most of the promised dowry, and with the stolen lumber they essentially blackmail him into marrying their lazy daughter. In the story, Žemaitė sets up a meaningful conflict in values. At first, her attention is on Petras and his concern only with money, work, and liquor. Eventually, however, the focus swings to his wife, and we begin to see Marcė in a new light, as a woman in love with another man, betrayed by him and sold by her parents to the highest bidder, Petras. Thus the author is able to demonstrate each of her main character's flaws and still show the interior world and longings of each one, ultimately bringing her solution of marriage for love into play.

"The Daughter-in-Law" is a different case. Again, the matchmaking is complex; Kotrė's father is captivated with the land his well-brought-up daughter is marrying into, ignoring the dirt and squalor of the family she will be joining, the laziness of the groom, the run-down cabin and surroundings. Žemaitė essentially emphasizes the class differences between Kotrė's family and her husband's; whereas Kotrė is a refined human being, her new family is crass and content in their filth. Her father-in-law is a patriarch of the old order: authoritarian, crude, indolent, even sadistic in watching his poor pregnant daughter-in-law fall off the hay wagon, laughing about it and not offering any help. Admittedly, the story is somewhat hyperbolized, dramatized, and rendered humorous in parts; the in-laws, the Vingises, close to caricature. Nevertheless, Žemaitė had a serious goal in mind: to show the cruel, even deadly, results of an antiquated tradition that disregarded the feelings of women and that were out of tune with the more modern attention to the individual and his or her desires. In a general sense, it was a movement away from collective, tribal thinking toward that which is more humane, leading to individual happiness; the vital importance of love, which seemed a salvation to her, the answer for women.[10]

The "women's question" was at the center of Žemaitė's thought and writings. There were many other stories in the five volumes of her fiction;[11] however, they are perhaps more of historic interest. Some were designated as anticlerical and gave rise to her being considered an atheist in a seriously Catholic country, but they have not aged well. They are not included here, though for the record, it needs to be said that those stories did not have the goal of turning people away from religion but, rather, focused on the clergy's hypocrisy in living well among great poverty, not practicing what they preached, or caring for the sick and impoverished. Again, during independent times, these stories harmed the spread of Žemaitė's works, yet during the officially atheist Soviet colonial period, they helped make her famous and her works classics of Lithuanian literature. The colossal statue of Žemaitė in the center of Vilnius, built in 1970 while still under the Soviet regime, attests to the respect she garnered. That respect is also reflected in the Soviet stamp bearing her profile and her picture on the Lithuanian one-litas note in more recent years, before Lithuania joined the Eurozone.

In this all too brief sketch of Žemaitė's life and achievements, I have tried to point out her uniqueness in contributing to the

---

[10] It is interesting that Žemaitė continued to believe in love and following one's heart, even though her own marriage seems not to have been a happy one. The class difference and level of sophistication/perception between her and Laurynas appear to have been insurmountable.

[11] Volume six of her works contains mainly Žemaitė 's letters.

evolution of humanity from the mists of slavery, oppression, and violence, both social and domestic. She needs to be broadly recognized as a secular humanist, a feminist, a revolutionary thinker and fighter by means of the pen rather than the sword. Despite poverty and antagonism, she achieved brilliance in identifying the ills of her society and in proposing viable solutions. Thus, she was able to challenge thinkers who in the eyes of the world were considered greater than she was. For these reasons, she continues to evoke a sense of wonder and admiration today.

ŽEMAITĖ'S AUTOBIOGRAPHY
(Unfinished)

My Relations

My father, Antanas Beniuševyčia, came from the gentry. My mother, Julijana Sčepuraitė, also of the gentry, always let it be known that she came from the upper class. Her father came from Vilnius, where he and my mother had many relatives, among them a canon, the Reverend Sčepura. But my mother's father, I don't know how or why, moved to Žemaitija. He lived there in great hardship; he couldn't even think of educating his children. As soon as they grew a little, the children became servants.

I knew one of my uncles, my mother's brother Aloizas, a potter, who made pots out of clay and lived in Mosėdis in the Telšiai area. Whenever he came to visit, he always brought presents of beautiful pots or little bowls.

Mother's sister, Karolina Sčepuraitė, was a servant in Liepaja, where she married some Russian—I don't know his last name because my mother disowned her for marrying a non-Catholic Russian.

That is all that I know about my mother's relations.

My mother was a servant in Mosėdis for a retired priest, an old man–I don't remember his name anymore. Next she ended up at Count Plater's of Šateikiai at his Bukantiškės manor as a housekeeper. She was supposed to receive a salary of ten rubles plus room and board for the year, which was a standard salary, but what she really got and how much–I couldn't tell you.

Mama didn't know how to write and could only read books, but she took great pride in her noble origins and the Polish language. She made sure that we, her children, spoke Polish; she made us read Polish books.

Father's relations were spread far wider. His grandfather had married three times and had three children with each wife; in all there were nine of them. My father and his two sisters, Ona and Barbora, who were the children of the third wife, were orphaned when their parents passed away. The first wife's older son was left the guardian of the smaller ones and the master of all the wealth and land. The older children could each earn their own bread. One brother entered the Dominican monastery, but he died young, so I didn't get the chance to meet him. Father's sisters, our aunts, married. One was Matienė, the other Norkienė; they'd come to visit us and lived in Telšiai. Father's brother, Uncle Domininkas, also lived in Telšiai and was married.

The oldest brother, Stanislovas, the guardian of the family's little ones, served Count Plater of Šateikiai as provisioner. He got rich while he was in service, buying Vinteliškės manor in Žarėnai parish in the Telšiai area. He married well–Albertina Abromavičiūtė. When my grandfather died, Stanislovas took the younger children into his house and placed the girls–Ona and Barbora–as servants with his countess and set up his brother, little Antanas, my father, with the count where he himself had served as provisioner and servant.

The bachelor count was old and sickly and never left his room. He had four servants–each one had his own duties. First, the valet, dressed the count; next, the assistant, fed the count; and the third had to clean the rooms; and little Antanas, the errand boy, had to be on call–in winter in the front entry and in summer on the porch. When the count rang a bell, he'd have to jump to fulfill his order–to hand him something or call some servant and once again sit down to wait in his spot.

The old count was very wealthy, ruling huge estates and vast counties with endless serfs and servants. No one knew the extent of his land, woods, and forests.

When the money collector brought the tribute that the people had paid in sacks from his other estates and smaller holdings, they put the money in bags and piled them in the count's room on the floor. Then the servants poured the money into small barrels without counting it. Instead they measured the money: they knew that a nine-liter barrel filled to the brim contained three thousand rubles. The servants also measured out the gold "imperials" and the five-and ten-ruble pieces. Then they would nail the barrels shut and store them in the basement under the mansion. The whole basement was piled full of barrels of money in rows.

When the old count died, all the treasure, the estates, and counties with their servants were left to the brother's sons, who were all Count Platers. There were four brothers who divided the uncle's estates and counties into four parts. Šateikiai with its estates went to the oldest, Pranciškus, who piled the barrels of money from the basement into wagons and told the serfs to take them to Riga where the count stored the money in the bank.

Upon his death, the old count left his servants an inheritance of a hundred rubles each and paid their salary a whole year ahead. Since he got a salary of ten rubles, after the death of the count, my father had one hundred and ten rubles. He put it in the Riga bank and received interest of four rubles a year. So with interest the sum grew, and at the end of a year he already had a hundred fourteen rubles.

Often Father would tell us stories about the old count's death, how they embalmed his body. They dissected his stomach, disemboweled him, and buried his intestines in the garden. They filled a barrel with distilled alcohol, dipped the count's body into it, and kept it like that for three days, then they pulled it out and hung it up to smoke. They say it got so smoked up and dry that it even rattled. Then they pulled it every which way, sewed up the stomach and made him presentable. Next they brushed him with oil paint, dried and dressed him, laid him out in the chamber, and put candles and grasses all around. Then they held the wake for three days.

First, they butchered oxen and sheep, then they boiled the meat and baked bread; everyone was given food and drink. For three days the serfs were free from work: they sang at the wake, ate and drank. Barrels of whiskey were rolled out into the courtyard; buckets and pitchers kept being refilled. They drank as much as they wanted, choosing whiskey or beer; they had bowls of meat to eat, which were always kept full, whole tables of sliced bread: they drank and ate as much as they could hold. Throughout the nights, they say, all the waysides were full of people, even women, fallen over, lying dead drunk. Supposedly, as the count lay dying, he had ordered this kind of burial feast to be held for his servants. This was to make up for his having wronged someone at some time or other or whipped someone who was not guilty. In this fashion, after his death he could compensate for it–he could fatten them up and give them drink.

After the count's burial, it took some guests a few days to crawl out from the waysides or the bushes to sleep it off, and there were even some who drank themselves to death. The count's burial was long talked about among the serfs.

Father's brother, the steward, had asked the young count to find my father some kind of service. The count allotted him the place of steward at the Bukantiškės estate, five versts from Šateikiai, in Plungė parish.

Father's older brother, who had served as steward, had bought an estate and a large parcel of land with woods farther away in Žarėnai parish. He had to look out for himself, build some buildings for himself; therefore, he stopped working for the young count.

Father's Wedding

Having taken up the steward's position in Bukantiškės, my father met my mother, who was serving as a housekeeper there. I don't know how long he'd worked there when Papa decided to propose to Mama. When she agreed, they announced the banns in church.

Father rode over to his oldest brother, his guardian, to boast of his coming marriage and invite him to the wedding. Learning of Antanas's intent, his brother almost spit nails, obstinately refusing to let Father marry that girl because she was poor and older than he was. Finally, the brother wouldn't let him marry at all, judging him to be too young and not yet man enough. My father was twenty-two, and Mother twenty-six or twenty-seven.

Some years later it wouldn't be so much Father who would tell us, his children, these stories as much as Father's sister Barbora, who at the time was brother Stanislovas's servant. Later she came to live with us. Often she would tell us: "As soon as your father rode over and told us that the banns with your mother had already been announced, his brother got so angry that he turned red as a beet, making his eyes look pale. All he could do was sputter: 'If you won't drop that girl, then get out of my sight!'"

Grabbing his cap, Antanas went across the yard to his horse as fast as he could. The brother's wife jumped up to make peace between them; she called Antanas back and sweetly began trying to convince him not to marry someone so old and so common. She promised to match him up with a wealthy, beautiful young noblewoman and give him their father's estate. She tempted him with the promise that if he got a good dowry, he could live on his own land.

The two of them went on lecturing relentlessly. Antanas just kept quiet.

Having talked their heads off, pounding him full of their wisdom and advice, they asked him: "Well, what do you think, Antan?"

"I'm thinking all's well," he replied.

"Well then? You agree not to get married?"

"As soon as I get back, I'm heading straight for the wedding."

They got angry again and started to curse and scold him every way they knew how. They tried to frighten him, renounce him, cast him away from the relatives, threaten to give him nothing, to fire him from his place at the count's, to sell his patrimonial estate–he had to listen to his older brother. Antanas just kept quiet. Having scolded him and threatened him, they asked again: "What are you thinking?"

Again he replied, "I'm thinking all's well. As soon as I get back, I'm heading straight for the wedding."

Enraged, the brother ordered his horse to be penned up and Antanas himself to be locked up in a small room to give him time to think overnight about listening to his brother's good advice.

In the morning they brought the deacon priest, who started in lecturing Antanas, too. The deacon, Father Senulevyčia and the brother and the sister-in-law took turns working on Antanas all day long, while throughout it all Antanas remained silent, as if he were deaf and dumb. They kept asking: "What are you thinking? Do you agree?"

He always answered the same: "As soon as I get back, it's straight to the wedding."

At wit's end, the brother called in two men and ordered some whips to be brought. He directed them to put down a rug and lay Antanas on it to be whipped. For, you see, he was a nobleman, so it wasn't proper to whip him on bare earth.

As they were getting ready to whip Antanas, Barbora said, "Ona and I were just screaming and crying, falling down on our knees at our brother's and the deacon's feet, begging them not to whip Antanas and to release him instead."

The deacon advised them to spare him at least overnight–maybe he'd change his mind. Leave the whips until the next day and, in the meantime, send an arrest warrant to the parish priest in Plungė, so he wouldn't perform the youngster's marriage without the brother's permission. Once again they locked up Antanas and his horse, too.

Having stolen the key to the stable from the driver, sister Barbora led Antanas's horse into the bushes, then helped her brother to climb out through the window. He mounted his horse and rode away into the night. Truth be told, as soon as he got home, they went off to get married, just the two of them. They hurried so the deacon wouldn't have time to bring the arrest warrant to the parish priest.

The brother couldn't do anything to Antanas. More angry than ever, he renounced his brother, took away his inheritance, and, even worse, sent his sister Barbora away. From then on she stayed with my parents and, in old age, ended her days in Žemaičių Kalvarija, in a home for pious old ladies.

Early Years at Home

My parents were employed at Count Plater's for more than twenty years: Father as steward, Mother as housekeeper. The serfs worked the fields, and then there were only my parents, a hired girl, and a shepherd who would watch and feed the herd in the winter. The four of them lived off their room and board. How much grain they got for their bread, I don't know. They planted potatoes in the field and sowed vegetables in the gardens—cabbages, beets, carrots, and the like.

Father kept some horses for himself. His salary was twenty rubles, and Mother's, ten rubles yearly. Father looked after the fields and the serfs; Mother, the poultry: she hatched chickens, ducks, and turkeys, and when they grew to size, she gave them up to the Šateikis estate. She milked the Bukantiškės cows, churned butter, and made cheese from each cow's milk, giving the estate a twenty-pound package of butter and sixty cheeses. There was no quota given for the fowl, so they tried to raise as many as they could, a hundred and more of each kind.

We were four girls. We didn't have a brother, there were just us: Emilija, Petronėlė, Julija, and Juzefa. I was born in the middle, after Petronėlė, on the 31st of May in 1845. I was baptized in the little church of Šateikiai by Father Golminas.

Growing up, from our early years we helped Mother with her work–tended the fowl and fed them. When we got older, we milked the cows and made cheese.

In winter, Father taught us to read and write in Polish. He made us speak Polish, forbidding us to speak Lowland Lithuanian (*žemaitiškai*). We were strictly forbidden from being friendly with the serfs' children who used to bring us food. We were not allowed to get together with serf kids or even talk to them.

When our parents taught us our prayers and the Commandments, we had to repeat them aloud morning and evening on our knees, and once I learned them by heart, they let me say them silently. In winter I'd say them at the end of the cottage where Father always hung his sheepskin on a hook. I would get under it and kneel there until Juzė finished saying her prayers out loud–then I'd get out and also say mine, but only silently. And in summer, when they would make us go to our prayers, I would cross myself and get down on my knees on the grass under the maple and after kneeling a while, I'd finish my "praying."

When I was learning to read–I remember: taking the primer, I'd have to cross myself and, turning to the last page, read the lines written there in Polish out loud:

The Holy Spirit commands that the switch should beat,
The switch does no harm to the health.
The switch pours sense into the head,
It teaches prayers and keeps one from indecent speech.

The reading of this hymn brought me the greatest displeasure; my face was usually covered in tears while I was reading it. One was not allowed to protest its reading, for the whip was always stuck under the beam waiting, and I would be forced to read with its menacing presence.

Having learned to read from the primer so the words rolled off my tongue easily, my parents started me on the prayer book. This was the greatest joy for me, since I wouldn't have to repeat the "Holy Spirit" prayer anymore.

My parents were God-fearing and strongly given to prayer, keeping us from evil deeds and bad words. I remember once, when wrestling with my little sister Juzė, I shouted: "Oh you Judas!" Hearing this word, my father scolded me fiercely; I almost got whipped for uttering it. As punishment he made me kneel and say three Hail Marys. Just imagine if he'd heard the words "devil" or "Satan" uttered; I don't know what would have happened. On winter evenings and at cock's crow, Mother and we girls would spin thread. Every morning and evening, while spinning, we sang various litanies, hymns, and other sacred songs.

No matter what the weather, every Sunday or holy day, my parents took the horse and wagon to church along with us, but there wasn't enough room in the wagon for all of us at the same time, so they took us by turns—one Sunday two of us, the next Sunday the other two. In summer we often walked. At church we had to pray, of course, and keep from looking to either side, looking only at the altar, the priest, and the book—reading the prayers and litanies.

I mostly said the rosary in church because after reading the prayers, I'd have to say ten Hail Marys, but as I was saying them, I'd always notice something: either a pretty scarf on someone's head or a nice skirt or a child in a colorful dress. Mother would elbow me: "Don't look around, pay attention!"

"I'm saying the rosary," I would retort. When I was going on seven, I had my first communion. The old priest, Golminas, who was much beloved by my parents, would come to our house often. When he visited, my hospitable mother would always make fragrant coffee as a treat.

Once the priest asked me: "Who created you?"

"Mother," I shot back.

I put the priest into such a conundrum, he started explaining to me about the soul, the body, and on and on. Of course, I didn't give a hoot about the priest's lessons, nor did I listen to him. Mother wasn't in the room; probably she was making coffee. On entering the room, she interrupted the priest's lecture and began trying to calm him down.

"There now, dear priest, why are you bothering your head with this silly girl—we are teaching her the Commandments. Something must have flashed into her head and she uttered some nonsense. It's not worth your while explaining or putting yourself out for her." She poured some coffee and the priest forgot all about me.

That old man listened to my confession for the first time in the sacristy. What I said to him or he to me–I don't remember any of it. Only afterwards he told me to bend down and beat myself on the chest–to repent for my sins.

The sacristy was paved in brick, and as I bent down, I saw a little round hole in the brick under the priest's chair. When I got home, I told my parents that in the sacristy floor there was a very good little hole–it was round, perfect for pounding nuts.

"How on earth did you ever see it?"

"Well," I said, "when I bent down to beat myself on the chest, I saw it under the priest's chair–such a nice, round hole, just right for pounding a nut."

They all started laughing. It seemed Father wasn't home because Mother began to scold me:

"What kind of confession is that? When you're supposed to feel sorry for your sins, to cry about them, you think about pounding nuts–it's a sin to do that: you're going to go to hell. You'll have to confess to it."

"Now how am I going to confess about a little hole? What am I going to have to say about that?" I wondered.

The Bishop Visits

I don't remember how old I was when we heard that the bishop was coming to Šateikiai. A short time later, the countess sent a message to my mother that she should bring all of us to the manor.

They were going to organize a group of girls to scatter flowers at the bishop's feet. It was an unspeakable joy, such an event! Emilka was already grown up, and we couldn't all leave, thus the three of us, the smallest ones, were chosen to go.

In Šateikiai there was a doctor's assistant, Bortkevyčia, who lived right by the church. He had four girls our ages, then there were the huntsman's girls, and those from other smaller estates; he assembled twelve of us in all. The countess divided us into pairs and sent her maids who were seamstresses to Bortkevyčienė's house, where they sewed white dresses for us, placing green wreaths on our heads and across our shoulders.

Flowers were ordered from the district—some to be picked from the field and others from the gardens. They put together a small basket for each of us and taught us how we'd have to do the scattering. We had to go in two rows of six in front of the bishop and scatter the flowers in his path. The taller pairs were to go first and the smaller ones would go right next to the bishop. They prepared us several days ahead of time, and we rehearsed every day.

The last day, first thing in the morning, while waiting for the bishop to arrive, they herded us all together, dressed us in white with all the wreaths, and there we sat holding our baskets.

From Plungė they sent a messenger on horseback to watch the highway: when he caught sight of the bishop's carriage, he was to fly back at once to announce his arrival. We sat and sat at the doctor's on the porch, the clock already striking twelve. It was almost late afternoon and we were still sitting, lined up in our rows ready to go.

The church was open; the pious ladies, girls, and young men were at work—sweeping, dusting, making wreaths, hanging them on the gates and crosses. The priest was walking around supervising everything. We were still out on the porch.

We were getting anxious and very hungry, and the little ones even started to whimper. Someone informed the countess. She told them to bring some milk and a roll for each of us–we snacked with relish. It was almost evening, the sun was starting to slip over the horizon, and that bishop was nowhere in sight. Finally, the messenger returned at a gallop, announcing that they were already going through Kadaičiai.

Such a bustle broke out. They lined us up in rows near the churchyard, placing a cushion on the ground for the bishop to kneel by the gate. From the church they brought out the biggest cross that had a lantern and a crown on each side of it. The cross-bearers were all in white vestments. The priest stood in the gateway, dressed in his stole, a ribbed cap on his head, the cross in his hands. Everything was in order, and the villagers had gathered from nearby. We were all standing on pins and needles, but still no sound of the bishop's carriage.

Again the messenger flew off on horseback to have a look. Returning at once, he told us that the bishop had stopped in Kadaičiai and was blessing the townsfolk.

We saw him coming at last: our hearts started beating faster. Six horses were harnessed to the carriage in tandem. The first pair on long straps was ahead by several feet, straddled by a boy on horseback. Such a carriage rider is called a *forišius*.

All the church bells were ringing. The driver snapped his whip and loosened the reins going uphill, but the *forišius* didn't manage to turn in time, so the horses came straight for us. Frightened out of our wits, we screamed and scattered out of our rows; the carriage came to a halt. The bishop climbed out. There wasn't enough time to get back in our rows. Encircling the bishop out of order, some in front, some behind, we just kept scattering our flowers. A priest came along at the same time, so we scattered some for him, too.

The bishop went off. He knelt on the cushion, kissed the cross, and then, getting up, he turned around and blessed everyone. Our priest was talking about something or other to him and led the bishop into the church. We regrouped into our rows by the church door.

Leaving the church, the bishop stuck his hand out so we could kiss it. Making the sign of the cross over us, he told us to go to bed, got in his carriage, and went off to the manor.

In the evening, they fed us and laid us down in a room on some hay scattered on the ground and told us to get to sleep because we would have to get up early the next morning. Sure enough, they roused us from our sleep early–we had to go to the mansion to escort the bishop to the church. Hurriedly they washed us, dressed us, thrust the baskets into our hands–we were going to have to run. Oh, no, look–the bishop was already in the churchyard. People were crowding around him, kneeling in front of him, taking turns kissing his hands. We rushed up too with our flowers, but there was no way we could get close. The bishop entered the church.

They told us the bishop was going to go to the rectory.

We regrouped into rows and waited by the door. As soon as the bishop appeared in the doorway, a crowd immediately mobbed him to touch his hands. Our rows scattered as they pushed us aside; we were nearly trampled. The bishop himself and the priests were pulling us out of the crowd, telling us not to barge in, to sit down somewhere near the fence, but we didn't listen. We ran off beyond the gate to the parsonage, reassembled into our rows, and waited. Running ahead, women with children started to kneel on the path, waiting for the bishop, but servants appeared, rattling canes, and chased them away.

For once we got to escort the bishop to the rectory in an orderly fashion. The bishop and the priests went inside, so we sat down on the porch. In a little while some priest or seminarian brought out a bunch of small pictures and, distributing one to each of us, said, "Here's a gift from the bishop." We sat there for another hour. When he came out, the bishop and the priests gifted us again with some copper coins–some got three kopecks, others two or only one.

We escorted them to the churchyard. We were told to pray outdoors. There was a throng of people, the church was bustling inside, so we were not to try squeezing in there.

We, the little ones, were happy with our little pictures and kopecks, the bishop's gifts, but the older kids were sputtering, "As if we were beggars–all we get is a kopeck!" They said, "I was going to throw it at his feet, but I was afraid of making him angry."

And that's all we got for scattering flowers for the bishop. At dinner time all the priests and the bishop went off to the count's manor house. The count's carriages drove them there. Toward evening a lot of people, including us, went to the courtyard of the mansion. We thought we might have to see the bishop off. But the carriage went right up to the porch, and as soon as the bishop was seated in it, away they went. The bishop blessed us from the carriage, and all the people in the courtyard crossed themselves, and so it was goodbye!

We girls talked about this great celebration of ours–the bishop's reception– for a long, long time afterwards. We kept the little pictures he gave us as a remembrance. Of course, we, the younger ones, weren't as bright as the older ones, who just spat on the gifts.

"If he couldn't come up with anything better than such beggarly gifts," they complained, "then he shouldn't have given us anything at all."

At that time they said that the bishop had persuaded the count to build a new church. The count gave his word that in ten years' time, he would invite the bishop to bless the new church in Šateikiai. They agreed on it and drank some champagne. The count kept his word and started building the church. He just swore at the bishop, wondering why he hadn't come ten or even five years earlier. During the construction of the church, the serfs were set free from their masters. There weren't any free workers left. Now they had to be hired–the cost of the church would be high. Earlier the serfs would have built it for nothing. In spite of that, the count did build a new church in Šateikiai. But Bishop Valančius didn't bless it in the end because he was moved from Varniai to Kaunas.

Learning to Read

Father taught my oldest sister, Emilka, to read and write a little. They couldn't spare her to go to school at all because she was indispensable at home as Mother's helper for the household chores. In the winters she was busy spinning and weaving a dowry for herself and the smaller ones. Sometimes matchmakers would drop by–suitors would propose to Emilka, but every time it would come to nothing. First, our parents didn't approve of the suitor, then Emilka didn't find him appealing; in the end they never returned.

It was the greatest disappointment for me that Emilka's wedding was nowhere in sight. And it so happened that I never did see it in my lifetime. Having lived some fifty years, she ended up in a home for pious old ladies and died an old maid.

Dr. Bortkevyčius sent my second sister, Petronėlė, to school in Šateikiai. They hired a teacher for their own children, so they added our Petrusė to the lot. I don't know how much they paid for her schooling, but she ate her meals at the manor from the second table. When my mother had asked the countess if she would take the girl in for schooling and boarding, apparently the countess had answered: "Let her sit at the steward's wife's table. Wherever she is, she'll be eating my bread, she might as well learn something while she's at it."

The teacher was a German lady, and my sister learned to read and write in the German language.

As for me, I learned from my father. I just loved to read, but we didn't have books at home: Father didn't buy any; all he had were old Polish prayer books.

He also had a Russian primer–I knew the letters and could read the words somewhat; I also had a Polish songbook. Moreover, he had some Lowland Lithuanian books: *The Life of Jesus Christ* and *Imitation of Jesus Christ* by Thomas à Kempis. So I read all those Polish and Lithuanian books in turn during the winter. Father also taught me to write on a little marble slate.

In summer I tended the fowl with those same books still in my hands. I pretty much learned them by heart.

The surroundings of Bukantiškės were very beautiful: a large garden, a pond nearby, a windmill at the bottom of the hill, fields, meadows, small paths running here and there, poplars planted all over.

Frequently, in the summer, the little counts and countesses would come over to walk and run around the grounds. They had a French teacher–they spoke only French to her and at the same time among themselves. I was curious about this and would ask repeatedly: "Why do the little counts talk like that, so it's impossible to understand them?"

Someone or other would explain to me: "This is the fashion among the nobility–to speak differently so the peasants won't be able to understand them. That's why the count brought over a young French woman to teach the children an incomprehensible language."

I thought to myself: "If our counts learn French here, then probably over there great gentlemen learn Lowland Lithuanian. Since that French woman doesn't understand either Lowland or Polish–then others there must not know that language. Well, when I grow up, I think, I'll travel to France and teach the noblemen's children Lowland Lithuanian so their people can't understand them. Then when I come back, I'll teach all our serfs French so they will understand what their masters are saying."

The Life of a Serf

I pitied the serfs a great deal. I heard about all kinds of injustices they suffered. They said that an educated man appeared among the Plungians, one who'd been many places far and wide, who'd seen much and knew many things. He started to incite the townsmen in Plungė, telling them not to pay tribute, to forgo the *corvée*, not to listen to the masters because it was the masters who contrived to oppress the people and to tax them. Moreover, he was told by the King himself that everyone had been pardoned. The serfs had been freed from all obligations, taxes, and the *corvée* by the King.

At that time, the estates, forests, and serfs all belonged to Count Zubovas. The master himself didn't live at the manor; only stewards, woodsmen, and huntsmen inhabited it. Incited, the serfs began their opposition to disobey the estate leaders and refused to pay their taxes. Soldiers were brought in to control the serfs' revolt, and they started whipping those who were to blame.

I don't know who brought in these soldiers, or how. Only our serfs related that the steward in Plungė was whipped to death and his wife got a hundred lashes too.

Many of the accused were beaten to death. There was blood all over the courtyard of the estate.

As I heard these stories, I sobbed because I couldn't understand why they whipped innocent people, why not the one who had done the inciting.

Another time, I recall Father returning home from somewhere or other. He didn't even want to eat, just sat there sighing in sorrow. Eventually, he started telling us that the Judgment Day had come to Gintališkės District.

The Gintališkės estates belonged to Count Ledakauskis, who lived in Vilnius. On the estate his stewards started to beat the people brutally, to oppress them harshly. The serfs conspired to complain to the count himself, and choosing four men from their midst, they sent them to Vilnius to explain to the count how the stewards were mistreating people on the estate. These men went to Vilnius on foot. The count received them and, having listened to all their complaints, declared that he himself would come out to investigate and rectify the situation. The four men returned joyfully. Alas, the estate leaders also found out that the count was coming and on which day he'd arrive. They summoned all the district's residents beforehand to tell them that the count was coming and instructed them to receive him festively. They released everyone from work and ordered them to gather for the count's reception, only to dress in their most expensive clothes–both men and women–so that the count would be pleased with his people. The gullible peasants obeyed and dressed in whatever they had–their best clothes: women in silk scarves and silk aprons, the men in homespun cloth; they even put on their dangling silver chains. The count arrived. The whole district–men and women–came out to greet and welcome him.

The count rejoiced, thanked everyone, and sent them home. Then he started to question the stewards about the peasants' various complaints, asking why they were beating his people and oppressing them.

Trying to vindicate themselves, the stewards replied: "If we beat the peasants, they wouldn't be so wealthy. Sir Count, didn't you see how dressed up they were, how expensive and beautiful their clothes were? Under you, Sir Count, they live like some noblemen."

The count circled around his estate–he had no time: not even for seeing his serfs any longer. On the way home, he paid a visit to the neighboring Count Čapskis and asked him to oversee all the affairs at Gintališkės estate, to improve the stewards' relationship with his peasants.

Of course, the stewards converged on Čapskis and portrayed all the peasants as rebels and liars and vindicated themselves.

Taking a company of Cossacks from Telšiai, Čapskis went off to Gintališkės to investigate the peasants' complaints. The stewards brought home a barrel of whiskey for the Cossacks and especially for Čapskis himself. When every last one had drunk his fill, they summoned the peasants to be interrogated, but they didn't listen to a word of what they had to say. The stewards and woodsmen just pointed to the rebels who were to blame. Whomever they pointed to, the Cossacks laid them down at once and lashed them with their whips.

First of all, they whipped those who had gone to Vilnius. They beat two to death on the spot; the other two were still alive, but since their flesh was coming off their bones, they would probably also die soon.

They beat others, too–scarcely a Gintališkės peasant was spared.

Father related further: "The Day of Judgment was upon us, with all the crying and screaming! The Cossacks' horsewhips just whistled, human blood splashed, flesh flew, women fainted!"

The count, who was dead drunk, his white eyes bulging, just kept roaring: "Whip them as hard as you can, whip them!"

Bursting into the thick of it, he poured whiskey down his throat and handed out more to the Cossacks to drink. The stewards and woodsmen just rubbed their hands together in glee and ranted: "These serfs won't be going back to complain to the count anymore."

Beasts, they're just beasts! And those poor peasants had to suffer at everyone's hands!

As Father told the story, mother's tears started flowing. Sobbing, I shouted out loud: "Why doesn't the Lord God punish such injustices? Why doesn't lightning strike that Čapskis dead, those stewards and Cossacks too? Doesn't He see what's happening? Why doesn't He take mercy on the serfs?"

I didn't get to finish, I took off through the door because father was reaching for the whip from under the ceiling, saying: "You little pig! You think you're going to use foul language against God, do you?"

Looking back to see if they were following me, I ran off to the hop-bine, then crawled into the thicket, shivering. I'm not sure if it was because of fear of the whip or out of anger against God.

My Mother's Illness

I'm not exactly sure how old I was, but I already knew my prayers when my mother got sick. The priest came by, and in the entry, the women were singing hymns. The doctor and his wife were there. Toward evening, Mother started to fade. They pushed us up close to the bed, made us kneel down, telling us to say prayers and beg for our mother to get well. Recovering somewhat, Mother told us to go to bed. Aunt Barbora always used to frighten us: "If you don't say your prayers, your mother will die. Papa will bring you a stepmother, then you'll see how she'll beat all of you."

I thought this over and said to myself: "It's not so bad, if Mother dies, Papa will bring home Mistress Domicėlė for a stepmother for us. At least she'll make me a little hat like she herself wears! Our mother covers her head with kerchiefs and makes us wear them, too."

But I didn't get to see either my mama's death, nor the stepmother, nor even the hat.

My Aunt's House

I wasn't ten years old yet, when one evening a stranger brought Father a letter. This was such an unusual occurrence that we were dumbfounded. After reading the letter, Father said sadly: "My brother Stanislovas, your uncle, has died. This is the invitation to his funeral."

Father left the next morning. Returning after a few days, he told us how festive the funeral had been, how many priests, how many guests, gentlemen, and hordes of people had escorted our uncle to the cemetery. What a lavish dinner there was after the burial, how much they drank and what they ate, and what they had talked about. So and so got drunk and quarreled. He told us so many stories. He told us that his sister-in-law, our aunt, had promised to come to visit us sometime, so she could get a look at us children.

The aunt had five daughters. The oldest was very well educated; she had graduated from a boarding school in Vilnius. She knew German and French and could play the piano. Now she was teaching her younger sisters what she had learned. Aunt Barbora had been a maid at the aunt's manor, so she knew the names of all the children and would always tell us: "The aunt's first two children were sons, but both of them died when they were still little. Then one right after the other she had five daughters who are all still at home: Apolonija, Valerija, Ona, Elena, Liudvika. Apolonija, the oldest, is one-eyed—one of her eyes got pierced, when she was little. That's the reason why her father sent that one to study in Vilnius."

"Maybe she won't be able to get married having just one eye," he said. "Let her at least get an education. She'll be able to teach her sisters, or she'll be able to teach somewhere else: she'll earn her bread." That was how uncle reasoned.

The aunt loved having guests over; she visited back and forth with all the noblemen and gentlemen living nearby. She'd be driven there and would invite them back to her manor and treat them royally, throwing fancy balls. Uncle wasn't very fond of any of this. Vinteliškė, uncle's estate, was close to a high road; therefore, guests stopped by every day. Uncle had bought some land farther away; he built a small estate in the woods and moved there to live. He called the new estate Šėmos—Posemy in Polish—because a stream called Šėma ran through the orchard. The side roads to get there weren't very good, and in some places you couldn't wade through the mud. Uncle thought he could hide there from all the guests, but he didn't succeed: even there, visitors often descended on them. Not far from Šėmos, uncle built another small estate, which he called Klibės.

Since uncle was very wealthy, he could have bought more land for himself, especially when he was still serving the old count.

There was no keeping track of his money. Uncle had always taken the count's district taxes to Kaunas. He would bring home bags of money and gave orders for them to be carried into his rooms. Untying some bag or other, the children would play, rolling rubles on the ground, until Uncle would take the money to Kaunas. And even when he had taken the rubles away, there would still be some scattered on the floor in the corners.

Thus Aunt Barbora would always tell us stories about Uncle.

I was amazed, even jumping up and down for joy, to think that I had such a cousin related to me somewhere, who knew how to talk like the little countesses, who studied in Vilnius and graduated from a boarding school. I kept dreaming and waiting for the day when she would come to visit us.

Unable to wait any longer for Aunt's arrival, my parents decided to visit her first, choosing to take us two middle girls along. You see, the oldest was needed to stay at home, and little Juzė was still too silly. And so we got ready to go.

Mama baked some cakes, killed some chickens; filled a whole small chest with cheeses, butter, and bread, and in another one she packed the clothes–our good ones, theirs and ours. After all, it was not a short trip–six and a half *versts*: that was no joke.

We wore our everyday clothes for the trip, as rain might pour down on us. Three horses were harnessed to the large horse carriage. A driver, Juozas Švelnis, a capable, loyal man, was selected from the serfs to watch the horses at night. We might have to stop and sleep a couple of nights on the road. Our rye had already been cut, set in stacks. By the time it seasoned, we'd be back home to put the stacks into the barn.

We got ready the night before–went to the sauna and washed our hair. The next morning at sunrise, Father roused us. We got up quickly, fixed ourselves up hurriedly, had a bite to eat, and, crossing ourselves, set out on our journey.

The day was hot, the horses were foaming at the mouth. Often they had to be given water, and they grazed at the waysides and along the bushes, so that they could feed a little. The surroundings were unfamiliar. We drove across the city of Plungė lengthwise–taverns, stores, after that estates, woods, farmsteads. It was so interesting to us. Father knew and told us whose estate it was, what the village was called, showed us a windmill–unseen sights and unheard-of names. We gazed around, awestruck. Even though we dilly-dallied, we got there just in time for dinner.

This was my first trip of any length: I was going on eleven years old.

When my mother asked for permission, the girls took us up to the attic to change our clothes. She said that there were guests who were eating their dinner. We prettied ourselves up and went downstairs.

All the rooms were crammed full of guests: ladies, gentlemen, young ladies, and children. Aunt was so warm and kind: she kissed us all over, caressed us, introduced us to her girls, told us to kiss each other, and sat us down to dinner. I really didn't like the food; I put my spoon down and ran off.

Hugging me, Apolonija, known as Poliusia, explained: "It's not nice to get up from the table while others are still eating. Even if you no longer want to eat, you have to sit until everybody has finished."

"We don't sit," I said: "Whoever finishes eating first, goes off first."

"At our house you're going to do it differently: you won't get up from the table first."

"Is that what they do in Vilnius?"

"Of course, they all sit still until the last one finishes eating."

"Well, well," I think to myself, "here's a new way of doing things."

Afterwards the guests' children and the hostesses' girls gathered both of us into their group. We ran around the orchard playing, having so much fun, if only our clothes hadn't gotten in the way. The other girls wore short skirts to their knees and thin-soled shoes, while my big leather shoes, made with enough room to grow into, and my long skirt tangling around my legs, prevented me from keeping up with the other children or from catching them.

While I was at Aunt's house crawling in the corners with the smaller girls, I noticed that they had an awful lot of books.

"Do you read them all?" I asked Anetka.

"Who's going to read them?" she retorted. "We don't have time; we have to do our homework that Poliusia gives us. In the summer it's vacation—we don't want to read then either—so they just lie there."

My Cousin Stasys

We drove home from church and found a horse harnessed to a wagon, standing in the yard. There was a guest, who said he was Father's brother Domininkas's son, Stanislovas. A handsome young fellow. We had already heard Barbora's story about

Domininikas's Stasys, whom his mother's brother, the Šiauliai attorney Paulauskis, had brought to his house when he was small and sent him to school. Stasys said that he'd been sent by the aunt to come tell us not to take me to study this fall yet. She couldn't take me in because even without me, there would be six students. Poliusia wouldn't be able to teach so many. She was leaving me for next year: I would be older and grasp the schooling better.

Whatever the aunt said, that's what we'd have to do.

This year even my clothes would not be a cause for worry.

From our first meeting we all loved Stasys and wouldn't let him leave. He told us how his Uncle Paulauskis wanted him to graduate high school and live with him and learn from him how to be an attorney. He intended to leave his house and all his possessions to Stasys, since the uncle was a bachelor.

But Stasys didn't want it: he was determined to go to Moscow University and study to be a doctor. The uncle got angry at his disobedience and sent him packing. Now he was at the aunt's house in Šėmos. He got fifty rubles from his uncle for his schooling in Moscow. Maybe he'd get more support from somewhere, and when he became a doctor, he'd return it all.

My father agreed to his studying to be a doctor, but he didn't approve of his disobeying his uncle.

"You have to think," he said. "Uncle is wealthy and single; you'd have your own house in the city, other buildings yet, maybe even some money–to reject everything for some idea about schooling–that's not practical."

Stasys quieted down, he didn't argue and that evening, there was no more talk about his uncle.

He said he'd left Šėmos very early, but he arrived at our house only toward evening: it was hard to make the horse go, he couldn't force him. It was a Sunday. I got curious as to where Stasys went to church today, in Žarėnai or Plungė. But I was too shy to ask. We were always told that on a holy day, it wasn't proper to do any work or set out on a trip. If we went somewhere far for the holy day, then we had to go to mass somewhere along the way. And if that was not possible, one had to say the rosary during the trip. Stasys set out in the morning and drove on a holy day for a long time. Where did he go to mass?–the question kept bothering me.

He stayed with us for a few days. We went for walks, ran through the meadows and the woods, picked berries, rolled around on the grass in the orchard. I got my courage up and asked:

"Stasys! Since you traveled here on a Sunday, did you go to church or did you say the rosary on the way?"

"What a stupid question." Stasys started to laugh. "I could scarcely get the horse to go with the small wagon, but if I had harnessed it up for church, how could it have pulled me?" Embarrassed at being made fun of, I tried to defend myself:

"Yes! The trouble is that we were taught that it's forbidden to travel without attending mass in church."

"And look at me, I arrived safe and sound without church and mass," he laughed, "and nothing happened to me."

"Probably you said the rosary, that's why?"

"Yes, I said the rosary by cursing out the devil, when I couldn't get the horse to go," he laughed. "You see, my rosary is better than yours."

I was horrified at Stasys's jokes: making fun of the devil. How come he wasn't afraid of going to that terrible place called hell? Stasys's jokes didn't sit well with me; I would observe him more.

Once we came home from picking nuts late, tired and hot from climbing the hazelnut trees, we hurried to get to bed. But you had to say your prayers. It occurred to me to see what Stasys was going to do. Through a crack in the door I watched to see if he was going to say his prayers. Wouldn't you know it! Throwing his clothes off, he fell into bed without even crossing himself. Sneaking up to his bed quietly, I whispered: "Stasys, you won't be able to go to sleep without your prayers. The devil will come at night and snatch you away."

"How stupid! He'll catch you with your prayers first. Off to bed with you!"

Going back to my bed, I imitated Stasys, quickly throwing off my clothes, falling into bed and going right to sleep. This was the first seed of godlessness in my life. Although the thought often occurred to me: what did it matter to God, if people didn't eat meat or drink milk? Or–what difference did it make to God if people wagged their tongues saying a Hail Mary or Our Father and other prayers? God must get bored hearing the same thing over and over again from so many people in so many churches. How could He even manage to fulfill all those requests? But you couldn't ask questions like that out loud, not even whisper them. It was a sin, you'd go to hell ... you had to go to confession for such questioning, and if you didn't stop, you'd get the whip on top of it. You'd hear such threats from your parents and from Barbora. And take Stasys; it wasn't enough that he made fun of me, and didn't even say his prayers, but on top of that he claimed that he'd never fasted. For him it was a fast when he couldn't find any food: and if he did get some, he'd even eat meat on Good Friday and herring on Easter.

After Stasys left, I became more daring about getting out of my prayers. During a fast, if I happened on some meat, cottage cheese, or sour cream, I'd hide and eat it. I wasn't afraid of being caught by the devil anymore. One fear did remain, though: What happens after you die? What will God say at the Last Judgment?

Fearful of that, I'd sometimes go back to praying. I was very good at getting out of saying my prayers. On a summer evening I'd kneel on the soft grass under the maple in the yard just to cool off. Bored with kneeling, I'd beat myself on the chest with my fist, kiss the fragrant grass, kiss the bark of the maple to which God's crucifix was nailed, then I'd roll around on the dewy grass and jump across the yard on one foot. Then I'd claim that I'd repeated the entire rosary.

During the winter, there wasn't anything for me to study. I could read in Polish and Lowland Lithuanian very well; I could read in Russian quite well already, and I knew the letters in German; I knew how to write and count a bit. And there was no use always writing the same thing over and over, just to mess up a pile of paper: "It all costs money," Father decided. So as not to waste time uselessly, they gave me coarse flax to spin until I learned how to do it and got used to the spinning wheel. When I got bored with spinning, I would knit socks with needles, and I also knit in the summer, as I was keeping the geese away from the crows. I was told that I had to know how to make everything for myself. I learned to sew, too. Mother told me that every girl has to know how to use the needle, to mend or to fix anything– not to rely on others. Supposedly, a dying tailor asked for a needle to be brought to him. Picking it up, he kissed it and thanked it for getting him into heaven. So, you see, sewing was not only necessary here on earth, but you could also be redeemed through the needle. Throughout the winter I spun, sewed, and knitted. In the spring, I was with the fowl again–feeding and tending them. In spring the aunt came to our house with her three little daughters and Stasys, all together. Since he was a student, he had a blue collar on. We were so happy and loved them to death, treating them to everything we had. The days were very hot, so we went swimming in the brook beyond the mill. When the mill was turning, the water ran across the stones swiftly. At night all of us, including the aunt's girls, slept in the barn on the hay. It was so much fun to run around with the girls and Stasys all day long. And I was most pleased that the bondsmen could all see what a rich aunt we had: she even arrived in a carriage. Now the aunt wanted me to come in the fall, when school was to start. She told Mother to make clothes for me, similar to what her girls wore—short skirts with bloomers. They counted up twenty-five rubles a year for my room and board. And father would bring me home to stay for Christmas, Easter, and summer.

The aunt and the girls left. Stasys stayed with us a couple weeks more.

What interesting and amazing things Stasys related from his journey back home from Moscow.

From Moscow to St. Petersburg, an iron road was laid out, smooth as a table and straight as a string, for wagons to roll along on. It traveled without a horse, there was just an iron furnace: they ignited it, made steam, and that pulled a whole row of connected wagons. And those wagons were bigger than the serfs' cabins, with ceilings, a roof, and windows. A wagon like that could hold more than twenty people: benches were made for them to sit on, and it went amazingly fast.

"Just think," he exclaimed, "from Moscow to Petersburg is a hundred *versts*, and it took us only three days on the iron road. It's such great fun. Whenever it stops, you can run out to the station or the town to buy yourself something to eat, some bread and cheese or other snacks. Several students were riding on it; they got something to eat, but there was nowhere to sleep, so at night they crawled under the benches and slept soundly on the floor. There were some young ladies who were also on board, but they were too timid to crawl under the bench, so they had to doze sitting up."

We listened with our mouths wide open at such wonders–a wagon with so many people in it rolling along without horses!

"If Stasys is telling the truth," said Barbora, "then the prophecies of the Judgment Day are coming to pass and the Antichrist has arrived after all, and he will soon drive around with his iron furnace and burn people. See, it's already happened! That's because there's so many people overflowing with sin!"

"You might feel sick, your head could spin going so fast," gasped Mother. "I wouldn't get into such a wagon for anything."

And I thought: "Just let me on it!"

Stasys had gone from St. Petersburg to Riga by boat–it was also great fun.

"You can't see land anywhere," he said, "It's just water, water everywhere. You bob up and down on the water like a goose and you can't tell if you're moving or standing in place. The wind just rocks you back and forth, sometimes it's a bit too much."

"It's such a long way," said Stasys, "but with good navigation, the trip took only two weeks, and I estimate the distance is about two hundred *versts*."

From Riga he came home by means of the Post.

Stasys brought many books with him and set them out on the table. He took others into the orchard and read them while sitting there. Touching those books, I was green with envy, but they were all in Russian, and I couldn't read Russian very well and understood even less of it.

Then Stasys made friends with our neighbor Endrijauskis, who had a collection of all kinds of books, mostly in Polish. Stasys would bring home several books and let me read them. Then, the next year, even without Stasys's help, I borrowed books from Endrijauskis.

My Friend Onikė, the Serf

Before Stasys's arrival, I had made friends with a girl my own age who used to bring food to the bondsman. I remembered it clearly as if it were yesterday. Norvaišienė died in the sharecropper's hut. We went to the wake to sing. I saw how Onikė cried, screaming and hugging her dead mother's feet. Someone came forward and pulled her away and led her off. Then, again she would rush in and collapse at her mother's feet, weeping and wailing. They told me to sing from the hymnbooks. As soon as Onikė let out a scream, my voice left me–the tears just streamed down my cheeks as I snuffled through my nose. I wasn't able to sing any longer–I pitied Onikė so much. Soon after, the bondsman's women were saying: "Norvaišas can't manage without a housekeeper, he is remarrying. Even though there's a small child left behind, it won't be a burden to the new wife." The women figured: "Onikė will watch the child and bring food to the *corvée*, but, of course, sometimes we'll have to rein Onikė in."

I hung around to see Onikė. When she brought the food, I asked her right away what her new mother was like, was she stricter than the one who died? When I questioned Onikė, her face turned red and her eyes filled with tears. Saying nothing, she ran off. When I went to the orchard to keep the crows from pecking the chickens, I burst out crying, as Onikė's tears stood before my eyes. How miserable she must be, I thought. When I asked about her mother, she started to sob. How can she possibly watch the child and bring the food? How that witch of a stepmother must scold and whip her. More than likely she doesn't give her any milk or butter.

Reflecting on all the injustices Onikė endured, I cried. Whenever I saw Onikė bringing the food, I hung around so that I could get together with her, to talk to her, and secretly I'd slip her some berries and apples. I was afraid to talk very long in case my mother caught me. I didn't ask Onikė about her stepmother again because I knew that she was bad-tempered and mean. No one had to tell me so, nor did Onikė need to confide in me, but she couldn't be a good stepmother because she was mean to Onikė.

Therefore, in order to comfort Onikė, I hastened to tell her of my own hardships: how I forgot to shut the gate when leaving the garden, how the pigs got into the dahlia patch and dug up the rue, how Emilka hit me on the back so hard that I started to cry.

Another time, when the rye was being brought in, I wasn't paying attention and the turkeys flew over to the barn and the horse stepped on a baby turkey. Mother scolded me something awful. I almost got the whip for not taking good care of the turkeys; but they were so nasty, it was so hard to watch them, and they run around like little devils.

Whenever I saw Onikė, I'd always tell her similar stories, so she'd know that I was as unhappy as she was. Besides that, I'd secretly give her berries, apples, and pears. Once in a while she'd bring me some nuts in her pocket.

Soon we became very close friends. Unfortunately, once while I was throwing apples from the orchard over the fence to Onikė, my father caught me. He led me inside and, holding me by the hand like a little thief, called Mother to come and ordered her to hold me down while he flogged me so hard with the birch whip for stealing that it really hurt.

"Now that you've started stealing apples," he said, "you'll begin stealing bigger things later. And worse than that, when we send you to work for strangers, you'll easily slip into a life of theft."

After my whipping, Father told me to kiss the whip and kiss him on the hand. While I was sobbing, Mother berated me as well. She scolded me and said that I should have been punished even more for such bad behavior.

"Father gathers apples, takes them to market, sells them, works so hard, and you steal them and throw them over the fence to the bondsmen's kids. You hang out with the shepherds. Have you lost your mind? You know it's a sin: every day you repeat the Fifth Commandment, don't steal. Another sin is to disobey your parents, so you have to go to confession, to better yourself. If I catch you running around with the shepherds and the bondsmen's kids again, I'll whip you myself until you bleed because otherwise you don't mind me."

After she finished scolding me, Mother sent me out to the fowl.

As I sat in the orchard, I pondered and wept: "Everybody says that God is merciful and just. Why doesn't God punish my father for whipping me when I'm innocent? Throwing rotten apples over the fence—what kind of theft is that? Piles of apples rot in the barn, we pick out the rotten ones, we dump them into the troughs by basketfuls. And those few that I threw out would have rotted, they would have been thrown to the pigs the same way I did for Onikė. God sees my innocence and doesn't punish my parents—why doesn't lightning strike them? They force me to go to confession, but how am I going to make up a long story about some rotten apples?"

Reminded of the confessional, I thought of another incident. One time they took me to Žemaičių Kalvarija. A place where miracles occur. It was on a great feast day, everyone had to go to confession. They took me with them, too. The priests heard confessions behind the altar. There were large crowds of people standing around, and they wedged me into the line with them by the wall. But, oh my, it was so warm, so suffocating, they pressed against me and pushed me; people blew their hot breath onto my head. Squeezed and trapped, I could scarcely breathe. I was thirsty, I needed a drink, or at least some water to rinse out my mouth, but Mama wouldn't let me leave the queue. I couldn't stand it anymore and started to weep and then sob out of control. Crying like that, I got shoved up to the front of the line right up to the priest. Getting out of the crush, I hurried to confess so that I could get some fresh air and catch my breath. Then how they praised me—I heard it myself, that I had cried and repented over my sins so much. Well, confession is confession, it just worked out better for me, I thought. But how would my parents be punished for their wrongdoing—for whipping me when I was innocent? They said that after confession, after taking communion, one was left without a blemish—you could ask God for whatever you wanted. When I went to confession, I thought that after communion I would pray to God and ask Him to pay back my parents. God would know how to punish them so that they wouldn't whip me again with the birch.

My Schooling Begins

With the coming of fall, when it was time to take me to school, they made my clothes and dressed me like Aunt's girls. They put extra clothes, underwear, and bedding into the green chest and tied it up with a sheet.

As I was leaving, Aunt Barbora hugged me, shedding tears. I was amazed as to why she did that. I was so beautifully dressed and could only be happy–what was there to cry about? They sent me with my whole dowry and left me there.

My schooling started then–it was no joke.

The schoolroom was in the attic. In the middle of the floor stood a table; along the walls were four beds and two cupboards where the books were kept. There were six pupils. The teacher, Aunt's oldest daughter, sat us around the table and chose a spot for each of us. On the wall, she pinned a paper with instructions for the whole week–what day our lectures were, what was happening before lunch, and what would take place after. Each week, one of us was designated to keep things tidy. Every day before beginning classes, we stood up, each in her own place, and the chosen one read and said the prayer out loud before school started. We crossed ourselves and all sat down; we had to sit as if in church. All the pupils were from last year; I was the only new one, the stupid one: they all made fun of me.

My questioning began: "What do you know?"

"I can read and write in Polish, I can read some Russian and just a little German."

"Who taught you?"

"My father taught me Polish and Russian and Petrusė taught me German. She studied with a German teacher and showed me the letters and taught me how to pronounce them."

"What books have you read?"

"Prayer books, primers, *The Life of Jesus Christ.*"

"Lowland ones!" The teacher was astounded. "Aha, that's why you speak Polish so poorly, because it's tainted with Lowland Lithuanian. You're not allowed to pick up even one Lowland book anymore, don't forget it!" the teacher threatened. "And you haven't studied any grammar, geography, or arithmetic yet?"

"I don't know any, no one taught me those things."

"So you can't even count to ten, you don't even know your numbers!"

They all started to laugh at me, and my forehead got hot.

"I can count to ten and I know my numbers," I said.

"And have you heard the French language or seen it written?"

"Yes, I often heard the little countesses speaking French and I saw a French newspaper. The countesses' teacher gave it to me to keep. The paper was big, it had pictures and the letters were all the same size."

"Good. What lecture comes next?" she asked the designated one.

"Arithmetic," she answered, putting down a marble slate for each of us to write on.

The teacher started explaining that singular numbers were written in single digits to 9, and tens were written with two digits up to a hundred, hundreds were written with three digits up to a thousand, thousands consisted of four digits. She explained it and told us to take note of it correctly.

"What are you telling me?" I was thinking, "I already know all that."

"Did you understand that?" she asked. "We understand, we understand..." they all replied.

"Now all of you write the number a hundred and one on your tablet and show it to me."

They all wrote 1001 and I wrote 101. Again she explained that this was four digits, a thousand and one. A hundred has to be just three digits. "You learned it last year."

They all puzzled over it and remained seated while writing. The teacher didn't show what I had put down, but not one of them had written it correctly.

"Aren't you ashamed of yourselves?" the teacher scolded, "Julka heard it for the first time and understood it and you didn't."

Later, other lectures followed: reading and writing were easy for me. I knew it better than all of them. I grasped geography quickly, too.

The hardest was studying grammar, especially French. I couldn't understand anything. Like a woodpecker I hammered the words into my brain, memorizing them.

As I've already mentioned, there was no shortage of guests at Aunt's. Not a day went by that someone didn't come to visit. While we were busy studying, we'd hear the rattling of a carriage, and the maid would come running, saying: "Little Miss! Please go join the guests, so and so has arrived."

Instructing us to go on reading and writing, our teacher would fix her hair and go out to greet the guests.

We got to know what kind of guests they were by how long they were staying. If they were guests from farther away, some ladies—we tossed our books aside right away, straightened our dresses, and combed our hair—we'd know that we'd have to see the visitors at tea or dinner. But if the guests were simple folk from nearby, we knew that they'd soon leave, so we'd stick close to our books. But how much we really studied—that was for us to know.

Sometimes no guests came for several days. Then we got so bored: we'd wait and listen, maybe someone would come rumbling into the yard.

Often Aunt herself went visiting. Our teacher always went along with her. She'd leave us lectures for several days ahead, for however long she meant to stay away. That sure was a happy time for us: we did whatever we felt like doing.

And when the teacher was home, on Saturday, it was only half a day of school. Right at the stroke of twelve, the teacher would read from the Bible, explaining a little about what it meant. We'd pray together, "The angel greeted us," and off we'd go to lunch. We had Saturday afternoon off. It was no trouble to figure out what to do on our own.

Often on Sundays we couldn't go to church because there were so many of us—we couldn't all fit in the wagon. The older ones went, and the smaller ones stayed home. Nonetheless, we had to say the rosary and recite the mass prayers, but we found time to play cards, too.

Aunt and all the daughters were very pious, firmly believing that you could get anything you asked for by praying to God. So all kinds of novenas, hymns, meditations, and all types of intentions took place. And in the month of May, every evening until well into the night, there were prayers at the Holy Virgin's picture, especially decorated just for the month. Aunt's girls prayed: one read aloud, and the others repeated in a whisper or answered the Litany by saying, "pray for us." This was torture for me: I just knelt and dozed, holding on so I wouldn't keel over. Every year this was how we suffered each evening throughout the month of May.

And so I studied like this for three years. I went home in the summer and for the holidays–Christmas and Easter. If the roads were good, my folks would come and get me, but sometimes I'd have to spend the holy days at Aunt's, too.

They taught us all about etiquette, manners, and even dances. They instilled in us everything that would make us better and warned us against evil ways, but they couldn't break me of the habit of lying.

From my youth, all on my own, I learned how to lie very cleverly; after doing something horrible–to deny it and weasel out of it. Even though Mother or my older sisters caught me lying outright, they would try to embarrass or shame me out of it, and I would promise never to lie again, to always tell the truth. But in no time at all, somehow, I wouldn't even be aware of it, I'd tell a lie about something or other.

My sister Juzė, who was smaller than I, was weak, sickly, and spoiled by Mama. I used to play all kinds of tricks on her: if she got some delicious treat, I would grab it and devour it, or I would turn her around and shove her. She'd start to cry and tell on me. I'd deny it all and lie my way out of it: "I didn't do anything; I didn't see a thing." It was the same when I was being schooled: lying was just a way for me to get what I wanted. Whenever I did something, I knew how to wiggle out of it wonderfully well. "I didn't see anything; I don't know anything about it; it wasn't me who took it."

Every summer, Dr. Solovjov's Russian wife and children from Telšiai would stay at Aunt's for several weeks. At the same time, other guests came to visit, the neighbors Underavyčiai, accompanied by their unmarried brother, Sirutavyčia. After convincing me to be her accomplice, Solovjov's older daughter, Maša, a girl of around fifteen, and I hid a stone in Sirutavyčia's coat sleeves. The coat hung in the entry. She made me promise that under no circumstances was I to leak a word about it or to confess to it. When he was ready to leave, the young master pulled and tugged on his coat, ripped the sleeves, and got angry. Our young misses and ladies and the doctor's teacher, Nadiežda Ivanovna, helped him to unroll the stone and apologized profusely for such an embarrassment. They promised to investigate and punish those responsible.

Both of us kept quiet. After seeing the guests off, they immediately flew at me: I denied it to save my life–"I don't know, I didn't see anything."

Suddenly like a ball shot out of a cannon, Maša shouted: "I, I did it, I did. The two of us, Julka and I did it," and she pointed at me.

And I had just denied everything. How do you like that? I was so ashamed, so disgraced, and so angry at Maša. No sooner did she forbid me to tell them than she went ahead and blabbed it first. What a traitor! Furious at Maša, I promised myself never to listen to such friends who told you to lie, but I swore to always tell the truth, whether I'd done something good or bad. But my friends didn't believe me much any longer, having caught me lying repeatedly. If I told the truth straight from my heart–they'd smile and ask: "How do we know you're not lying?"

But I heard Aunt defending me, "What can we expect? She grew up with the little peasants. She was friends with them, so how could she learn anything decent? It's lucky she only learned to lie and not something worse."

*

Later, Aunt's daughter, our teacher, took ill. She could teach us only a little because mostly she had to attend to the guests, and then she had to waste time visiting, so there wasn't any time left to teach us. Aunt hired a Polish lady teacher from Vilnius, from the Vizitkos Convent School, to replace her. At the same time, she took in three new pupils from outside, and there were still three of Aunt's little ones, for a total of six pupils, which had been the agreement with the teacher. There wasn't any room left for schooling me. However, Aunt didn't allow me to leave her: she told me to read, write, and learn on my own. Sometimes the teacher took it upon herself to explain something to me. At other times Poliusia, our former teacher, would show me what I asked—when she had the time. Besides my studies, I often helped around the house.

Slowly I grew into a little miss, a servant, a housekeeper, a messenger, and a seamstress all at the same time. Anybody could count on me for anything: if somebody was late with some job, I had to pitch in. If guests came, I had to serve them; if they were staying overnight, I made the beds and got everything ready. Sometimes I had to prepare the dinner and sit at the table as well. If something needed to be bought, I hurried to the village or to the women sharecroppers' for butter or sour cream or to bring home some eggs. Then, on my return, inevitably some different job awaited: pick apples, dry them, see to the bees, make preserves. You never knew from which direction some job would jump out at you. Not to mention, sewing the shirts, mending for everybody, again it was my job. I found time to read and write only in the evenings, when the days got longer. And at other times when there was company, then the evenings were taken, too. If some young people came, I had to play and dance at the same time. Many a time, leaving the dancing, I had to pass around a tray with berries and preserves for the guests, for you see, it was not proper for Aunt's girls to do the serving–it was my job because the chambermaid was too little, only about fourteen years old, so it was up to me to carry out her duties, too.

But I enjoyed myself, and I was happy. In summer we ran around berry and mushroom picking with the young people, wearing ourselves out. At home we still had to learn how to dance and play games afterwards. We played cards until they called me to do some job or other. Sometimes in the summer I'd go home to my parents, but not for long: right away Aunt would be writing for me to come back–there was something important coming up. Father harnessed the horses and took me over.

In the summers, while staying at my parents' together with Stasys, I often got to read some books borrowed from the neighbor, Endrijauskis. His little estate, close to us, was also called Bukantiškės. Being a very educated old bachelor, he read newspapers, so he'd come over to our house and tell us all the news. I can barely remember the time when Endrijauskis came over and informed us about the war in Sevastopol. How the French were dropping bombs on the Russkies, shooting their cannons, and mowing down the Russkies like sheaves of rye.

The Russkies were starving, eating horse meat. One time he came and told us some very big news: that Tsar Nicholas I had died. The Russkies lost the war and left a lot of people behind, lying there dead. Although I was still quite young, nevertheless, I remembered it well.

Endrijauskis owned a lot of books and lent them to me to read. They were all in Polish; mostly I borrowed books by Kraszewski.

I remembered one more event from my young days.

One time some men came from the manor to fish in our pond. There were many of them by our pond. They pulled out large fish and tossed them into a barrel full of water. We were watching them. All of a sudden, one of the men jumped into the pond with a splash. Wading in deeper, he cried out: "I'll drown myself first before I get drafted."

The men on the shore sprang into action; some ran to the other side of the pond, others climbed onto a raft. And my mama, standing right on the edge of the pond, started shouting: "Mykol, Mykolėli! Save your soul: just think, if you drown yourself—you'll go to hell. Don't drown yourself, come on now, wade back out, can't you see the devil is egging you on, he'll snatch your soul—cross yourself! You're much too young—you'll do your twenty-five years of army service and you'll still have a life after that."

Either that shouting of hers helped change his mind, or Mykolas came to his senses. Wading back to shore, he submitted to being tied up. They brought the tied-up Mykolas back to our cottage and we boiled the fish. Mykolas announced, "If it wasn't a mortal sin, I really would have drowned myself."

I had heard the bondsmen saying that "they're out capturing recruits" and drafting them, but now for the first time, I saw someone caught, tied up, and handed over to the recruiters. Crawling behind the stove, I couldn't stop crying for a long time: I felt so bad for Mykolas being turned over to the recruiters. A long time passed, and I'd already grown up a little. I was studying at Aunt's when Mykolas Jonušas returned from the army. By then there weren't any bondsmen left on the estates. As it turned out, Mykolas married a pretty girl.

The Uprising Begins

After that more restless times followed: they freed the people from their masters. Although Aunt didn't own many serfs, even the ones she had started to scatter far and wide.

There was the driver, Stasiukas Blažiniauskiukas; the pig herder, Pranukas, raised on the estate from his youth–that one abandoned the pigs and went off somewhere right away, without so much as a by your leave. Stasiukas also refused a place, even though they offered him a salary, but he didn't want to be a slave anymore, so he left. Those freedmen who had their own land and went to the *corvée* stayed where they were: they had some land measured off for them. Aunt had just a few of those kind of bondsmen; I believe there were only the two brothers Kiaurakis.

Mostly Aunt had built small cottages on the estate's land, and those were already inhabited by Jews. There were all kinds of tradesmen there–butchers, shopkeepers, merchants. The Jews had a tavern and a school, and they managed a little land as well. For that reason, not much of Aunt's land was divided up and given away.

Afterwards the ladies started to dress in mourning: they all dressed in black. Everyone talked about it, and the newspapers wrote about beatings and demonstrations in Warsaw and elsewhere in Poland, about how the Russkies shattered a Polish cross during some procession and, while they were dispersing the procession, murdered five people. All the ladies dressed in mourning to honor those five fallen victims.

They started praying and singing hymns in the churches. During some feast day or mass, the organ would fall silent, and immediately the ladies and gentlemen would bleat out the hymn in Polish, "God Save Poland." The people in the courtyard and those scattered around the edges laughed. "See how the masters are howling at the loss of their people. They want to get their serfs back."

To tell the truth, the masters did become anxious. Get-togethers upon get-togethers, meetings on top of meetings, there was no end to it. Outdoing each other, they went around in their carriages, on horseback, even on foot to meet. They'd discuss, consult, and write to each other, sending messengers back and forth. Then they'd drink, scold, kiss, sing hymns and patriotic songs: "Then masters and peasants will all be equal" or "You'll get pieces of land, just stay out of the sand. Those who destroyed us, destroyed lots of churches." All kinds of new songs appeared.

We started to befriend the hired girls and sing with them. We'd bring them into the piano room and learn Lithuanian songs and tunes from them. I had the upper hand here as well, because from my youth, I had learned a lot of songs and I also knew the melodies. And at this time, freedom and equality became fashionable.

It's too bad my Onikė is so far away, I thought to myself. Now nobody would keep her away from me.

During that winter everything was stirring like yeast, rising and foaming: they discussed and consulted, always in secret, always in whispers. A number of committees made up of masters and priests sprang up, and ladies' committees, too. They started to talk about war more and more loudly: "All the young masters and adolescents will go into the woods. They'll lead bands of peasants to beat the Russkies. The ladies and young misses will stay home and care for the rebels' food. Some will take bread, meat, and milk to the forest, others clothing and underwear."

Everyone agreed to do everything so readily because no one thought that they would have to wait long in the woods as rebels: the French would come to their aid very soon. Together they would capture and beat up all those Russkies, pin them down like frogs and throw them out of Poland and Lithuania. Then we'd all enjoy freedom and equality.

All those meetings of the masters, all those decisions were always made in secret: they kept the young people–especially the girls–far away from it all. We overheard only a phrase here, or a word there. We were so curious because it was so important to find out: we really wanted to take part in such great, important work–defending our homeland from the Russkies.

Spring was approaching. The month of February was warm, even hot in the daytime. The birds were flitting about; the insects were humming; the frogs were croaking. Some years it wasn't this warm even in May. God was providing all this for the war! During the ancient rebellions, as far back as old people could remember, the springs were warm. That's the way it was this year–an early and warm spring was a good omen for winning the war. God was helping the Poles, that's why He was providing favorable weather. We rejoiced and waited for the beginning of the war with trembling hearts. "For the homeland, for the holy homeland."

And when it starts, conquering the Russkies won't take long,
To chase them out of our land with a song.
Then masters and peasants will all be equal
And for the last time we'll sing together:
From the Austrians, Russians and Prussians
We'll take back our dear homeland!

We sang these songs and similar ones with the girls who worked outdoors. We taught them patriotic songs, but those were mostly in Polish, and the simple country girls understood only Lithuanian.

Somewhere there were committees formed, which drew up lists of young men eager to join the war–to go into the woods. They started to say that this one and that one had signed up; among them were many young gentlemen whom we knew.

Aunt had a hired man named Juozas (I no longer remember his last name). He knew a bit of Polish and grappled with a few words like *vego počego*–meaning, "why did this come to pass?" He said he was a nobleman from Tytavėnai. The girls told us that Juozas had signed up for the forest fight. We didn't say anything: after all, it was a secret, but we took good care to send him off properly. We sewed him some new underclothes, two changes, some socks, and Aunt bought him some new shoes. We waited for his departure.

One night the dogs started barking without ceasing; somebody was knocking on the door. Juozas was leaving, saying he wanted to say goodbye. We got wind of it in the attic, and all of us flew headfirst out of bed and down the stairs. We looked around–across from the porch the yard was full of men with several horses. They said they had come to take Juozas to the camp.

Our hearts were pounding, our arms and legs shaking, tears even came to our eyes from joy to see real Polish patriots, fighters against the Russkies. We gave Juozas all his gifts, and he ran off to get dressed. Meanwhile, we didn't know what kind of hospitality to offer those Poles, what to give them to eat. But they turned down our treats, not wanting anything. They were in a hurry to reach the encampment before dawn.

Juozas got ready, gathered up all his clothes, tied them up in a bundle. He even had a rifle of sorts—some kind of stick. We said goodbye, blessed the heroes, kissed them with tears in our eyes. They were valiant, and this was how they carried on:

"What are Russkies to us? We'll pin them down like frogs! As you see us standing here, each one will take down five Russkies. And if we take ten, there won't be one parasite left."

We saw them off, we blessed them—you had to admire such dedication greatly. We couldn't go to sleep until dawn. Our heroes stood before our eyes, their determined words rang in our ears—to kill off the Russkies.

People started to talk: one came upon a Polish encampment here, another somewhere else. The Poles surrounded the Pušinės tavern. They looted everything they found at the Jewish owner's and carried it off: whiskey, beer, bagels, cheese, eggs. At another place they stopped at a village and demanded food. The Poles had hung Pušinės's steward; his wife was left with five children. He had been a very decent man. It wasn't only the country folk who pitied him, but the committee ladies also mourned him and were angered at the Poles' deeds.

That's how the uprising began.

The police sprang into action, too: they arrested the suspected noblemen whose sons had disappeared into thin air and kept them until they revealed where their sons were hidden. They especially took note of those who were singing hymns in church.

There was an officer of the gendarmerie in Telšiai named Brandtas, who made it his mission to follow the rebels and catch them. He did this eagerly and endlessly, following those who sang in church and spying on the suspects.

Once during the Feast of St. Anthony in Telšiai, the masters and ladies, as always, started singing during the mass. That gendarme stood up in church and was writing down the names of the ones who were singing. That day someone in particular by the name of Petrulevičia took over the role of self-appointed guardian. Seeing the gendarme writing, he went straight up to him and poked him under the nose with the knob of his cane: "Kneel!" The man didn't listen, so he ordered him again: "Kneel down!" When he still didn't listen, Petrulevyčia grabbed the gendarme by the scruff of his neck and pushed him out the door! Then he waved to the people in the churchyard to throw him out. And there were a lot of people there. The people pounced on him; immediately bricks and rocks started to whistle past the gendarme's ears. He ran and fell on his knees, barely making it out of the churchyard. Later, when they interrogated Petrulevyčia, they asked: "What right did you have to throw the gendarme out of church?"

"That's my service," he replied, "that's my duty—to watch the church during the Consecration, to make sure that everyone is kneeling. If someone disobeys and won't kneel, no matter who he is, the police or whoever, I have to throw them out."

"He's Russian Orthodox, not Catholic—he doesn't have to kneel."

"Then he shouldn't come to our church," he answered, "and if he does, he has to follow the rules like everyone else."

"And why are you acting like the guardian of the church? You serve as a deacon—you're in the civil service, why are you engaging in work that isn't yours?"

"During confession the priest made me repent for my sins. I am carrying out my penance."

Having lied his way through the interrogation and weaseling out of it, he came home. At our house–that is, at Aunt's in Šė-mos–all hell had broken loose: there wasn't a night that some-one didn't come knocking. Several Poles, as we called them, would appear at night or come riding on horseback with papers and orders from the camp: deliver such and such here, so much bread to such and such a place, or so many shirts to some other place.

One had to feed these messengers, but you couldn't really trust the hired hands to do it. Aunt woke us up: one of us heated up the samovar, another boiled eggs, sizzled meat and bacon in the pan, another served food to the Poles. And they hurried to stuff their faces while the tea was brewing. At the same time, they'd tell us their deeds: how many Russkies they'd pierced and killed, where they'd attacked their camps and twisted the heads off of all the enemy they found. We were dumbfounded, we hadn't heard anything. But they explained that things like that were not to be repeated; the Russkies were being destroyed quietly like so many bedbugs.

We tripped all over ourselves to treat such heroes in the man-ner they deserved.

The papers that were brought had to be delivered to the prop-er place. And the documents were always sent to the committee. The committee was composed of the ladies who took care of the food and clothing: Mrs. Goštautas in Kegiai, Mrs. Gudonis in Vambutai, and my aunt in Šėmos. The other ladies were farther away and didn't tell us who they were: the first three lived right in the neighborhood. Aunt would read what the documents said. She'd tell us to carry them to Vambutai and Kegiai. It was six versts to each place.

After a sleepless night on account of serving the guests, we then had to carry the papers six versts. It was not safe to send any of the hired help. Sometimes one of the committee ladies would come and tell us what they needed, however many shirts to take here or there.

"Girls, get to sewing. Here, I've even brought you some cloth." She'd hand us a whole roll of linen or cotton.

"Just hurry because they need it right away," she'd command.

There were six girls, but only three of us knew how to sew; the two older ones and the little one didn't know how, and so the three of us would sit hunched over for three days, sewing. We hadn't seen or heard of sewing machines yet, so we'd keep pricking away with our little needles and always as fast as we could. Realizing that we wouldn't be able to sew what had been ordered in time, we had to sit around the table by candlelight and work the entire night. If we were lucky, the Poles didn't detain us, but if they showed up from somewhere, we'd have to feed them and put the samovar on. It was such a waste of time and took us away from our work.

We would just manage to cut and sew one roll of cloth, when the committee ladies would already be delivering another roll. Again they urged us to hurry and sew it up. The number of shirts we made—not even the angels could count. The number of nights we went without sleep—only the devils could figure that out.

The Magpie Wedding

Aunt's daughter Valerka, the second oldest one, was getting married to Grigorius Ulinskis–it was an unusual wedding. You see, it was a year of war and mourning. Not only did the wedding have to be without music and dancing, but the wedding guests' attire had to be patriotic, too. Before the wedding the young misses and the ladies got together and agreed to all dress the same in Polish *kontush*, which had come into fashion, a dress with double sleeves. One set of sleeves was narrow, tightly fitting the arm; the second set was long and wide, not sewn together, attached only at the shoulder together with the sleeves, hanging like wings, called *viliotai*. These loose sleeves were lined in black or white silk, depending on one's preference. The *viliotai* hung down at the sides or were thrown over the shoulders so that they hung down one's back.

All the helpers at the wedding were in black with white *viliotai*. On their heads they wore four square-horned confederate hats, also in black and white: they looked like magpies–black bodies with white under their wings.

The men didn't have a particular style: outer coats and tails, students in uniform, whatever anybody could muster.

Aunt knew countless people from far and wide, and she had even more relatives. The invited guests filled the whole manor, not leaving any room even for a mosquito.

It was Sunday, so the whole wedding party–as many as a dozen or so carriages–drove to the church to attend mass. The wedding ceremony was right after mass, performed by the Reverend Deacon Senulevyčia, who was specially invited to perform it.

The vicar, Father Bernevyčia, climbed up to the pulpit and gave the sermon. After the ceremony the whole wedding party went outdoors–and the rest of the guests shoved to get outside behind the group of magpies. The whole church was in an uproar; no one was listening to the sermon. The vicar shouted: "All you who don't want to hear God's word, just pushing and shoving, be damned! You'll go wherever the devil takes you–straight to hell." He continued with similar threats and curses.

The wedding guests heard the vicar's cursing, but it wasn't until they got home that they started laughing. During the dinner, who should pop in but the vicar. Oh my goodness! How the masters took to teasing him! They started in on him; whistling, clapping their hands, shouting *"valio!"* The vicar barely managed to escape through the door. Hopping into his carriage, he rushed away from the magpie wedding.

The most prominent guests at the wedding were Aunt's relatives the Citavičiuses–two brothers and two sisters who no longer had their parents. One of the brothers, the elder Zigmantas, had finished his service in the army, but the younger one, Kazimieras, who was still serving as an officer, came to the wedding in a Russian uniform. The other guests, especially the students, gave the young officer dirty looks, made fun of him every way they could think of, and called him an enemy of the homeland. But others, particularly the older masters, held the Citavičiuses in high regard: both brothers and sisters were always placed first among the magpies–as they called them–everyone walked around the Citavičiuses on tiptoe.

"They'll be sure to come! They'll show up!" everyone predicted.

The Citavičiuses were the first to leave the wedding–all the invited guests and those from home saw them off. At the little cemetery in Dargeliškės, everyone drank champagne and said their goodbyes, wishing them a good trip. The remaining guests returned to the wedding.

A couple of weeks after the wedding, we found out that the Citavičiuses had gathered a large regiment and had led them into the woods. The elder Zigmantas, the leader of the regiment, appointed the little officer as his helper. We got our own back: we made sure to keep pointing this out to the students, especially to Stasys: "Who is the greater patriot, you who sit at home doing nothing, or him you call 'the enemy of the homeland,' who throws off his Russian uniform and goes out into the forest to torment the Russkies?"

We didn't rejoice for long—in a few weeks we got news again: a messenger arrived with a letter reporting a great catastrophe—the Russkies had attacked the Citavičius encampment in the Tytavėnai forest. They scattered, beat, and captured all of them. The Russkies stabbed the elder Citavičius, the leader, to death with bayonets; the younger brother, who jumped into a tree, was left alive. Having finished up their work, the Russkies left; then the younger one dragged his brother's corpse back home.

They invited us to the funeral. How many tears flowed, and what sorrow it was for us.

"You see, we said our goodbyes after the wedding, they drank champagne next to the cemetery, we saw them off, and now it's turned into a real cemetery! The little Dargeliškės cemetery was a bad omen. Who could have foreseen this?"

Day and night we mourned, honoring and lamenting them.

Aunt went to the funeral with her oldest daughter. When she came back, she described the solemn fashion in which they had buried the hero: the casket was all covered in white roses and lilies, mobs of people escorted him to the cemetery. The deceased had so many wounds you couldn't count them: his face alone was pierced with seven jabs.

They buried their leader; the regiment was beaten, scattered, or captured. They arrested the younger brother, too, but they didn't recognize him. They questioned him and interrogated him as to who he was. But he didn't reveal his identity; he was afraid that they would shoot him immediately as a deserter from the army. They beat him and tortured him until they found out who he was. He lay like a corpse from the torture for a whole month. When he got somewhat better, they sentenced him to be shot. But because of public concern and high connections–through the influence of family who were generals and ministers–the court lessened the death penalty to twelve years of hard labor.

The third brother in the Citavičius family, the middle one, also had deserted from the army and joined his brother's encampment. He had fought against the Russkies but managed to escape without injury. As a consequence, he couldn't show himself at home.

He went into hiding at Aunt's house. But it wasn't safe for him to stay here for too long. Aunt's brother Abromavyčia lived near Kartėna in Aleksandravas, almost on the very border with Prussia. Aunt came up with the idea of sending the guest to her brother's. Our teacher and I rode in the carriage as young ladies, and the "guest" Citavičius became the driver–we went to Aunt's brother's manor and left him there. Then he crossed the Prussian border and traveled farther. Later, on occasion he would write to us from Paris.

At that time you had to get a permit from the army leader to go to a different town or village. When we traveled, we had permits because my teacher was going to see her uncle and I intended to see my parents. Someone stood guard at every town and often in the villages, too, looking out for where people were moving about. How our legs shook when the guards stopped us to look at our permits; we were afraid they'd stop our driver. But after all, the guards could see that young ladies had to have a driver–they couldn't travel on their own, so no one thought to ask about our driver's permit. Still, we were frightened to death.

Stasiukas Gets Injured

One night, a group of maybe ten Poles showed up with a horrible ruckus; they had agreed to join a camp. They stopped in at Aunt's because Stasiukas was going to go along. He had been in service for a long time at Aunt's manor as her serf; when freedom came, he went his own way. Now, en route to the camp, he and all his friends came over to say goodbye. Stasiukas needed shirts and new shoes. But where was there to buy some? We gave him shirts and underwear and at least some money for shoes. We treated the whole regiment: they finished off a whole samovar of tea, drank up all the milk that had been milked, ate all the bread that had been baked, and put away a whole side of bacon. We saw them off, wished them good luck, and blessed them.

After a few days we looked out in the evening–someone was trying to light a lamp in the sauna, which was beyond the fir trees by the stream.

"There's something unusual going on there," we exclaimed.

Making a foray, we went off to investigate. Why, it's our Stasiukas! His head was bound, and his hand swollen like a log.

"I'm as hungry as a wolf," he growled. "I haven't had a bite to eat since yesterday morning. After I was injured, the camp dispersed, and I've been wandering around all by myself."

We scurried around like little mice! One rushed to bring some food, the others tried to remove his outer clothing. There was no way we could get his sleeve out; when we pulled on it, he screamed. They hurriedly brought some milk and bread. Alas, he couldn't eat anything, he just drank a little.

When everyone had gone to bed, we brought him to our rooms. We cut the coat sleeve with scissors, but the shirt was all soaked with blood, dried up and stiff. His head wasn't too bad, only his face was covered in wounds–he couldn't move his teeth or open his mouth, and it was difficult for him to speak. We washed and cleaned him up, gave him some more tea, and helped him back to the sauna. Aunt told him to lie down on the straw in the sauna–at daybreak she'd somehow try to get him a doctor.

Not far away in a cabin, the Jewish woman Maušienė lay ill. Aunt called for the horses, and Maušas brought Doctor Pšibilski from Telšiai. After calling at the sick woman's cabin, he came over to the manor. While walking around with the young ladies, he also visited the sauna.

Stasiukas's face was not seriously injured, just burned by the gunpowder. His eyes were all right too, only his eyebrows were singed. But his arm! When he was holding his arm out to shoot his revolver, the enemy had fired and the bullet entered through his fingers, exiting through his shoulder. The path of the bullet had turned his whole arm blue.

The doctor cut the skin all the way down his arm, cleansed the wound, and bandaged it, saying that if it had been left just a little bit longer, gangrene would have set in.

What a frenzy it was for us, what with running around for warm water, rags, cotton batten, medicine. We'd bring one thing, and they were already clamoring for something else; we had no choice but to rush around and hide ourselves.

At last the doctor finished attending to the patient and promised to send him medicine by way of Maušas. He showed us how to bandage the arm, how to cleanse the wound, which medicine to put in the water, and which to put on the wound.

We took care of Stasiukas for a couple of weeks—every morning we brought warm water, soaked his arm, threw away the rags, washed the arm with medicine. The doctor had sent over some powder that we put on the wound and bandaged the arm exactly the way the doctor had instructed.

Having been cared for and fed well, Stasiukas decided to go deeper into the forest—he didn't stay in the sauna in the daytime, he'd come back only at night to eat. If we got there first, we'd just leave his dinner out. He'd eat it when he came back and then he'd go out again. No sooner did we bring back the dishes than we'd have to worry about the dinner again. Most of that work fell to me.

Our Stasiukas was already feeling better—his arm and face had settled down. One night several Poles came again—one was always the commander, the others just foot soldiers. They told us they were from the regiment that Stasiukas had abandoned. We began asking how Stasiukas was getting along. "Poorly," they informed us, "he was injured, and we don't know where he is now, but he was injured because of his own stupidity."

"How so? Did you fight with the Russkies? What happened?"

"Go on!" the Poles say, "On their way to joining the regiment, Stasiukas and all his friends went to the tavern and got drunk like pigs. Dead drunk, they came to the forest. The guards met them and asked, 'Who goes there?' They answered, 'Our own.' The suspicious guards wouldn't let them into the camp. They started to curse in Russian and a commotion ensued. Hearing the Russian language, they thought the Russkies were attacking the camp. They grabbed their guns in fright and fired in alarm. Immediately the drunken ones who'd also arrived shot their revolvers. By the time they'd figured it out and recognized who had come, two from the camp were slightly injured and Stasiukas seriously because they had burned his eyes.

"The colonel ordered Stasiukas to be hanged for disturbing the peace, but he hid somewhere—we couldn't figure out where he had disappeared."

We didn't tell the Poles where Stasiukas was hiding. But in the morning, we started to tease him endlessly and tell everyone how he got so drunk that he started a hullabaloo and almost ended up hanging from a branch.

Stammering, Stasiukas defended himself, but the same day he disappeared from the sauna; he didn't even come back to eat.

Later on we found out that he was at his sister's—hale and hearty.

The Wounded Stranger

I came across another wounded stranger in Medingėnai. The Poles brought an injured man to master Šiukšta's and left him in one of the rooms. Šiukšta was frightened, so he ordered his horses to be harnessed and left for Telšiai to tell the officials to come and get their man, who was lying unconscious in his house. In the meantime, Šiukštienė sent a message to her brother Underavyčia, asking him to help the wounded man escape. She was afraid the Russkies would come and take him away and kill him. Underavyčia rushed to Aunt's on horseback; everyone sprang into action. Right away they harnessed the horses and put straw in the wagon. Ulinskis, Aunt's son-in-law, and Underavyčia got in. They needed a third person. While the two of them were carrying the wounded man, someone had to watch the horses. Who's going to go?

"I will, I will!" I jumped up, volunteering, "I'll go as long as you'll take me."

In a flash my kerchief was on my head and I was in the wagon. We moved at a gallop, as fast as the horses could carry us, hurrying to get ahead of the Russkies. The sun went down, the night was dark. There were still about two *versts* to go, and we were racing along a pitted dirt road, rocks flying, the wagon jumping from side to side.

We got close to the manor. There were no lights visible anywhere—everything was quiet. My masters wound their scarves around their faces and heads; only their eyes were gleaming. They broke off some short sticks to use for revolvers and laughed: "If the Russkies got the injured one, we'll have some fun with Šiukšta: we'll take him to hang or to be executed."

Once our horses cooled off; one lash of the whip, and we galloped up to the porch. They threw the reins to me and both jumped out of the wagon. One hammered on the door while the other knocked on the window. They talked and shouted in unison; you'd think there were ten people out there.

"Who is it?" someone from inside asked timidly.

"Open the door! Let us in! If you don't, we'll burn the place down."

Šiukšta pried the door open: pale, with hands trembling. Even the candle he was holding flickered.

At the same instant, my masters pressed their sticks into his chest, and both cried out in unison: "What did you do with the injured Pole?"

"He's l-l-lying inside the r-r-room. Take him."

"Turn the light on!" They stamped the ground with their feet. "Help us carry him out, or we'll hang you."

Holding onto his dressing gown, first Šiukšta, then my masters, burst into the rooms. All of them lifted the body and carried him out straight away. The injured man was bloody, muddy, frozen with one leg shot entirely through and a bullet lodged in his shoulder. They put him down on the straw, his head on my lap. We took off.

They didn't say anything else to Šiukšta, afraid that he'd recognize their voices. Once again we feared running into the Russkies. We couldn't move quickly because the victim shouted with pain. He said the lady gave him food and drink, but no one attended to his wounds. He wanted to be taken to his uncle, who lived in the woods near Žarėnai.

It was dark, and we didn't know the roads. We made a racket riding through the tree stumps, rocks, and bogs. When the horses came to a stop, the man was moaning. Day broke and the sun rose before we got to our destination. The people were old. When they saw the injured man, they gave in to despair. Without saying a word, my masters carried the sick man inside; then when they returned to the wagon, we rolled off. Neither the old people nor the sick man knew who it was that came from out of nowhere to rescue him from the Russkies' hands.

We didn't hear any more about the man's identity, whether he got well, where he disappeared to—nor did anyone seem to care.

Only Šiukšta complained that the Russkies came and, when they didn't find the injured man, almost tore him to pieces, threatening to hang or shoot him. He defended himself by saying that a whole regiment came in the middle of the night and took the man away.

"Did a lot of Poles come to get him?" Underavyčia asked Šiukšta on purpose.

"Who could count them—they invaded the whole manor," he related heatedly. "They almost broke the door down, nearly shattering the windows, they poked their revolvers into me—a whole regiment—by wagon, on horseback, on foot: who could account for all of them—it was pitch black."

The Poles at the Camp

So that was the extent of the injured who I saw during that summer. However, I came across many healthy Poles. Once one of them came in the evening without his weapons and said that there were more of them in the bushes by the barn. The Russkies had attacked their group in the Pušinė forest. They didn't have a commander and didn't fight; they just ran off and hid. They had gathered together in a group in search of a larger camp. Now they were dispersed and didn't know one another's whereabouts. Now they were hungry because they hadn't managed to get even a bite of bread anywhere. They were afraid to go inside anyone's house.

When the family had gone to bed, aunt invited all of them to come inside and eat.

About six of them entered–four were decently dressed, but two were ragged and dirty: nothing but tattered shirts on their backs. They complained that they had been wandering around for many days. Perhaps ten of them had banded together, but they had no leader and didn't know where to find a larger group. Wherever they begged for food, they managed to get only half a loaf of bread, but they were chased away from other places and left empty-handed.

We fed them with whatever we had. We gave the ragged ones clothes and newly sewn underwear. Halfway through the night, we saw them off. They intended to press on toward the Papilė forest, where there was a large encampment led by Commander Pisarskis. Maybe all the scattered fighters would unite there.

In the morning the hired girls were laughing and telling us: "Young ladies, take away the pile of dirt that the Poles left behind the barn."

"We haven't seen any Poles, nor are we interested in their rot," we shot back.

But we were still concerned as to what was left behind the barn–maybe it was an injured Pole or a dead one.

Taking the long way around, we went to take a look from the orchard side. Why, it was a pile of clothes and rags–dirty, worn-out shirts. We came closer and found that they were full of lice, just creeping and crawling in heaps. My friends ran away, sick to their stomachs. I picked up the vile heap with a stick, dragged it off, and threw it in the pond–I disposed of the rags and drowned the live critters with it.

We kept avoiding the family, who acted as if they saw no one or heard anything. But the family, along with the hired girls, kept laughing at us. They observed every one of our steps and took note of everything we did. How could you hide anything from those you live with?

Once Gudonienė, who I thought was the chair of the committee, arrived in a fancy carriage, she sent her driver off to the post office. She had loaded the carriage with bread, meat, and pickles. She had received word that Jablonauskis's camp was spending the nights in the Karstėniai woods and provisions had to be delivered there at night. We piled in every bit of what was in the wagon and what Aunt added in the form of bread, meat, and a little barrel of milk.

"Who will take everything there?"

Gudonienė said that she had to go to meet with Jablonauskis herself, but she didn't want to go alone. She decided to take our teacher along for company.

"And who's going to show the way? Who knows it?"

"I do, of course, I do. I know how to get there, and I know the road."

I wanted to see the encampment in the worst way. This was a golden opportunity. My ladies were getting the wagon stocked.

More cigars, matches, a candle. Slowly, slowly they got it ready—finally they were done, and we were on our way.

The new moon was shining, so we had to hurry before it slipped out of sight.

I was familiar with the Karstėniai wood, but it was big, and we had no idea where the Poles were spending the night. We were on the road to Žarėnai. Before we knew it, the Karstėniai Lake was glistening. The tavern was already close by. Without any warning, two armed men jumped out of the bushes and blocked our way.

"Who goes there?" they asked in Polish.

"Freedom and unity," answered the ladies.

The men raised their caps. The ladies told them that they'd brought provisions, which had to be taken to the camp.

"We expected them for supper," said the Poles, "but now it's late. We think the men went to sleep without eating."

One of them whistled, another one ran up, and they told him to take us to the camp to unload the wagon. Taking the horses by the muzzle, our driver led them off the road through the bushes, then he turned them to the right, then to the left, then set them on the narrow path, and said: "Go this way, the camp will be straight ahead."

We drove along. It was dark in the woods, and the horses didn't want to budge. The ladies were accusing me angrily of not knowing how to drive. I gave the horses a hard whip, and they trotted downhill into a dip in the road. Suddenly we heard a clanging sound: ding ding! as the wheels got stuck and finally wouldn't move at all.

Getting out, Gudonienė struck some matches and, lighting everything up, stared in amazement: a weapon as large as a log lay under our wheels. Immediately some people surrounded us. "Who are you? Where are you from? Why are you here? Arrest them, hang them."

My ladies tried explaining who they were, telling them where they came from. A commotion arose, more people appeared from the woods. Another man came running. You couldn't see what he looked like in the dark, but you could tell that he was older because all the others got out of his way. He butted in and started swearing at my ladies: "You filthy sluts, you stupid night owls, you drag yourselves here and then light up your matches." Lowering his voice, he muttered, "Isn't it enough that you give people no rest, but you want to bring the Russkies down on our heads, too?"

He cursed us out with the most vulgar words, mixing us up with all the devils there could possibly be. During his sputtering, I said to the others, "Take the provisions out of the wagon, empty it."

They descended on the wagon like a flock of ravens—grab, grab, grab! One pulled out the bag with meat, another the barrel of milk, a third helped himself to the bread, another to the cake: they yanked everything from the wagon and disappeared with it.

My ladies were stammering, making excuses, but all that the angry man could shout was: "Get out! Get the hell out of my sight!"

He ordered the guards to turn the horses around, take them to the road, and chase them away.

They turned my horses around, and two men led the horses, one on each side, while another two men walked alongside the wagon. And it took no time to get us onto the road by the tavern.

"Russians," they cried out and disappeared into the bushes. My ladies caught their breath. "Are we going to take everything back with us? It's a pity."

"What do you mean!" I gasped. "There's not a crumb left in the wagon–they removed everything."

"We didn't get a chance to ask if that was the same Jablonauskis who was so rude to us. As soon as they saw us, they thought we were Russkies."

"Who could have predicted such impertinence?"

"We have to write to the central committee. They need to know this."

Feeling downcast as if we'd accomplished nothing, heads hung low, we headed for home.

I never had the opportunity to see another encampment.

The Visiting Soldiers

We ran around like that all spring. We fed anyone who showed up and brought food to the woods for whoever needed it, but when we took it to the designated place, they would take the provisions away at the roadside and wouldn't let us into the camp. We kept on sewing underwear. The ladies from the committee would deliver fabric to us and take away the things we'd finished: they knew who needed it.

And we kept waiting for the French.

"When, oh when will our saviors arrive?" we sighed. "That will be the end of the Russkies!"

One month went by, and another, then a third and a fifth. There were no Frenchmen in sight.

One evening after sunset, someone whistled in the fir trees beyond the stream, then whistled again.

"Those are our men!" we winked at each other. "It's the signal we agreed. The Poles are letting us know that they're coming tonight."

Dusk fell. The family went to bed after supper, while we waited and got ready for the company. We heated up the samovar.

"Why do you need the samovar?" one girl asked on her way to bed.

"We're going to wash our hair," I replied, "We need hot water."

We sliced the bread and meat and cut up the bacon. When everything quieted down, we lit the candle and placed it in the living room window as a signal that we were expecting guests. Shortly after, someone knocked on the window. We opened the door—the porch was full of men, some still in the yard. When fifteen came in, the blood drained from our faces. They were completely different from our ordinary Poles. They were all in uniform—their jackets were grey, they wore tall black boots with spats, purple confederate hats, wide leather belts. They were all dressed the same way. Greeting us politely, they asked to speak to the lady of the house.

Aunt came out. She spoke to them, asked them to sit down, and in the other room we hurriedly not only set the table but also filled the glasses with tea. We opened the door. Aunt saw that supper was ready and invited the guests in to have some tea.

And how happy they were. They thanked us, saying they were hungry and hadn't seen tea in such a long time.

The soldiers complimented, praised, and flattered us in turn, while they kept on eating and eating. We kept filling the samovar, putting in coal, and at the same time we were so happy that even our hearts beat wildly.

Having eaten their fill, four of them got up, thanked us politely, and went outside to take over from the guards. Another four entered; again we sat them down and found room at the table for all of them to eat.

These four were clean and polite as well. They were all young and handsome with elegant manners. And one of them, whose hands were small and white like some young lady's, was so very young. Not a one of them was like our ragged Poles from the woods.

No one asked them where they came from or where they were going. It was not the custom to ask, especially when it came to such a high-class contingent; in fact, it was unthinkable to question them at all. Obviously, they were very patriotic, talking big about the war and showing no doubts about beating the Russkies. Among other things, they kept repeating: "Any day now the French will show up and we'll give the Russkies a sound thrashing! We'll rattle their bones but good, so they won't sit on our backs anymore."

They hurried to finish eating and inquired about what towns were nearby, what farms and manors were close, and how to get straight to the Pušinės woods.

They talked only to aunt and heaped generous compliments on us, calling us patriots.

We fed them until they were stuffed, gave them lots of tea, and filled their pockets with apples and even pears.

After the guests left, we wondered: "Where did they come from? Probably from the depths of Poland, because you could tell from their speech that they didn't belong to our parish."

As she got into bed, Aunt mused, "Maybe French messengers are making their way around the encampments?"

"Mama really guessed it right," we all agreed.

Lying in bed, we started up lively discussions as to who was the handsomest of those Poles and also about who liked which one the best.

"That tall dark one who sat by the window is the most handsome—remember his eyes! It seemed like they pierced you all the way through."

"Well, no, I disagree, wasn't the blond one with the long hair more handsome? His eyes were such a heavenly blue, so lovely... how aristocratic were his manners."

"The handsomest was the one with the curls."

"Sure he's the most handsome! His nose is crooked, it turned to the right!"

"I liked the one who had his spoon tucked into his belt... obviously it was silver."

"When all is said and done, they were all noblemen, young dukes, not common gentlemen. Could they have been French?"

"It's a pleasure to befriend the likes of these, a privilege to serve such heroes. They're not like our regular ragamuffins."

"These nobles are certainly devoted to their country. I really fell in love with the dark-haired one. I was ready to go off with him."

"Aha! You fell in love with him because when you were serving him his tea, he kissed your hand."

"Didn't the curly-haired one kiss your hand, too?"

"Wonder where they are roaming now, the poor dears?!"

"Tomorrow or the next day the French will pull in. Then we'll..."

"Katrė said the bread flour is almost gone, Mama has to send us to the mill! We may need more flour."

"Tonight they ate two and a half loaves of the family bread, half a ham, three cheeses. And we didn't even put the butter out!"

"There wasn't any churned, where were we supposed to get it from?"

"That's not decent, maybe they wondered–tea without butter, nothing but meat, cheese, and black bread. Those light blue eyes must have done it."

"And those black eyes, dark and deep! Hair like velvet, and the golden ring on his finger."

"He's probably married?"

"How can he be married, so young. His beard is barely coming in."

"And the one with the spoon in his belt, his whiskers are curled like King Poniatowski's."

"They probably have servants at home to take care of them, while here they have to go on foot in the night."

"They didn't use their last names at all, they called each other by their first names–Otto, Bruno, Myroslav, Ceslav, Zigmunt, Myron. The long-haired one is Myron. That's the same as Myroslav."

"Myroslav is the tall one with the big nose."

"My dark-haired one is Zigmunt."

"No, the little one is Zigmunt. Didn't you hear them calling to him: 'Zigmunt, hurry up'?"

"Maybe you mean someone else, I heard the brunet call Zigmunt by name. If only I could meet him somewhere or kiss him in a dream."

"Your brunet is Jurgis."

"No, it's your curly locks who's Jurgis, mine is Zigmunt."

"Oh, Zigmunt, dear heart, it's delightful when we're together."

Arguing away, we started singing and reciting.

"Maybe they were French?"

"But they spoke like Poles do."

"We should have invited them to eat in French: 'Monsieur, je vous prie à table!' Then they would have started using their own language."

I didn't hesitate to start a song:

Oh, Ziggy, my darling,
We are in heaven,
When we're together.

Our sleep dispersed: we chattered until dawn.

Waiting for the French

We had to rise and wash the dishes before the servant girls got up. Then there was the sewing to be done.

After she got up, Aunt wrote a letter and told us to take it to Kegiai.

"Who's going to take it?"

Julka, of course.

"Who'll go with me? I don't want to go by myself."

"Liudka will."

Liudka was younger. We talked as we were running: "If we'd just hear the French cannons trilling. How happy we'd be!"

Mr. Husca from Paminijis was visiting at Kegiai. Having read Aunt's letter, Mrs. Goštautas gave it to her guest. When both of them had read it, they exchanged knowing glances.

They started interrogating the two of us as to the appearance of the night visitors, what they'd talked about, where they'd gone. The two of us gave a heartfelt description of the brunets, blue eyes, and curly locks. They set out a whole dish of pears for us. We ate our pears and told them how the guests had assured us that the French would appear tomorrow or at least by the next day and would smash all the Russkies to pieces. It seemed that we were babbling on so heatedly and Mr. Husca just listened and smiled, but he didn't look at all happy.

After resting a while, we began the journey home. The hot sun was baking us, but we were thinking only about the French.

"When the French come, we'll shower them with affection and give them the best we have. Why, they're our saviors and defenders against the Russkies–if only they'd show up! Then the Girdvainis and Stankus boys wouldn't sit home; they'll take off for the forest. You can't talk them into it now; the father won't let them go. Juozukas would like to join, but he can't get away from his father, and Zenukas is still a shepherd. And it's not enough that Stasius Komaras won't go to the camp himself, he even makes fun of others that go–the scoundrel. Well, well, he'll catch his comeuppance from the French, they'll send that kind off to fight. It's his duty, after all."

We were nearly home when, behind us, we heard a trill from the west, a sound as if erupting from underground–rumble, rumble.

"The French!"

Instantly we headed for home as fast as our feet could carry us. We ran straight past the hay barn, breaking our necks to announce the important news that the French cannon could already be heard. We almost bumped into old man Rumpas coming from the brewery.

"Well, well, little lassies!" he said, "Why are you scurrying around like that: you're so heated up, you'll catch cold. The rain's not coming that fast, the thunder is still rumbling far away."

It was as if the old man had poured a bucket of cold water on us. We looked up and noticed dark clouds rising like a wall from the west, where lightning was crackling, and thunder was rolling in.

We wiped the sweat from our brows, fixed our hair because now we could see horses in the courtyard. Someone had come visiting.

Mrs. Gudonis had come; she was asking about our night visitors. Speculation about them had raised much hope.

"Messengers are making the rounds of the camps, which means the French are close by. Any minute now we'll see the Russkies retreating. We'll tear down their jails and release our men, bringing them to safety."

If not for that ray of hope, you might as well hit your head against the wall.

The End of the Uprising

In fact, the Russkies were bombarding us like mad. Our men couldn't hold them off anywhere. Word was that they beat the Citavyčius camp, took away their weapons, dispersed the fighters, tortured their commander, and pierced him to death. Soon the news came that the Russkies attacked a camp at Kaltinėnai, killing many Poles on the spot. The Russkies beat the Poles again at Papilė. And those they had taken prisoner were carted off every day by the wagonload–they drove the injured ones in wagons and forced the healthy ones to go on foot. All distressing news, but they'll get their own yet.

Worse still: we heard that they arrested the noblemen of the manor–Pilsudskis, Gromčiauskis, Vaišvila, and the reverend Moncevyčia, the parish priest of Telšiai. They carried them off in a covered wagon to an unknown location.

"Here's a bit of sausage for you, dog!" Everyone knew that all these gentlemen had been members of the committee.

"Who turned them in? Who betrayed them?" we wondered and grieved in disbelief.

Soon we got more bad news. In some forest the Russkies arrested Father Noreika in a fight. Before they captured him alive, they said, he felled five Russkies dead on the spot. Father Noreika was the Žarėnai vicar, our acquaintance, a tall, stout priest. Once again we were full of anguish and tears.

The following was the story told on the same day of the arrest of the gentlemen of the manor and the priest.

The masters' committee drew up some kind of documents, announcements, and reports addressed to the central committee in Warsaw. Those papers had to be hand-delivered there. It was not safe to send them in the mail. They delegated Count Čapskis to take the papers to Warsaw in person. They entrusted him with all the documents bearing all their signatures.

Čapskis traveled through Vilnius. Nazimovas, the governor of Vilnius, invited Čapskis to his house for dinner, and after getting the Count drunk, got hold of all the documents. It was likely that Count Čapskis wasn't over his hangover yet and was still sleeping after his dinner with the governor when the Russkies captured all the committee members at home and stuffed them into covered wagons.

Having failed so badly in his mission, Čapskis was terrified to return home. The governor offered him soldiers as guards to escort him there. But the count didn't dare to go home to Beržėnai. Instead, he hid at another one of his estates on the other side of Telšiai. Nevertheless, the Poles visited Beržėnai every night bent on hanging the count. And since they couldn't capture the count himself, they robbed the manor blind until there was nothing left but the walls and the bare shelves.

Another harsh piece of news penetrated us like a cannon shot: "Duke Oginskis is dead!"

All our hopes and aspirations had been placed on the shoulders of the duke. Ever since the beginning of the war, everyone claimed that Oginskis had signed a document in Warsaw that, together with his whole county, he agreed to provide as many men as he had—young and old—arm all of them and send them to join the rebellion as soon as the French made their appearance. Carefully recorded were the number of wagons with weapons, carrying guns and cannons, and the innumerable times the duke had brought them from Prussia.. We knew that there were close to several thousand men in his county, and we needed all of them. As soon as the French showed up for battle, the duke's army would join them for the forest fight, *Valio! Valio!* We would all rejoice at such good news.

But the duke died suddenly, so all the hopes and aspirations of the poor Poles vanished with the wind, and we were crestfallen.

There were all kinds of stories about the duke's death. Rumor had it that his death was announced on purpose and some beggar was buried with considerable pomp in his place. Evidently, the authorities had found out about his preparations for war with the Russkies, but in the meantime, Oginskis escaped to Prussia–otherwise he would have been in deep trouble. Ten or more years later people, were saying that Oginskis was still alive. He came home to his manor from time to time dressed as a Russkie and would leave again after a week or so.

As fate would have it, in the thick of the forest fight, Oginskis's death struck a deep blow to the poor Poles, who were counting on his backing. All of a sudden their hero vanished like a burst bubble.

They shot Father Noreika during the Parcinkulis Feast Day. When they drove the priest outside of town to shoot him, there was a huge throng of people there for the feast day. Crowds of people escorted the priest to his death. The priest shouted to the people from the wagon: "Brothers, don't weep! Have courage! They will shoot me, as they will slaughter and hang dozens of others like me, but in the end death will come to the Russkies. The Poles will conquer them, they will squash those executioners and cleanse our soil."

We weren't present, but those who were there saw it and heard it.

Father Noreika was shot on August 2, and they shot another priest, Gargasas, on September 8, in the same location, in the Telšiai pasture.

Some they shot publicly and paraded them in front of the people, but no one counted how many they killed secretly in the jails or how many they hanged as Polish rebels.

Toward the fall, when it got cold, the scattered Poles started returning from the woods and one by one retreating closer to home. Those who had parents and could manage to come back home in one piece escaped somehow, but those who were injured, even with healed wounds, were stuffed into jails at the first sight of their scars. No one wanted to take those who had gone to the camp into their homes, nor those without parents, or anyone without a home, or the hired hands, because the master was held responsible for sheltering rebels. Aunt's Juozas, whom we saw off with such fanfare and whom we treated more than once in the summer, boasted at that time that he needed to get only two more to make him an officer. That is, if he killed two more Russkies, he would become an officer. He came back in the fall and asked Aunt to hire him again. But Aunt was afraid to take him back because everyone knew he had been in the camp. Although she felt sorry for him, she just couldn't take him in. The poor man left, devastated. I never had the chance to find out where he ended up.

And there were many more like him! Having nowhere to go, most gave themselves up on their own—surrendered to the authorities! There were announcements that said: "Those who give themselves up of their own free will and confess to fighting in the rebellion, these men will not be court-martialed."

But we had no way of knowing how the government treated those who surrendered.

Most of those who returned from the forest surrendered to the Russian army of their own free will. They replaced their brothers or hired themselves out as mercenaries for those about to be drafted. Some poor Polish rebels were found frozen to death in the woods.

Siege at Paežerė

One young man, my mother's relative, who joined the Russian army in place of his brother, told the following story after the rebels were dispersed from the woods. While he was in the camp near Tvėriai, evidently under the commander Niemojauskis, the order came to pass over to Laukuva parish in Aukštagirė. They had to bypass the lake's end, past the village of Paežerė. They traveled along the woods and fields–no one bothered them. There were about fifty men in that camp. Arriving at a small pine grove beyond the barn of the Paežerė manor, they sat down to rest. Several of the braver ones went to the manor to ask for bread. Suddenly they spied a group of Russkies approaching on horseback down the highway from Laukuva.

He said we couldn't run away or retreat–the forest was left far behind and there were only fields around us. We fell to the ground and lay low, hoping they would ride by and just not notice us. Not on your life–the cursed ones saw us immediately and started shouting: 'Polacks, sons-of-a-bitches, kill them! Charge!' You see, the pine grove was thinned out, the boughs high up, you could see clear through it. Right away the commander gave the order, and they started in pummeling us with bullets. Jumping up, we started shooting back, but the Russkies stood tall, and our men were falling, one on top of the other. Surrounding us, the Russkies slaughtered our men. I could see, he despaired, that not a one of us will be left. I threw my hat onto a branch and rolled into a hole under a fir tree and lay there limp as a log, desperately hoping that maybe they wouldn't shoot at a dead person. The Russkies shot and killed some; they wounded others. Some fell to the ground, but others managed to get away across the fields by hiding in ditches and holes. Not one was left upright on the plain. The Russkies kept on firing, shouting 'charge' three times as they mounted their horses and took off in the direction of Varniai. Some of our men lay still, as dead as doornails. Others who were wounded rolled around in their own blood, sobbing and moaning, pleading to God. People gathered around us. At first a few men approached timidly, then more and more gathered, some carrying axes and sticks. Women and shepherds appeared as well. They cursed us, kicked the dead, and slaughtered the wounded—cursing and swearing all the while.

"You masters, you Poles, get to the devil with you! You Satan's noblemen—see how you've beaten the Russkies. You'll bring back serfdom only to skin people's hides. Well, stick it to you, masters; we the peasants showed you. You just piled hardship on the backs of us peasants. We'll have to bury all you swine, before your rotting corpses smell up the forest."

"It's a good thing the devil brought those Russkies along," the old women rejoiced, "We would have had to feed those pigs. They were already begging for bread. The Russkies kicked the hell out of them and saved us the trouble of stuffing them."

"Throw the weapons and guns in a pile. We'll have to surrender them to the authorities."

They got it into their heads to pull the clothing off the dead soldiers. If someone was still moving, they'd whack them on the head with their ax or slit their necks with a knife. It made my skin crawl. I thought for sure that it's going to be the end for me. Lying down, I look around. If I run across the field, they will see me. They'll be furious, they'll catch and kill me. Getting up on a lower branch, I jumped onto a fir tree. Slowly, branch by branch, I made my way higher. The branches of the fir were dense, so maybe they wouldn't see me. I could see them, however. The women were busy ripping the clothes off the fallen, picking their pockets, grabbing a watch, yanking the rings off fingers—they were happy. While looting, they started shoving and arguing with each other.

"That's plenty for you—you've already taken a pile of clothing home."

"And isn't that enough loot for you? You picked out the best booty for yourself."

"And you, you just clean out pockets, and when you find money, you hide it from us."

"Stick it up your nose! And what did you end up with? You grabbed three pair of pants and all I got were patches."

Arguing back and forth like that, the women dragged home bundles of clothing. The fallen were left almost naked, only rags hanging from their bodies.

The men discussed among themselves: "What should we do? The police will come and find the dead fighters robbed, and we'll be in trouble. The women will spill the beans."

"Let's dig some graves, pile the dead ones in, so nobody sees them. We'll say those are the ones we found shot, the others ran away."

Having agreed, they got down to work: brought some tools, drove some women and shepherds with spades to the gravesite. They worked hard digging on the wasteland, egging each other on all the while:

"Let's hurry, the Russkies will boast of it in Varniai, soon the authorities will arrive."

"You order others around, but all you do is stuff your pipe."

"I keep thinking what it will be like, when the souls of the dead come looking for their clothes and start strangling the womenfolk."

"No, their souls flew away with the bullets: they can't scare anybody anymore."

Within the hour they started to carry and drag the dead into three long ditches that they dug, laughing all the time:

"Hand over the naked ones first. Then we'll put the dressed ones on top."

"Here's a gentleman so soft and white--he could have used some serfdom for sure."

"Here's a mister gentleman with whiskers, many a time he'd wallop a peasant on the ear. May the worms get you, you bastard," and so on and on it went.

They lined up the dead in rows inside the ditches, covered them with dirt from the sides, and laid others on top. They filled all three ditches this way. Nothing was left on the forest floor except a pile of dilapidated guns; the men selected the better ones for themselves. Since the sun was about to set, they decided to go for supper. They'd have to station guards at night, so the dogs wouldn't start dragging out the dead. They figured the police wouldn't come at night.

The men and women went their ways; the children stayed behind to gather papers, cigars, cigarette stubs and little boxes from the ground.

When the battlefield grew quiet and twilight fell, I came down from the fir. My arms and legs had gone to sleep, I felt light-headed, so I went off to the side and rested a little while, then I headed out for the big forest. I became so frightened of people that I felt I would be more terrified of meeting a man than coming across the fiercest animal. It seemed to me that all human beings had turned into the Paežerė wild animal people. I thought I could almost feel their axes and knives ready to strike me over the head.

It got dark, and I became tired and weak. I remembered that I had not eaten a crumb since morning. I couldn't walk anymore, my legs gave way, my mouth tasted bitter, and my tongue became stiff. Reaching the woods, I crawled into the bushes and collapsed on the ground. If only I had a drop of water. I was afraid I'd have to die right then and there. And that was fine with me; at least the end would come.

Crammed into the ditches, my friends lay before my eyes.

How much energy, how much strength, how many dreams, ideals, and noble ideas vanished! We were determined to put down despotism, establish freedom and equality. How much torment and suffering were piled into those ditches. And how many tears those who remember them would shed: sisters, mothers, beloved ones will mourn. Who will recount your deep suffering in dying, dear brothers, and who will explain how ruthlessly they shoved you into the ground! He recounted, I was overwhelmed by pain, heartbroken, so that tears started rolling down my cheeks. I wept lying face down in the grass as if I'd been whipped by my father. After I cried, I felt somewhat relieved, but I couldn't fall asleep. I hadn't stopped shivering from fear. The sky started to turn blue as the stars disappeared. I got up on legs that felt like wooden sticks. I started looking for water in any stream or ditch. My hat was gone, and I remembered how the Russkies shot at my hat hanging on the branch. I stumbled through the woods. I heard the skylark suddenly singing his song. It seemed to me that frogs started croaking not too far away.

There's got to be water here, I thought, and walked in that direction. I found some kind of a pond or bog with water. Taking off my shoes, I waded in deeper. I drank and drank, sifting the muck through my teeth. I looked up and saw—right there in front of me—some chained horses, grazing. Frightened, I looked around, thinking that there must be some people close by.

Well, all at once I saw three herdsmen sleeping on the pasture, face up, their noses in the air. Some charred bonfire remains were still smoking; their caps and coats were thrown around helter-skelter. Coming closer, I saw that they were all just young fellows. If they woke up, they probably wouldn't kill me.

I scrounged around to find a nice cap for myself and put it on. It fit just right. I picked out one of the better coats and put my black jacket in its place. Wearing the wool coat, I headed for the woods again. In the coat pocket I found a jackknife and a bit of bread. I ate it as hungrily as a beggar on a feast day. Drinking some more water, I crawled into a thicket and fell asleep.

Later, I slept in the woods during the day and walked during the nights, steering as far clear of villagers as I could. Coming to a village, I went to the Jewish shops to buy bread, since I still had some money. So through trial and tribulation, I made it home. In the fall my brother was drafted, but I went in his stead. They accepted me, and off I went to serve the Russkies.

Pranas related these events to me in the Telšiai army dormitory, where he served as the army doctor's assistant. As he told me his story from the Polish war, he kept sighing, and at the same time tears the size of beans streamed down his face.

Just as in spring we had rejoiced at the war's beginning, so by the coming of fall we wept bitterly at its end.

After the Uprising

The war ended, but only in the woods and forests. When the cold came, our cherished Poles, huddled up and famished, wandered in all directions, looking for shelter: a place to rest their heads. They no longer dreamed of killing the Russians; they just desperately tried to keep themselves alive.

On the side of the Russkies, the war went on.

They shot some of the army commanders, hanged the others. Many were the people they sent to concentration camps, many the courts held those freshly captured, and the numbers of inquiries and interrogations!

Throughout the winter the commandants and army courts were kept busy. Day after day fresh news reached us: so-and-so was gone, someone else was deceased, one disappeared without a trace, another joined the Russian army, one was arrested and another beaten, someone else died in prison.

All we did was sigh and sob. We pitied our heroes who didn't live to see a Polish victory, but if not this year, then next year or some years later, the Poles will surely defeat the Russkies.

Aunt had all kinds of worries: she had to contribute to the Polish central committee, her taxes weighed her down, she had to pay the Russkies taxes on property and pay fines on the acreage. She had no choice but to pay up. If she didn't have it, they'd get it from her one way or another.

While the Poles asked you to do your patriotic duty politely, the Russkies took it by force.

Aunt cried and tore her hair out by the roots. Even though some kind Jews came to her aid, lending her money, in return they took the two and three-year-old cows away so that there were none left to milk. They led away the mares and ponies, one after the other. The stalls remained empty, the barn echoed, the basements and pantries were emptied. There was nothing left to feed the Poles, nor anything to put into one's own pot. Only the bare shelves on the walls were left at my kind Aunt's.

It was bad enough there was no bread or porridge–there were no seeds either, nor any workers left. Freed from their masters, they ran off in every direction. Spring was coming; it was bad enough there was no seed, but there was no one to plow the soil or anything to do it with it. Horses would have to be bought and workers hired, wages paid. There were no more people of one's own to send out to work. We sighed at people's ignorance, their ingratitude: they had lived and grown up at Uncle's, then at Aunt's, they had lived so well. The estate fields weren't too large; they could do all the work quite easily. Besides, those who were at the manor house were well fed and cared for. As soon as they heard "freed from the masters," they left the house and ran off without any thanks. The ignorance and ingratitude! If only the Russkies had been beaten! Having suffered so much, fought, and sacrificed, our Polish heroes were now being hanged, shot, and tortured like criminals. The old "Granny" kept laying out the Kabbalah cards, and these always predicted that the Poles would win. All of us said so many prayers, fasted so many novenas, and there's no counting the litanies or rosaries we repeated. God should have heard us after all this, or at least the Holy Ghost. He should have inspired the French to come to the aid of the Poles. After so much hope and anticipation, toward fall everything collapsed but didn't die out entirely.

"We didn't succeed this summer," we comforted ourselves. "Spring will come, Garibaldi will show up with a flurry. The

Poles will rise anew, and they'll stick it to the Russkies, so the dust will fly."

At least we kept hope alive in our hearts and convinced one another that up there in His Heaven, God wouldn't be just if He didn't help the Poles conquer the Russkies.

My Job at the Manor

In the meantime, we were hungry, and it was everlasting emptiness at the manor. Aunt's son-in-law moved to another one of her estates to live; another daughter went to some relatives, and they found me a good place at the estate owner Gorskis's near Telšiai, in Džiuginėnai. They agreed on a yearly salary of thirty rubles. They hired me to take care of the Gorskis's little daughter, who was being breast-fed by a hired woman; as soon as the little girl was weaned, they'd hand her over to me to raise. In the meantime, my job was to serve the master's sister, an old maid. We had two rooms on the upper floor; my mistress slept in one of them, and the second one was given to me.

There was very little for me to do. I had to make my lady's bed morning and evening, help her get dressed. During the day I had to embroider or fix or mend something. The girl swept and washed our rooms every day, I just had to dust them. The food was good, all from the masters' table. The orchard was big–all kinds of fruit and berries; you could have as much as you wanted. It was much better here for me than at Aunt's.

Žemaitė's Autobiography

The lady and I got along; we went to church together. I ended up not taking the child, as I preferred to serve the lady.

There were many servants, two valets in the rooms and a little valet besides those. There were two servants for the mistress—one to do the sewing, the other to serve the lady. I took care of the old maid, and there was one more common girl to serve the two of us. A male and a female cook, a steward, a huntsman—they all had rooms in the other house. Two drivers who were served by a younger servant lived in the third house; also, there was a night rider for the horses, two girl cooks, and a third who tended the fowl.

The fieldworkers just worked the fields; they lived separately from the farmhands and didn't mix in the manor where the official ladies and gentlemen and their regular servants lived. At any time, the manor was full to overflowing; it felt like it was crawling with people. It was impossible to tell who was in charge of whom or what job they were supposed to be doing.

I felt right at home at the manor; it was fun, the work was easy. Nobody sent me here or there, packing me off like at Auntie's. Here they gave me something to embroider, to mend, or to fix. When I got tired of sitting, I could slip out to the gardens to explore.

When the masters had gone somewhere in the evenings, the steward, the servant, the cook, and the huntsman come around to our sewing room and we drank tea together. We also invited the female cook. Well, they told all kinds of jokes and stories, which sometimes were so funny that we'd laugh our heads off. Other times they'd talk about sad occurrences or painful experiences, then the tears would roll down our faces.

Mr. Laurynas, the Huntsman

The huntsman, Mr. Laurynas, knew how to relate his experiences as a young boy especially well. He was the son of peasant serfs who had been assigned to do the *corvée*. He was taken from his parents at a young age to live at the manor. The farm was a separate property that was run by various stewards. But the larger estate, where the master owners lived, was a few *versts* away. The lady in charge was a widow who had one son. As his father's heir, he was designated next in line to inherit all the wealth, the estates, and the serfs. But until he grew up and came of age, the Jew Mr. Abromas was the steward and caretaker of all the estates and the serfs. He had been either assigned or hired by the lady. No one knew if the lady was a German or a Jew, only that she came from Prussia and didn't speak any Lithuanian.

Laurynas's parents had a whole bunch of children: five sons and three daughters, so they were very poor. Since the father was sick, the children were forced to become laborers at a very early age. They could barely afford a hired hand to work the *corvée* for them.

The manor wouldn't accept someone weak or young. Whether you could afford one or not, you had to come up with a strong worker for them. If you couldn't produce one, then out of the farm with you, and someone else who had a strong worker for the estate would take over.

At home, the children were small. As much as they were able to, they worked the land, sowed and reaped, flayed and ground grain, but often there was a shortage of bread and seed. Once, while making the rounds of the estates and farms, the steward,

Mr. Abromas, dropped by at Laurynas's parents'. He was so awe-struck and delighted at the sight of so many children, he even patted little Laurukas on the head.

When he left, the parents, especially his mother, became very worried that nothing good would come of this visit, mostly be-cause the Jewish man had patted Laurukas on the head, foretell-ing that something unusual was about to happen, probably some misfortune.

A mother's heart guessed correctly: a week or so later the vil-lage elder arrived and announced: "Take Laurukas to the manor right away, and if you refuse, it will go badly for you."

The mother was weeping, the father was cursing, but he was getting ready to go.

In Laurynas's Own Words

Remembering the past, our Mister Laurynas liked to retell the events of his young days, and we, especially the girls, liked to listen to him. We would ask him to remember more and tell us the stories. Sometimes when we asked him, he told us not only about his estate but also about the goings-on of other masters.

(I will now write in Laurynas's words.)

Mama said: "Let's take the older boy Beniukas, at least he's finished his tenth year, but Laurukas has barely started his ninth year. Without someone caring for him, the lice will eat up such a little one."

"And if they don't take Beniukas, we'll have to drive the distance a second time," said the father. "So let's take both of them, whichever one they turn down, we'll bring that one home with us."

Coming to an agreement, they herded the two of us like lambs into the wagon. Mama was crying all the way there, and Benis kept wiping away the tears from time to time until we arrived at the manor.

The lady gave orders to bring us to her. Mama took both of us over and presented us to the lady. Mr. Abromas came along, too. After mumbling something to the lady, he put his hand on my head and said: "You'll make a good servant, if you mind. You'll be loved, stay at the manor," he told me and left.

Crying without ceasing, Mama fell at the lady's feet and begged her to let her child be raised at home, at least until the age of eleven or twelve. Then, when he was bigger, they'd give him up to the manor. The lady wouldn't hear of it and did what she always does, clacking her tongue: "*Tugu, tugu! Tugu tugu!* Mister Abromas ordered it, that's the kind of child that's needed at the manor. The boy will get used to working, but at home he'll just learn to laze around and play pranks, *tugu tugu!*"

Still wailing, Mama kept falling at the lady's feet, pleading with her to take the older one. The little one was only eight years old; he wouldn't be of any use to the manor. He didn't know how to do any work at all. He couldn't do any herding.

"He'll learn at the manor, he will, *tugu, tugu!*" the lady retorted, "Mister Abromas picked him, so he's the one who has to stay. And if you don't obey—you'll regret it," she finished and ran off to her chambers.

We left the lady and went back to the wagon. Mama rushed to the lady's cook and to the head cook, begging them to look after me, at least to make sure I had food. She promised to come to see me as soon as she could. While Mama was sobbing and Benis was hopping up and down, they departed.

Left behind, they said, I just sat by the kitchen door. The dogs wandered around: one licked my hand, the other my nose and mouth. I didn't chase them away for fear of getting bitten. I had some bread and a small piece of meat that Mama had put in my pocket; I broke the bread into pieces, pinched off some meat, and threw everything to the dogs.

The dogs licked me and lay down around me, so I sat in the sun and dozed.

In the evening, the family and hired hands began to gather for supper. There were lots of men, girls, and shepherds. They took me inside, poured some porridge into a little bowl for me, and told me to eat. As the family ate, the men especially made fun of me in any way they could they think of: "What the hell kind of servant is this? What kind of work are they going to give you? Cutting logs?"

"Of what use to anybody is a little bugger like him?"

"It's that Abromas's idea, that filthy Jew, wouldn't you know it? If he gets a chance to bite somebody, he will. They have so many kids. The Jew is jealous, and just had to take one of them, sending the poor child into hardship."

"At home he'd grow up to be a fine worker, but here he'll turn into a thief and a liar: you can't be a manor servant without that."

I could hear what they were saying about me, but I didn't understand much of it. They all went their separate ways, and I ended up outside again, sitting on the foundation, except I couldn't snooze anymore, because I was so cold. The girl called to me: "Hey, kid, you can't sit there all night, go inside the cabin to sleep."

As I went inside, I saw that another child had lain down on the bench by the wall. So I, too, took off my shirt and, putting it under my head, lay down on the bare bench under the window. It got chilly at night, when the wind rattled through the window, the cabin got cold. I awoke trembling and groped around looking for the stove, but that was already cold too. I crept behind the stove, where the dogs were snoring, and curled up next to one. Warming up somehow, I fell asleep. I felt the dogs climbing over me; waking me. I heard the men talking in the cabin. I crawled out from behind the stove. The men started making fun of me again: "So you're sleeping with the hounds; soon you'll learn how to bark at the rabbits."

"Go wash your face: you can't eat at the manor unless you've washed up."

I washed my face. The hired hands sat down to eat. I remembered that at home Mama didn't let us eat before we said our prayers.

I knelt down on the dirt floor and said my prayers; even though I didn't know them very well, still I said them, as much as I could remember. Seeing this, the men laughed again: "Go ahead and pray," they said, "Abromėlis will send you to become a priest."

Someone else chastised them: "Don't make fun of prayer, don't pester the child, he was raised right."

Herding the Geese

When day broke, the housekeeper set me to herding the geese. We drove them to the fallow fields. The goslings were still so small, so she told me to watch for crows and not let the goslings get into the pond. The pond was by the manor orchard so the animals could get to it from the field. They didn't wade across the pond, but if the geese were allowed into the pond, they'd end up in the orchard right away. After telling me to keep the geese away from the pond, the housekeeper warned me: "If you let them in there, you'll get a hiding."

I herded the geese, driving them closer to the bog, next to the water. Praniukas drove the pigs there. It wasn't so boring when the two of us herded together. He brought a dog, which he sicced on the pigs to pull on their ears. The dog also scared the geese away from the pond. We rolled around on the fallow field, warming ourselves. We went for lunch, bringing back bread for the afternoon snack, which we shared with the dog.

While the sun shone, everything was fine, but when it started raining, there was nowhere to go. Squealing, Praniukas's pigs headed for home with Praniukas following behind. And my geese covered their goslings, but I got rained on; it ran down my collar, and everything got wet. Dripping, I walked home behind the geese, who fed their young. I locked them up in the barn, but there was nowhere for me to go. I cried, shivering from the cold. Feeling sorry for me, the girl told me to take off my clothes, wrung them out, and hung them up to dry. Then she only gave me a long shirt to wear. Fearing the men's laughter, I crawled behind the stove by my friends, the dogs.

As long as the goslings were small, without wings, I could more or less herd them. But toward summer, when the goslings grew up, and there was a large flock of them, they spread out over entire fields. When it got hot, the water dried up in the marshes, and the geese couldn't find any water to drink. Then they headed for the pond, and there was no way I could hold them back.

Praniukas and I drove the pigs and geese over to the other side of the field. It was no problem with the pigs, which were happy to roll in some mud. But it seemed that the geese could smell where the water was. Rising up over our heads, they fluttered off to the pond. Open-mouthed, the goslings ran along the ground after the oldsters, flapping their wings. There was a multitude of goslings. If I got ahead of them from one side, they were already far off on the other side. In a panic, I ran among the goslings, yelling and waving at them, brandishing a stick. Suddenly, bang! The stick fell from my hands right onto the gosling's head; and there the bird lay, fallen over writhing. What's worse, the old geese were already in the pond. Out of breath, I fell on the ground. Meanwhile, all the goslings escaped to the orchard.

Shouting and cursing, the gardener sicced the dogs after the geese. The housekeeper came running and grabbed me by the neck. She knocked me to the ground and lashed me with the whip. Noticing the kicking gosling, she got furious and tore the clothes off my back until I was naked. Then binding my hands behind my back, she tied me to a tree: "You little bastard, you'll learn how to herd the geese instead of beating the goslings," she said.

Leaving me there alone, she drove the scattered geese to this side of the pond. The wasps and horseflies and other bugs converged on me; they began to chew my bare back. I screamed with as much voice as I had in my head. I screamed so loudly that

Žemaitė's Autobiography

I ran out of breath. Mr. Abromas stopped in his tracks and came tearing down from the highway, carrying his whip: "Horrors! Who's screaming like that?"

Finding me tied up, naked and bloody, he jumped back. "Who tied you up?" he asked.

"The housekeeper," I gasped.

Right away, he cut the rope, which had been cutting my hands and drawing blood, while I was twisting and turning. Catching sight of the housekeeper, he bawled her out and cursed her, and swore at her, threatening to take not only her, but the lady herself to court for this kind of brutality. He told me to go to the tavern and promised to give me a ride to my parents.

In the morning, after driving the geese out, I immediately boasted to Praniukas that Mr. Abromas had promised to take me to my parents. "I'd run to him now," I declared, "but I don't know where the tavern is." Praniukas walked me along the highway and showed me the tavern roof. "When you decide to run," he said, "run directly past the mill and straight to the tavern along the highway. There you'll find the grey-haired Jew."

After herding the geese home in the evening, I took a slice of bread from the table and headed for the tavern. Seeing Mr. Abromas, I kissed his hand. He told me to lie down on the straw in the stable. When he was ready to go, he'd wake me up. Joyfully, I threw myself onto the straw. The next thing I knew he was waking me up. The horse was already harnessed, so we got in the wagon and took off. The sun rose as we came to the Aunava bridge, at the count's estate. We got home just in time for breakfast. My folks were both frightened and amazed to see us.

The Jew told them why he'd brought me home, how he'd found me tied up and naked, scarcely alive. He was trying to talk

Papa into taking the housekeeper to court without fail. He even offered to be a witness.

They told me that I ran around the house with the kids, so happy. Everything was the way I left it, except that the barn was full of hay and the other barn full of rye. In the garden the carrots had grown really big. Pulling them out, I threw an armful into Abromas's cart. Digging up a basket full of potatoes, Benis also poured them in for the Jew. Father thanked Abromas himself, and Mama also thanked him and gave him some white bread. My folks were very happy that the Jew took pity on their child and brought him home. At the same time, they were worried about what would happen when they found out at the manor. They keep asking me for details and I told them everything—how I ate, where I slept, how I couldn't herd the geese anymore, because they flew to the pond. My folks raised some questions: "But maybe they let him go on purpose, since he couldn't herd the geese?" They listened to what I told them and wondered what would happen next.

Mama combed my hair and washed it, heated up the sauna, bathed me, and scrubbed me with leaves because my head was full of lice, not to mention my shirt, which also had handfuls of them inside. In a few days the manor boy came riding up. Finding me at home, he ordered me to return to the manor immediately. Then he turned to me and said: "Well, now you're going to get a beating. Praniukas told us that supposedly you were going to drown yourself. We searched the whole pond, looking for you everywhere, and you were here the whole time, you runaway!"

Return to the Manor

Mother held me again, crying and sobbing. As soon as we arrived there, they took us straight to the lady's, who ordered them to call Mr. Fokas right away. She asked me: "Why did you run away, *tugu tugu?*"

I could only cry, trembling so hard that I couldn't utter a word. Mama fell at the lady's feet, sobbing. She started making excuses for me and complained about how they had tied up her naked child in the sun for the bugs to feed on. Feeling pity for him, Abromas had untied him and after releasing him, had brought him home. The lady ordered the Jew to be called without delay. As soon as he came, he started to mutter away in Yiddish, pointing to my back and demonstrating with the end of his finger the size of the bugs that were eating me. Most likely he complained about the housekeeper because the lady called her to be brought in too.

They all argued, speaking jibber-jabber. Then Mr. Abromas proclaimed, "Well now, Laurukas! For running away you'll get fifteen lashes on the rear end. Mr. Fokas is already waiting for you in the stable."

Rushing to Mama, I screamed in a piercing voice, so that even the lady took fright. "Don't be afraid! *Tugu, tugu,* he won't whip you for the first offense," she assured me.

Once again she started jibber-jabbering to Abromas. Mama begged the lady to allow me to go home, but Abromas commanded me to stay. "If you hadn't brought him," he said to mother, "you'd be cast out from the farm by tomorrow and blessed with the whips." Then he ordered me to beg the lady for forgiveness and promise not to run away again. "And if you do try to run away again," he threatened, "it's fifty strokes for you and a boot out of the farm for your parents!"

What could they do? Once again they left me there for the lice to feast on.

This was the time they let the geese out into the summer fields, including the rye fields, farther away from the pond so that it became easier for me. You didn't have to sit and herd, you just had to send them off, and in the evening they'd come home by themselves. Then you'd just have to shut them up in the barn. As before, I rolled around with the dogs. I got into the habit of hanging around the kitchen to catch a morsel of meat or a piece of white bread from the cook. I took some to Praniukas too, and he taught me how to wheedle some more. The kind-hearted cook didn't pay attention to a few crumbs, but two of the junior cooks, catching me snacking, hit me on the nape and on my back. How can you protect yourself from the likes of such serpents?

I hung around like that until the cold winter came. I couldn't step outside the kitchen at all because I had no footwear. I was barefoot, my clothes were all tattered and torn, the knees of my pants had fallen out. I just hid behind the stove so no one would send me anywhere.

On winter evenings the serfs' children and even the manor shepherds had to come from the farms to tear up feathers. About ten or twelve of us children would gather. The housekeeper would bring out a bag of feathers for us to work on. Seating us around the table, she would measure out a tumbler each, stuffed full, and scatter them on the table in front of us. "Here's some for you and some for you," she'd measure the tumbler out, saying: "you have to tear them up tonight, she says, otherwise, I won't let you go to bed, so the sooner you finish, the earlier I'll let you go."

While the housekeeper kept her eye on us, keeping her whip ready, we ripped up our portions. If someone started to doze off, smack! she lashed him with her whip. Everybody struggled to stay alert, to keep from snoozing. But those feathers went on forever–you kept pulling and tearing at them, but there were still piles and piles of them left. Praniukas and I figured out a way to get around this: while we were busy tearing, we stuffed some of the untorn feathers down our shirts and into our pockets. Then running outside, we shook them into the wind. And we had to run outside often, pretending that our tummies hurt. After doing this several times, our pile was soon all done. Then I crawled behind the stove once again.

The farm kids were driven to the manor every evening until we finished ripping up the feathers off all the birds–the geese, the ducks, the chickens, and the turkeys, which had been killed over the summer.

Hanging around with the dogs behind the stove, I got covered by horrendous lice: they crawled through my shirt and over my head in rows thick as ropes. My head got covered in itchy scabs, which I kept scratching until it was all bloody.

Household members, including the men, started shouting at the housekeeper to provide me with some clothes to change into: "He's going to give all of us lice. We're going to complain to the lady," they muttered.

"They must have brought the child to the manor," they murmured, "just so the lice would feed on him."

Through the head steward, the housekeeper let mama know about the lice. She came over, washed my hair, combed it, and scattered the nasty critters by the handful into the fire. Mama felt so sorry for me that she cried, and I whimpered, too. It really hurt when she pulled the scabs off my head.

The housekeeper gave mama some cloth to sew me new clothes. But the manor cloth was so pretty, so fine, that mama took it home and made flour sacks out of it and ended up making me clothes from her own coarse cloth.

After Christmas the winter cold set in with snow flurries and freezing temperatures. At night the cabin windows were so iced over that you could probably drive a sleigh on them. Because we were frozen stiff we couldn't even sleep at night until they started a fire or got the stove going in the morning. In the daytime they kept sending me outside to bring in wood, or to summon someone. I rushed barefoot through the snow. I began to cough horribly, gasping for air. Falling down on the ground, I coughed so hard that blood began to spray through my nose. I didn't want to eat. Moaning and crying, I couldn't even get up. Learning of my condition, the lady ordered me to be taken to my folks. They wrapped me in a fur coat and horse blankets, carried me to the wagon, and drove me home. They said that I was sick for a long time and that Benis and the other children got sick too. When pointy pustules appeared over our whole bodies and inside our mouths, they said it was the measles. Mama was so thankful that they brought me home when I got sick. "At the manor he would have died behind the stove with the dogs," she pronounced.

I stayed home until spring, when the geese hatched. Once again they called me to return to the manor.

In the summer Praniukas and I herded the pigs and geese as before. We herded them in different fields–farther away from the pond where I didn't have so much trouble. Except that when

Praniukas and I returned to the manor, we both got covered by lice and my head got all scabby again. The scabs on our heads itched and hurt. I scratched them off so that the blood ran down over my eyes. Once we found a soft cow pie with bugs crawling around on it. "Let's feed the lice," we exclaimed, "the bugs eat the cow pie, the lice will too."

We smeared the manure all over our heads and dried it in the sun until it got stiff. Our heads looked like the Jews' yarmulkes: it hurt horribly, but in spite of the pain, we let the lice eat their fill. We suffered all day long. In the evening we ran to the pond, stuck our heads in the water and kept them there for a while until our yarmulkes came off along with all the scabs and lice. We washed our hair, bathed all over and our life became much easier. Later I noticed that the young women were smearing their calves with some kind of porridge to get rid of the lice. I asked for some and they rubbed it along my ears. My scalp stopped itching, and gradually healed. Somehow or other we got rid of the lice.

Again in the winter I hung around behind the stove, half-naked. One time the lady appeared in the kitchen without warning; I didn't manage to hide myself, so she saw me. "Where did that child come from?" she asked.

The cook reminded her about me.

"*Tugu, tugu,*" she said, drooling, "why do you keep him around with nothing to do? He's already grown, so he can do some work now instead of eating bread for free.

"*Tugu, tugu,* he can scrub and wash the pots or carry messages. Make sure," she emphasized to the cook, "that he doesn't fritter his time away."

"I don't want to send the likes of that kid anywhere–I'm embarrassed to send him naked and barefoot," argued the cook.

"When they see him, people will say: the manor doesn't even provide clothes for its servants."

"*Tugu, tugu!* I'll get them to find some clothes for him."

Soon they came up with a sheepskin coat, shoes, and a warm hat for me. Since the sheepskin had been lying around for years, it was stiff and moldy. Warming it up in front of the fire, I brushed and combed it until it got a little softer so I could put it on. The shoes were stiff also and too big. I smeared them with fat in front of the fire. Because they were so big, my feet turned in them, but at least I was able to wade through the snow with them on.

Even Praniukas was jealous of the way they dressed me. He only wore wooden clogs or moccasins. They didn't even give him a sheepskin coat for outside.

No sooner did I get the clothes than some other trouble came my way: they started sending me out at night. There was nowhere for Mr. Abromas to sleep at the manor, so he lived separately. He fixed up some rooms for himself in a cabin beyond the small pine grove along the Dubysa River.

During the day he would hang around or go somewhere; in the evening he'd always be at the lady's for tea. He'd sit there all evening talking, then go home to sleep. In no time, the maid would show up at the kitchen with a slip of paper. Dragging me out from behind the stove, she would tell me to put on my shoes, get dressed, and take the slip to Mr. Abromas. "The lady ordered me to send you," she said, "hurry! If you don't get over there, you'll catch a whipping."

Rubbing my eyes, I got ready, then waded through the snow with the note. Once I arrived there, I banged on the door, left the note, and returned. I lay down, and no sooner had I managed to get warm, than, again, the maid sent me back to get Mr. Abromas to come to the lady's. If Abromas listened and came the first time, then I only had to go once, but if he didn't come quickly, I had to run over a second and even a third time. It wasn't too bad when it wasn't cold, but sometimes there was a big chill or a howling wind with the snow swirling down. Then I could scarcely pick up my feet against the wind, and my nose and ears even curled up from the cold.

I waded through the snow to get there. If I didn't get an answer to my loud knocking, I had to stand by the door, stiff with cold. Letting me inside, Abromas read the note and, lying in bed all the while, asked: "Well, Laurukas, did you get very cold? Here, have a drink."

He poured me some whiskey from the bottle always stashed under his bed. Filling a glass, he told me to drink up. "You'll get warm, you little pig, you."

Shivering from the cold, I drank it up, even my soul revived.

After I downed the drink, he bellowed: "Dance, drunks always dance."

If I didn't feel like dancing and I didn't obey him, Mr. Abromas would quickly grab his whip and start turning it in his hands: "If you don't dance, you'll get whipped on the behind."

Without a bite to eat, I did the Cossack dance until tears streamed down my face and my head spun, but Mr. Abromas just lay in bed, snorting with laughter. If Mr. Abromas dragged himself off somewhere, then nobody woke me up. But when he was home, every night I had to run with the note, and when I got there, he forced me to drink and dance.

Everyone in the entire manor hated Mr. Abromas, fearing him like the devil himself: he had total power over the whole estate and its people, even more than the lady herself. All the people in the manor and the other masters, even the Jews, called him Abram Gorski. The number of his victims, the lady's serfs, whom he had ordered wrongly whipped couldn't be counted. If anyone made him angry or argued with him, he'd send them to Fokas right away without the lady's knowledge. In the barn, Fokas would make the man or girl screech in terror.

I was afraid of Abromas and hated him, but I despised the steward Fokas even more. That German Fokas never let go of his whip, so he'd strut around waving it and just waiting for the lady or Mr. Abromas to hand over some poor soul to whip. Such a horrible German—with bulging red eyes, the torturer of the estate and its people.

If anyone was blamed for any little thing, someone would snitch on them to the lady, and without wasting any time, she'd respond: "*Tugu, tugu!* Get them over to Mr. Fokas."

That poor person already knew what was waiting for him. Without checking to see if they were guilty or not, that brute Fokas whipped them without mercy. We heard the victim screaming in the barn. Running into me once, Fokas waved his whip and laughed: "Rue the day, Laurukas, when you get handed over to me in the barn to taste some of this."

Even the sight of Fokas would turn my face red hot with anger.

"When I grow up," I thought to myself, "and you get old, just wait, I'll get back at you for everybody. I'll order them to lay you down and whip you so hard that you'll kick the bucket. Not only that, I'll pour whiskey down Abromas's gullet and make him dance until he collapses. Then you'll know how good we have it!"

On occasion they sent the farm girls to clean the rooms. While washing the windows, one of them accidentally broke a pane of glass. When she saw this, the lady shouted immediately: "*Tugu, tugu,* call Mr. Fokas."

He showed up quickly, took the girl into the barn, and whipped her, following the lady's instructions of fifteen lashes for the broken glass. After her whipping the girl didn't return to work. The others called her and looked everywhere for her. Finally, they saw her hanging from the rafters by a rope. One man jumped up and cut it. Barely alive, the girl revived somewhat. Because she tried to hang herself, they dragged her to the barn and thrashed her until her voice was gone. She couldn't get up anymore, so they took her home scarcely alive. In the morning she died. That's how much a woman's life was worth at that time: less than a windowpane.

Later, rumors spread that Gendrutė's ghost was wandering around on the estate, supposedly tapping on the lady's windows at night. Then the ghost appeared under Fokas's windows, scratching the glass. One person claimed he saw her, another one ran into her. The maid heard her scratching at the windows, and yet another person saw her in the pine grove walking toward Abromas's room. When it got dark, everyone, especially the girls and the shepherds, were afraid to stick their noses outside the door because they feared meeting Gendrutė's ghost.

The men claimed that if a person's soul was driven from the world at the wrong time, it never forgave its murderers. There was no room in the next world until the appointed time, when the soul would have died a natural death. The ghost would wander and knock around on the earth, taking revenge on its executioners. I kept waiting for Gendrutė's ghost to strangle Fokas, Abromas, or the lady, and in the evening I too was afraid to stick my nose outside the door.

There was nothing for me to do in the kitchen: the cook's helpers licked and scoured the pots. In the daytime, I wandered here and there around the estate, ending up at the gardener's. He and his helper were making some straw covers for the greenhouse in preparation for spring. I tried to pitch in and made some, too. They liked my work; the old man praised me and encouraged me to work more quickly, to help him more often. Soon I got the hang of it, making a cover as fast as the experienced ones. When it got a little warmer, the gardener asked the lady to send me over to work with him. The lady agreed; as if it made any difference to her where she put me. She just picked on somebody else's child to tend the geese at the manor.

Now the old man and I, the two of us, worked away in the garden.

The serfs hammered up the boxes for the greenhouses, hauled in the manure, dumped it on the soil. All we had to do was even it out, rake it, sow the seeds, water, and cover the beds.

The Young Master, Mykolas

When the weather turned warm, the nanny started bringing the young master around to the garden, and he came to me right away. I liked the boy; he was dressed up in white, such a dandy. He was called Mykoliukas after the old master, who was Mykolas. When I met him, I was almost twelve, and the young master was going on six. I seated him in a wagon and drove him around or carried him piggyback, or like a horse, I ran with him straddled on my back. The nanny was happy that we were playing; the gardener was laughing. Later the child got so used to our play that as soon as he went outside, he came to me. They couldn't hold him down in the rooms even if they tried.

The lady caught sight of me carrying the master piggyback and started scolding: "*Tugu, tugu,* you're just a common peasant, how dare you carry the master around? *Tugu, tugu,* it's indecent!"

She scolded the nanny too, for letting the master come to me. She intended to take him away, but he screamed, threw a tantrum, fell to the ground, kicked, and screamed–they couldn't separate us. As much as the lady wanted to break the child of his habit–coaxing him sweetly or threatening him angrily–she didn't succeed in the least. When she didn't allow him to come to me, he fell on the ground and started kicking and screaming. She decided to send me back to the geese, but the gardener wouldn't hear of it, explaining: "Laurukas does the work of two workers for me. Besides, throwing tantrums will make the master sick."

Concerned for the master's health, the lady no longer minded the master going to me. She only told the girls to bathe me and wash my shirts often, so I wouldn't spread cooties to the master.

We played together throughout the summer. Things went very well for me, and I couldn't help loving the master. The only trouble was that I couldn't communicate with him very well. The master didn't know Lithuanian, and I didn't know Polish. They told me to learn to speak Polish because the lady wouldn't let him speak the peasant language. Thus we spoke one word one way, the next word the other way, and by pointing, we understood each other. When they told me to weed, he rolled around in the soil. If I watered the flowers, he got all wet and muddy.

And when it was a cold, rainy day, they had trouble keeping him indoors. The master cried and fretted until they called me in to play with him. He gave me some white bread, and I ate the cake and meat that he didn't finish.

As soon as it was winter they sent me to the kitchen to bring water for the dogs and scour the pots. They brought a young German teacher for the master, hoping that he would attach himself to him as he did to me. Not on your life! As soon as he escaped from the chambers, whether it was cold, raining or snowing–the master came running to me in the kitchen.

The nanny and the teacher had trouble keeping an eye on him and catching him when he slipped away. Once more they resorted to sending me like a dog to Mr. Abromas to deliver notes at night. Same as before, I had to drink and dance like a madman.

Trying to distance me from the master, the lady assigned me to the mill as helper and messenger. They didn't tell the master where they'd put me, and since it was too far for him to run to me, we didn't get together anymore.

But I felt right at home at the mill: nobody sent me out at night. I didn't run into Abromas and Fokas very often, so it was peaceful. In spring the master found me out. From then on, every day he slipped away and came running to me in the mill, getting flour all over himself. Again this brought trouble for the servants and anxiety for the lady.

At long last, realizing that she couldn't do anything about it, the lady gave up trying to separate us. She sent me back to the garden, where the master and I became inseparable once more.

Whipping the Serfs

One day, as I was running around in the garden, Mykoliukas heard a person crying out in terror. "Who's screaming there?" the master wondered.

"Probably Fokas is whipping some poor soul," I told him.

"Whipping someone? Let's go see."

Before I knew it, he jumped over the fence, with me at his heels. I tried to hold him back, but he shot forward like a bullet, heading straight for the barn. Getting closer, we heard the whip whistling and someone counting the blows. I could see my master running up to the doorway and kerplunk! he fell over.

Beating a hasty retreat, I ran back along the fence to the garden, hiding myself in the cucumbers and weeds. Sweat poured off me, I was shaking with fear, thinking that the blame would fall on me, and then I wouldn't escape Fokas's whip. In the barn I heard loud noises, followed by alarmed voices. I raised my head and saw that the driver was bringing the master home in his arms with Fokas following behind. Waving his whip and looking around, he kept calling; "Laurukas! Laurukas!"

I tried to get closer to the ground. Near the porch I heard the nanny, the lady, and the maid cackling like hens: "Sweet Jesus and Mary! The master is dead!"

"What happened?"

"Where? Where did he get beaten?"

"Who hit him, who hurt him?" They all shouted, one over the other.

Fokas tried to explain and kept on mentioning Laurukas, but no one was listening to him, only choking up as the lady shouted:

"Get the doctor! *Tugu, tugu,* doctor!" Like wild horses they rushed to Šiauliai for the doctor. "Put him to bed, to bed."

Lifting him up, they all carried the master inside. Fokas headed back, swearing, but the gardener blocked his way.

"What do you want with Laurukas?" he started cursing him out. "He's been in the garden weeding since morning. You yourself are to blame: the child has never seen anyone being beaten. He could die at the sight of it. You're going to be held responsible."

Fokas rushed off, spitting. At last my heart started beating again. An hour later I suddenly heard a woman's voice start calling in the orchard: "Lauruk, Lauruk! Yoo, hoo!"

Jumping up, I headed toward the voice.

"Get indoors," urged the maid.

My body froze, my heart kept beating, and my hands and feet were numb.

"Did the master die? It's not my fault… I couldn't…" I kept making up excuses.

"Stop blathering and just come quickly."

They brought me into the master's room, where he was lying in bed, tossing and turning, shouting feverishly: "Fokas with his whip… blood all over… Laurukas is dead…" He jumped out of bed; the nanny and the lady could barely hold him down. I started feeling sorry for the master, as the tears rolled down my face.

"Hush, don't cry, don't be afraid," they comforted me, pushing me toward the bed. Then to reassure the master, they showed me to him, "Here's Laurukas, Misiuta! He's here beside you, hale and hearty. Lie still, nobody beat him; just look."

Spying me, the master cracked a smile, saying, "Sit beside me here on the bed–I won't let Fokas whip you." The master fell silent for a while, calmed down somewhat, and then again his mind started to wander and he jumped up, shouting: "He beat him up! Fokas killed Laurukas." Once more they pushed me to the bed and pointed to me: "Misiuta! Misiuta! Laurukas is standing beside you. He's right here!"

They brought the doctor. After examining him, he ordered the master's head to be covered in ice. Afterwards he took me outside and started questioning me. I trembled and whimpered so that I couldn't get a single word out.

"Don't be afraid, nothing will happen to you," he assured me, stroking my head, "just tell me the whole truth as to what happened to the master."

Gathering up my courage, I told the doctor the whole incident from beginning to end, without a single lie. The doctor sat through the whole night and kept putting ice on the master's head. He told me to stay close by, so I curled up at the end of the bed and dozed on the ground. The lady didn't leave the master's bed either, she continued whispering to the doctor. During the three years that I was at the manor, I kept hearing Polish and was told to speak it, so I already understood the language. I didn't get every word, but I caught the gist of what the doctor was saying to the lady: "Madam, you order people to be whipped, you ruin their health, because of that your Ladyship's child fell ill. His nerves are young and weak—he can't stand the sight of human suffering. It's possible he'll get a brain infection. In that case not even a hundred doctors can save him. Or when he gets well, if he sees this kind of brutality again, he could even lose his mind."

The lady just snuffled. "*Tugu, tugu,* I didn't know anything about it. It was Fokas's fault. Misiuta, Misiuta, why did you go there? I swear you won't have to see it again."

I felt sorry for the master, but it was a good thing for the lady. Yes, it was a good thing! She wouldn't ever give that order again: "*Tugu, tugu,* take them to Mr. Fokas!"

The master got well, but they wouldn't let him leave his chamber: I had to show myself every day to prove that I was hale and hearty. But if he hadn't seen me for a long time, he started shouting all over again: "They killed Laurukas–Fokas lashed him to death with his whip."

After the master's illness everything took a turn for the better. First of all, the lady called Fokas to her and threatened him that if he ever hurt anyone, even so much as that person's finger, she would immediately drive him away from her service and out of the manor. "Without my knowledge, God save us, whipping is now forbidden!"

In this way, the lady put Fokas in his place, breaking his power over us.

All the manor servants and the hired hands danced and rejoiced.

In the winter they brought the master another teacher and a lady governess. Because they employed more people, they needed more servants, so they hired a valet.

By bringing in so many teachers, the lady thought that the child would calm down and wouldn't run to me anymore. But not a chance. He spit at the teachers, kicked the valet, and wouldn't let them near him. As long as one teacher or another kept him close by their side, the master stayed indoors. But if they went off somewhere, for instance, when guests came and everyone mixed together, the master slipped away and came running straight off to me in the kitchen.

Guests always came, but Mr. Tiškevyčia from the Kurtuvėnai estate was a constant guest. If he missed a day, then he came the next one.

Mr. Tiškevyčia loved the master dearly. As soon as he came inside, he picked him up immediately and set him on his knee—kissing and caressing him as he carried him around. During the master's illness, Mr. Tiškevyčia was always at our house; he brought the doctors and ran errands. It was said that from the time the lady first came here, he was always over. They all laughed that the master looked so much like Mr. Tiškevyčia. The more he grew, the more he resembled him. In fact, he was the spitting image of Tiškevyčia. In order to calm the master, he persuaded the lady to move me, Laurukas, into the chambers. This way, the child could no longer run around without permission.

They brought me to the chambers so I could help the valet. They dressed me in clean clothes and gave me some shoes. While the master was doing his lesson with one of the teachers, I had to work: washing the floors and stairs, shining the candlesticks, and polishing the valet's shoes. In the morning I had to start the fire, sweep the edges of the rooms and the hallways. As soon as the master was done with his lessons, my work got interrupted, as the master immediately ran out and led me to his room, where we'd spend the whole evening together. That was how they moved me around: in the summer outside in the orchard, in the winter inside the chambers. Well, at least it was not with the dogs behind the stove anymore! Often I was sent to the kitchen or at other times to the barn, to Mr. Abromas's, to Mr. Fokas's, or to the housekeeper, where at least I'd hear some manor news. As soon as I found out that someone was guilty of something and that Fokas was complaining to the lady and getting ready to whip someone, I would take off for the master. "Little master! Fokas is intending to whip so and so. He's complaining to the lady about them."

The master in turn ran to his mother: "Mama! It's forbidden for Fokas to whip people! Mama! Don't allow him to whip that person." He'd cry and carry on, shouting at his mother until he persuaded her to call Fokas and stop him from whipping anyone. Thus through the master I succeeded in saving someone from being lashed several times.

Fokas and Abromas started putting two and two together and figured out that this was my work. One day they cornered me. "Laurukas, just remember that you're going to catch it for that tongue of yours. The lady is afraid that the master will get sick, but you tell him everything. If you make him sick, then you'll really be in trouble. I will personally take you by the ears to Fokas and we'll both thrash you on the behind."

While Abromas was laying down the law to me in the sewing room, the master, who was in the dining room listening to Abromas's threats, ran to his mother straight as an arrow. "Mama, why is Abromas going to whip Laurukas?" he shouted. "I heard it: he wants to take him to Fokas," he cried loudly, creating a scene.

The lady went to Abromas right away: "*Tugu, tugu!* Who thought up such a thing–to whip Laurukas?" She scolded: "*Tugu, tugu,* you'll make the master sick. I don't want to hear a word about whipping anymore."

Fokas in turn inexplicably cursed out the master: "Such a little bastard, see how he shows his will–he leads everyone around by the nose. Give him and Laurukas at least fifteen lashes each– that'll settle them down."

And so the serfs' screaming in the barn came to an end. If someone did something really bad or absolutely had to be punished for thieving, Fokas would very secretly whip them somewhere in the hay barn so no one could hear anything, and the master wouldn't find out.

Once, while running to the kitchen, I noticed that our neighbors, the people from Usnėnai, had come. One of them was related to me, he was my uncle. I inquired, "What have you come here for?"

"Why," they answered, "the steward complained about us to Mr. Abromas, so he ordered us brought to the manor. We're probably going to get it, even though really we are innocent. Someone snitched on us."

I could see Abromas, his nose in the air, jabbering to Fokas. I took off, and, finding the master, I babbled something to him privately: "They're getting ready to whip our neighbors from Usnėnai. My uncles are good people, they're innocent. The steward turned them over to Abromas out of spite."

Without hesitating a moment, the master charged to his mother. "Mama, are you going to allow innocent people to be beaten?" he started shouting. "Do you, Mama, know them, do you know... did you see?"

"Misiuta, Misiuta, settle down! *Tugu, tugu!* Abromas knows that they're guilty; the serfs have to be controlled."

"Mama, you're going to order them to be whipped? I won't stand for it; I won't turn them over," he screamed and didn't let up. "Mama has to find out who's guilty, not Abromas. He should be beaten, not the serfs. I won't allow it! It's forbidden! They're my people. I won't hand them over for whipping."

When all attempts to calm the master failed, the lady had all the informers and the accused brought to her. Abromas, Fokas, and the steward arrived, all the while complaining to the lady. The accused party presented their side and fell at the lady's feet, trying their best to get out of the lashing.

Once again the master shouted: "I won't surrender them! I won't allow them to be whipped!" Jumping up, he quickly grabbed Fokas's whip and cried, "You're not going to lash my people!"

The teachers, nannies, and the servant ran in, interested to see who was going to win. In an attempt to calm the master, Abromas leaned over him and talked to him in German. With the back of his hand the master socked Abromas in the teeth. The master continued to spit and make faces at him. The lady cried out: "Misiuta, Misiuta! *Tugu, tugu.* This time I forgive all of you! The master is adamant, he won't allow you to be punished, and so I pardon you, too."

The people rejoiced, kissing the lady's and the master's hands and feet. They left, and the informers slunk out also. Sticking around, Abromas reproved the lady for spoiling the accused serfs even more by not allowing them to be punished. He told her that they didn't want to abide by the rules of the manor anymore and that he wouldn't be able to control the serfs. Hanging onto Abromas's coat tails, the master shouted frantically: "Abram, get the hell out, Abram, out!" and shoved him outside.

"Misiuta! Misiuta! *Tugu, tugu,* that's not at all polite!" declared the lady.

Laurynas, the Valet

Some said the lady was German, others that she was Jewish, except that she was born in Prussia. The old master was Catholic, so the child was raised Catholic, the same as his father. Since the teacher was also Catholic, he taught the young master his prayers and the Ten Commandments. When the masters gathered at teatime or in the evening, the conversation sometimes turned to religious matters. The young master would begin to argue adamantly that no one would go to heaven after death except peasants, workers, and serfs.

"How do you know that, Misiuta?"

"I just know. When a master, a nobleman, dies, he'll knock on the gates of heaven, and St. Peter will ask, "Who's there?"

"A Polish nobleman, mister," he'd say.

"You're not allowed in here!" St. Peter would answer.

So they had to head to hell.

And when Abromas dies and knocks at the gates of heaven and gets asked: "Who's there?"

He'll answer: "A Jewish merchant!"

"Go to the devil and burn in hell!" St. Peter will retort.

When he German mother dies and knocks, and when St. Peter asks, she'll answer in German: "Ich."

"We don't need any of those in here," is what you'll hear St. Peter say and she'll have to step aside.

And when Laurukas dies, knocks at heaven's gate, and gets asked, "Who's there?"

He'll proclaim: "It's me!"

"Oh, that's one of our very own," St. Peter will shout and let him into heaven.

All the masters would laugh and laugh, the lady would also be happy that her little master was so clever.

"And you, Misiuta, when you die and are asked who's at heaven's gate, how will you respond?"

"No question. I will cry out, 'it's me, me, me, dear Peter! I'm a Lowlander.' The gate will burst open for me and St. Peter will receive me: 'Come, come forward, you Zemaitish Kukutis, native bird, at least you'll chirp for us.'"

The master studied at home until he was twelve, and I kept being moved around in the chambers or to the gardens. Then I ended up as the master's valet. He wouldn't let anyone except me serve him. I was ordered to speak only Polish, but I kept trying to get out of it, saying that I didn't understand it and didn't know the language at all. This made everyone laugh. They called us peasants and other names when the master and I spoke Lithuanian, but the master paid no attention.

One time a Jew brought some meat to the manor. I was crossing the yard, and the Jew was shouting in Polish: "Maybe you need some meat?"

Forgetting myself, I answered loudly in Polish: "We don't need any!"

I didn't even notice that the lady was close by, and she shouted back in turn: "*Tugu, tugu!* You've learned Polish already! For that you won't be Laurukas anymore, but Wawrzyniec in Polish."

She went with me to the sewing room and told the valet and the maids that the peasant Laurukas was no more, but they were all to call me Wawrzyniec and talk to me entirely in Polish, not a word of Lowland dialect.

The lady's order was announced everywhere in the chambers and the kitchen. The master was the only one who didn't want to obey. As soon as we were alone, naturally we broke into Lithuanian. Nor did he change my name–as far as he was concerned, I stayed Laurukas.

The master's uncle, the deceased old master's brother, who had been the master of the Šaukėnai estate, died a bachelor. The estate was to be left to our master, who was the closest successor. But a more distant relative, the old master's cousin's son, appeared and started traipsing around from court to court, scheming to get Šaukėnai for himself. He hired lawyers to represent his case; the lady in turn hired them for herself. At one time one won the estate, at another time the other. And so it went, the case dragged on, and the master kept pleading: "Mama, stop carrying on! We don't need that other estate!"

In the meantime, the master had to be taken to Vilnius to some institute to finish his schooling. The master was twelve and I was eighteen. The master asked his mother to bring me along as a valet because he didn't want to be served by anyone else.

So they took the two of us to Vilnius. They rented us an apartment, got all the necessary household items together: some were brought from home. We settled into some rooms and a kitchen.

The master would study at the institute all week and he'd eat there too. My only job was to bring the master home Saturday afternoons and take him back Monday mornings. On Sundays I had to prepare him breakfast, lunch, and dinner or buy him food and prepare anything he liked. Of course, at the same time I took care of food for myself.

All week long I just had to cook for myself. That's how we lived. I had time for myself, since there was hardly any work at all, except getting my meals and keeping the rooms clean.

The master gave me as much money as I needed. On Sundays, when the master was home, I would try to make the best meal I knew how, since his student friends would come for dinner.

One of them played the violin wonderfully well, another would bring his guitar, yet a third one his flute. They would play and sing, while others danced. They'd raise such a ruckus that even the neighbors upstairs would start to yell and try to quiet us. And when the weather was nice, we'd all go to the hills outside of town for walks, or we'd hire drivers to take us for rides.

When we were alone, the master and I talked and planned how we would live on our return to the manor. We'd fire Abromas and then send Fokas packing. We'd hire a good steward, but we wouldn't need a head steward, as the master would look after everything. He always promised to give me the windmill. Talking and dreaming this way, we set our future life and forged our destiny.

Mykolas Gets Ill

Once I went over on a Saturday to get the master, waiting until he came out from school looking pale and changed, his precious hands trembling. Frightened, I asked: "What happened, dear master, what took place?"

Žemaitė's Autobiography

"Nothing," he replied, " I just don't feel too well, I feel weak, my head is spinning. I have a bad headache."

After we went out into the street, I called for a driver.

"It's not necessary, it's not necessary!" the master protested, "I want to walk, you understand, breathe some fresh air and get my energy back."

I barely got him back home. I undressed him immediately, put him to bed, and ran off to Dr. Kopickis, whom the lady had put in charge of seeing to the master's health. Suddenly a bolt traveled through my heart–ping! The gentleman who was battling my lady for the estate was sitting at the doctor's office. I felt as if someone had pierced me through. Should I say that the master had been taken ill or should I run to find another doctor? Seeing me, Kopickis asked, "Why did you come here, has someone taken ill?"

"Yes," I said, "the master is not well for some reason. I put him to bed."

"Okay, okay," he said, "run along home, I'll come straight away."

I ran home; it felt like my heart was being squeezed with pain.

Dr. Kopickis came in the evening, wrote out some medicine, instructed me how to give it to the sick youth. Returning in the morning, he examined the patient and wrote a prescription for another medicine. He came three to four times a day, prescribing new medicine each time, always ordering me to get the medicine at the same pharmacy.

My master kept getting weaker. I couldn't even talk him into a drop of tea anymore. The doctor was worried and said, "It's most unfortunate, but our master has scarlet fever. I sent a message to the lady to come."

I was sick at heart. I asked the doctor to call in more doctors to save the master. "It's not necessary," he replied, "it's not necessary, the lady will be here soon."

He gave me another new prescription and told me to get the medicine right away. I high-tailed it to another pharmacy and asked them to give me the medicine quickly. Looking at the prescription, the pharmacist inquired, "Who is sick, how old is the patient?"

When I told him, the pharmacist swore through his teeth, "That horse doctor!"

I took note of everything carefully. The master looked worse each time. My heart was breaking, I didn't know what to do. I could only wait for the lady.

The lady finally arrived. She saw that the master was scarcely alive. He couldn't even recognize his mother anymore. Immediately she called in three more doctors. Kopickis was the first to arrive. Lying on her son's breast, the lady was fainting and crying pitifully. All the while the doctor was busy twisting and tearing all the prescription labels from the medicine bottles.

Three more doctors gathered. They examined the patient and consulted one another. All the time they kept writing down something, then they grabbed their hats and left. I let the first two out; the last to leave was the old doctor. I fell at his feet in the front hall, weeping and wailing, begging him to save my master. Stroking my head, he uttered: "I'm sorry for the child too," he continued. "But unfortunately it's too late, there is no remedy. The child has been poisoned. What a pity!"

I felt like I had been hit on the head with an ax, even my eyes went dim. The lady called for me and told me to run to the pharmacy with the doctor's prescription. I brought home the medicine and rushed to the master's side—he was lying there, looking as if he was dead. The only sign of life was his heavy breathing. The lady was pouring medicine down his throat, but alas, he couldn't swallow, and it ran out of his little mouth. Beside herself and sobbing, the lady tried to get him to talk, kissing him, but she couldn't bring him to. Some ladies, young misses and acquaintances, arrived together to visit the patient. They led the lady into another room and tried to calm her down. Sitting by the master, I didn't leave his side.

Come night the lady finally calmed down: she may have fallen asleep. The visitors left, and everything turned quiet. It started to get light and the patient began to move. He managed to raise his hands a little. Kneeling by the bed, I grasped his hands and asked him: "Maybe there's something you want?"

I offered him a drop of water, just to moisten his mouth.

Raising his eyes, he looked around, then fixed his gaze on me, barely whispering: "Laurukas! Are you by me?"

I was so happy to hear him speak. Kissing his hands, I said: "Yes, dear master! Anywhere you are, I'm always with you."

He seemed to want to sit up. Embracing him, I attempted to hold him up, but falling back on the pillow, he squeezed my hand, pulled me to himself and quietly said: "I am dying... I am the only one who's happy. All of you left behind are the unhappy ones." His dear gaze became fixed, it seemed that all he was still able to whisper was: "Mama..."

Frightened, I jumped up, and stumbled to open the door to the other room, calling loudly: "Lady! The master is asking for you!"

The lady rushed in; the master scarcely took another breath before he faded. With the first rays of the sun his soul flew away!

Žemaitė

After the Master's Death

Every time Laurynas told the story of the master's death, he could never finish it without crying, causing his listeners to shed tears themselves.

Then he continued. The lady collapsed on the ground by the bed. I didn't know what to do. I ran to Dr. Kopickis's: everyone was still sleeping; I almost broke the doorbell ringing it. Finally the doctor got up and ran out, I called to him from a distance: "The lady's become very ill, please come right away." I rushed off and found Miss Keršnauskaitė; I immediately told her that the master had died, and that the lady had collapsed. I rushed home at the same time that the doctor came huffing along. If I could have grabbed a gun at that moment, I probably would have shot the doctor: that's the kind of anger that burst out of me as a result of the master's death. Opening the door I shrieked out loud, "The master has already died, glory be to God!"

I was about to say to the wicked doctor, you can rejoice now. But he threatened me angrily: "Hear, hear, stop talking nonsense or you'll end up at the Bonifratres Cemetery yourself."

I crawled into my little room and, falling into bed, wept and wept, remembering his last words: "I'm dying happy and all you who are left behind are the unhappy ones!"

While crying without respite, I must have fallen asleep. The next thing I knew Miss Keršnauskaitė was waking me up. She told me to get ready to go to Kaunas.

Preparing myself, I went in to the lady's. She gave me a letter to take to the lawyer in Kaunas. She gave me money, told me to take the postal carriage without delay and deliver the letter to the lawyer and tell him that the master had died.

I paid 15 rubles at the post and rushed off. At every stop I gave the drivers a tip so they'd go faster, but still I only reached Kaunas toward evening.

Straight away I went to the lawyer's. Several gentlemen had gathered there for a visit. As soon as he saw me, the lawyer pulled out a paper to show me: "See," he said, "the estate really does belong to our master."

"There's no need now," I retorted, "the master has passed away."

The lawyer and all the other gentlemen stopped dead in their tracks. Astonished, they asked me how it had happened, what disease he died of. I told them all about it.

"I see," said the lawyer, "that is such a great misfortune. After winning the case, I'm holding a party for all the leaders and those who were involved in it. Anyway, all the guests have been invited. Maybe you could help me entertain them?"

"I can't," I replied. "I'm returning home now, to be by my master, even if he is dead." I left that place. I returned home as dawn was breaking. My master had been dressed and was already lying in his coffin in his room with the catafalque they'd made, surrounded by candles. Two priests were reciting prayers. The wake lasted two days and the priests, taking turns, didn't stop their prayers day or night.

It was a solemn burial: we took him to Rasos cemetery in a procession accompanied by a small orchestra. It was as if they buried my heart at the same time.

After the funeral, the lady started selling and getting rid of his things. Since they were no longer needed, the rooms would have to be rented.

I had a feeder pig that I bought at the market when it was small. I intended to butcher it and roast it for the master. It was so pretty that I had felt sorry for it. I started feeding it milk and bread; I built a pen to keep it in. When it got bigger, I bought potatoes and flour for it. The master had been so happy. We had agreed to butcher it on St. Mykolas's–the master's name day.

"We'll have a party for my name day," the master had declared gleefully. "We'll invite lots of guests to partake of the fresh sausage–it'll be a big party."

My piglet grew into a good autumn pig. The butchers started to bid on it, but I had held onto it for the master's name day.

The lady noticed the pig and asked, "Whose pig is that?"

"Mine," I replied, "I bought it when it was small and raised it. The master and I intended to butcher it. Now I'm going to sell it."

"*Tugu, tugu,* it's not your pig, but mine," she said, "You're not going to sell it. Call the butcher."

He came right away, and she sold it to him for 15 rubles. They had offered me 18 rubles. I cried, protesting that I'd bought its feed with my savings, but to no avail.

"*Tugu, tugu,* you're my man and your pig is my pig."

She should at least have paid me half a ruble for my work, since I had to clean the manure every day and buy straw for the pallet. The lady clearly demonstrated that a bonded man had no rights, not even over his own work.

The lady gave notice to rent the rooms. She had sold most of the contents and was getting ready to leave. My heart was quaking with fear. I thought to myself: "She'll take me home now and put me into the hands of Fokas and Abromas!" I expressed my fear to my acquaintances. One of my good friends offered me service at an old retired general's who had two official day servants. He hired a third as a valet, a free man. The master was a bachelor with no relatives. He'd be leaving Vilnius soon for Russia, going somewhere far away.

"You'll leave and no one will ever know what direction the wind blew you to!" my friends advised me. "Even if the masters want to, they won't be able to find you, and even if they do find out, they won't dare to take you away from a general."

I intended to play a trick, to run away from the lady and Abromas. If it wasn't to the general's, then as far away as my legs could carry me.

Laurynas, a Free Man

In the morning the lady's lawyer, the one who took the inheritance case, drew up a paper. The lady called me and gave it to me, saying: "You were a good servant to me, you obeyed and loved the master. We lost the master, such is the will of God! It's in his name that I give you your freedom, I free you from your serfdom. As a free man, you can go wherever you like; you don't have to ask anybody's permission. Here is the evidence, confirmed at the lawyer's and notarized. God help you. I'm not going to take you to the manor anymore."

I couldn't believe my ears, the lady's final words—it was as if a rock had been rolled off my heart. I fell at the lady's feet and thanked the lawyer and the lady and she and I both cried.

Going into my little room, I pulled out the paper, kissed it, and pressed it to my heart. I jumped up and down with joy. "Here's my fifteen years of salary! I didn't get even a kopeck, but I got my freedom, my freedom!"

I set out my things and thought: "I'll leave Vilnius with the general, get far away from Rasos cemetery. Maybe my heart won't hurt so much anymore. If I don't go with the general, I'll go somewhere else–a free man. No one can call me 'my man' anymore, as if they're saying, 'my dog.' Nobody would seek a runaway peasant. Even for the likes of a general, I could stick this paper under his nose. I was going into the wide world a free man."

In the evening I found out from my friends that the general couldn't hold onto his help. His last servant hadn't lasted more than three days and ran away.

They related an incident when they ran out of tea at the general's. When they told the general, he immediately pulled out 25 rubles and ordered the servant to buy a pound of tea for the whole amount. The servant went to the biggest tea store and asked for a pound of tea for 25 rubles. He paid for it, brought it home, brewed it until all the rooms smelled of tea. He poured it and gave it to the master. The general looked at it and began swearing and cursing. Grasping his stick, he accused him of theft: "Was that you, you scoundrel, who bought the tea for 25? I won't drink such dishwater. Take it back at once and don't rob me of my money, go buy me some good tea; otherwise I'll teach you a lesson!" Bringing the newly torn package of tea, he went to the same store and the owner wanted to know what was going on. The servant explained that the master had sent him to exchange the tea: "You gave me the wrong one for 25 rubles. He's accusing me of theft."

"Who is your master, whom did you buy it for?" they asked him at the store.

He told them the general's last name.

"You should have told us right from the start whom you were buying it for."

You see, they knew what kind of tea the general drank. They gave him a pound of tea and 24 rubles in change. They kept the ruble for the other pound and for tearing the first one. He took it home, brewed it black like tar, and pouring it for the master, carried it in to him, trembling. The master shouted, "See there, scoundrel! You tried to steal my money–it didn't work: you had to pay the whole amount for some good tea."

The general couldn't be without tea even for a minute: the samovar was on day and night so that a pound of tea was used up in a week. He gave you 25 rubles for a pound, but you only paid 75 kopecks–wasn't that a nice profit? So getting 24 rubles for three days of work, the last one took off from the general's.

I didn't agree with that way of making a profit, but I didn't know of any other place to go, so I would have to try to get service at the general's anyway.

Laurynas Ends His Stay in Vilnius

While I was thinking about this and getting ready to leave, a messenger came from the hotel with a note. Some master was inviting me to come to him at the hotel.

"Well, what's this all about?" I wondered: "Some master is asking for me."

I went to the number indicated and rang. The door opened, and I saw the same gentleman whom I had seen at Dr. Kopickis's during the master's illness. The thought ran through my mind: "Evidently, he's still hanging around Vilnius, but he didn't show his face at the master's funeral, neither at home, nor in church. You see his conscience wouldn't let him appear."

"You called for me?" I asked.

"Yes," he replied, "I heard that you're a good and loyal servant. Now having buried your young master, you're left without a place."

"That's not a problem," I said, "I'm intending to work at a retired general's and go to Russia with him."

"You have no right to do that," the master was quick to say.

"I have the right. I'm a free man," I retorted. "The lady let me go. She gave me a notarized statement to that effect."

"But I'm not going to let you go. I'm a nobleman."

"I don't have any master sitting on my neck and I won't obey," I grabbed my cap and stomped out the door.

"Wait, wait! Don't get excited," the master interrupted. "Let's talk some more."

I stopped in my tracks, but my hands and legs were shaking with anger. That's the way the masters are! He wants to put the yoke on me again?

"Sit down," the master said. "I'll explain things to you." The master sat down, and I did too.

"You're still young, you don't understand yet. You state: 'The lady let me go.' In what way? You don't belong to her, but you're a man of the estate. As long as the young master was alive, there was an inheritor of the land and the wealth, including the father's serfs. As long as he wasn't of age, the mother controlled all, until he came of age. Now that the son is gone, the mother is no longer the lady for the estate and its people. In the end, the lady will be let go from the estate because she has no document. Her letting you go free is just worthless paper and you're still a peasant like before."

"Even if I'm still a peasant, I can decide for myself whom I will serve," I replied. "After being taken away to the manor for fifteen years without a penny for my labors, I've had enough hardship. I don't have to serve like that, not even in the tsar's army. So long."

"Wait, don't rush off," urged the master. "I want to advise you like a friend. If you go away to a distant land, your parents and all your relations remain here. There everyone is a stranger; you don't know them. In case of trouble you can call on your own people, but far away, among strangers, you'll just be in the master's hands. You don't know his whims or his dishonesty. In a few years he can send you away again without a penny or accuse you of something and give you up to the recruits or stick you in jail. Who's going to stand up for you, who will acquit you? You're better off going with me to my estate."

"Estate!" I repeated in amazement. "And be under the steward's whip? No, thank you, sir, and goodbye!"

"No, no!" the master contradicted. "Wait, please be patient and hear me out. There won't be any steward or whip. As it turns out, your estate was in foreclosure. It's going to be taxed, so until someone buys it, there will be an administrator."

"Aha, so you see how low Mr. Abromas's management brought it?" I interrupted.

"But I don't mean to go on about your estate. I'm hiring you for a salary as a free man for my estate. There is no whip at my place, so you'll be free and protected by me. At my place there aren't very many masters: I'm a bachelor and I have only two sisters. I heard that you're good with a rifle. Do you hit the mark well?"

"Yes," I boasted, "the young master and I were both taught how to shoot by officers, and we were already hitting the targets."

"Well, that's excellent, I'll make you the huntsman to take care of the woods. We can hunt together. You'll be well taken care of; I'll give you a salary of thirty rubles a year. Besides that, there's not too much work to be done."

The pine groves along the Dubysa, where I used to set traps for the rabbits while I was at the estate, flashed before my eyes. The master tried to convince me: "I advise you as a friend to listen to me; otherwise you might regret it. I'll give you until tomorrow to think about it. If you accept my offer, come over tomorrow morning because we're going to leave in the evening. But if you don't come, I'll know that you aren't accepting it. I'll be forced to make other arrangements then. Goodbye for now!"

On my way home I ended up in the Bernardine Gardens. Sitting down on a bench, I pondered the master's words. I was so overcome with sorrow that the tears started to flow. I felt regret that my joy and freedom had ended so suddenly. Now again it was hardship, and a master on my back. Once more the word "recruit" passed before my eyes. The master's words, "I'll be forced to make other arrangements," rang in my ears. I began to wail as if Mama had whipped me. While I was crying, my good friend Juozapas wandered by.

"You might as well stop your weeping," he started scolding me, "your tears won't wake the dead one. You have to take look out for yourself. You're a free man now, you can choose a good job."

I started telling him about the general and about the other master's offer, about his promises and his threats. After some reflection my friend advised me, "You know what, brother? I like that master's offer better than serving the Russian. Here you're in your own country at least, near your parents, relatives, a familiar place. If it doesn't suit you, you can always leave. You don't owe anyone anything; you're free. If your folks don't need a worker at home, you can get a job at another estate. A bird in the hand is worth two in the bush. You're better off! You can get a salary anywhere, even at a peasant's, if you choose. That's better than under the Russkie's fist and at the mercy of the whip. The hell with the general! If I were you, I'd go right away. You'll even get the trip for free, at least you'll get to see your folks."

In the evening some other friends also advised me to steer clear of the general because they'd heard that he got angry at his valets and immediately sent them to the recruiters. Why get involved with a devil like that!

After talking to everybody and thinking about it overnight, I went to the master's at the hotel in the morning and announced: "I agree to go into service for you, sir."

"Very good, a wise decision," replied the master, "you won't be sorry."

He took me to the Jewish drivers to find out who was going to Telšiai and to hold a place for me and my belongings. The master was still going on to Warsaw.

He continued: "When you get to Telšiai, you may be tired of sitting, so you can go to the estate on foot. It's only three versts from there. Leave your things in the hotel at Maušas's until they can bring them to you at the manor." He gave me some money and a letter to show the mistresses, his sisters, so they'd know who I was.

The very same day, I found a Jew who was going farther than Telšiai with four passengers. I was to be the fifth. We were to leave the next day. I went home to collect my things but found that my lady had already sold everything and was on her way out. We said our goodbyes, and both of us cried. I told her where I was going to serve. The lady praised me for returning to my native area.

It was totally bare in our rooms: all the furniture had been taken away, even the corners were empty. Not a trace of the young master left. In the sweepings on the ground I noticed a silver teaspoon the master used for his tea. I was so happy to find at least that much to remember him by. To this day I still keep it on display.

I piled all my meager belongings into a carrying case. Everything fit—a few little things like a razor and some blades. I couldn't find my good shoes anymore, probably somebody made off with them during the funeral or during the auction.

I took my valise to the Jew's place and I still had some time before the trip the next night. At nighttime and during the day, I said goodbye to all my acquaintances. I even went to the Rasos cemetery with my friends to visit the young master's grave for the last time.

And so three years of my life in Vilnius ended. The master's death cut off all our dreams and aspirations like the blow of an ax.

Laurynas at Telšiai Manor

I rode in the Jew's carriage with two young gentlemen and two Jewish passengers, going farther and farther from Vilnius with each roll of the wheels.

My suspicion as to who was responsible for the master's death was strongly confirmed when I arrived at the manor. At first the young misses liked to question me repeatedly about the master, especially about his death. They were curious to know all the details. I, of course, related everything willingly and sincerely when asked. As soon as the misses brought up such talk, the mister left the room immediately or sent me off somewhere else. And once, when I mentioned the old doctor who said that there was no help left for the young master because he had been poisoned, the mister jumped up and suddenly appeared from the other room, crying out: "Maybe you were drunk or that old doctor of yours was completely crazy?"

From that time forth the misses stopped questioning me about the master's death.

It was already the seventh year of serving the new master. During this time both the young miss and the master got married. I attended two weddings and even made it to the master's daughter's baptism. I worked faithfully everywhere, trying to please everyone and satisfy their needs and wants. But I was destined for loneliness in my young days; a gnawing emptiness filled my heart.

The abolition of serfdom came. I spent my time in Poland happily.

Laurynas Visits His Uncle

"After visiting my folks for a while," I said, "I went to my uncle's, who lives near the Lykšelis estate. While wandering around the fields there, we came upon an old, dilapidated hay barn that belonged to the manor. Uncle took off his cap and crossed himself."

"Well, Uncle," I said, "'what is this–a church or a grave?'"

"This, my child," he replied, "is an even holier place. The amount of blood and tears that flowed here, the suffering and torment that took place here speak for themselves. This is a place of human torture since the time of the Bogušai. There, in that hay barn," he went on, "they whipped many to death. They took away their health or sent them to their grave before their time or brutally tortured them to death. The tools they used to torture people are still here. When the workers return from the field, it's deserted here." he added, "Then I'll show you."

At this time, Uncle and I sat down on the boundary of his field and went on conversing. Uncle explained to me: "The masters Bogušai of Lykšelis estate were extremely brutal with their serfs. They beat and tormented them for the smallest infraction without mercy. The lady of the manor especially was incredibly evil and mean. If some man or woman was ordered to be whipped for the slightest offense, she herself would most often rush to the hay barn to count the lashes to make sure that they were whipped the required number. If the master was doing the counting, then they'd whip the person until the latter started cursing. Whenever the beaten one did a good job of sending the master to the devil, the master would release him sooner. Evidently the master liked it better if the man cursed him out.

But if the beaten man suffered patiently, offering his suffering up to God, he'd whip mercilessly and keep waiting for him to start swearing. Once he whipped a poor man to death. At first they lashed him a few dozen times and let him go. The man prayed, 'Lord Jesus, I offer my suffering and my holy wounds up to you!'"

Hearing this, the master immediately shouted, "Beat him on the same wound!"

Again they whipped him several dozen lashes more. They let him go, but the serf started in again: "God, I offer my holy wounds up to you!"

The master sent him back to be whipped one more time. They whipped him until the man lost consciousness. But they couldn't force a curse out of him.

"The lady herself," said Uncle, "went around like that all day long, boxing the hired girls' or serfs' ears or sending them off to be whipped. She poured some dry peas on the floor by the cradle for the nanny and forced her to kneel on them on her bare knees. Afterwards the nanny couldn't go to sleep at night because of the pain."

Uncle continued: "Another time the serf girls were shearing the estate's sheep. Somehow one of the girls accidentally cut off a ewe's nipple. Witnessing this, the lady immediately told them to hold the girl down, grabbed the scissors and cut off the tiny nipple on the girl's breast. That devil's wife had no heart. That's what she was like. Drinking their fill of the serfs' blood and tears, the two of them, one after the other, died off, leaving their children nothing but debts. The children divided up some little bits of land at the margins, but most of the large estate was auctioned to pay off the loans. The people caught their breath under a new master. Even though a military person bought the estate, nonetheless, he didn't whip the people anymore, and the hay barn was left abandoned."

Toward evening when there were no workers left in the fields, Uncle and I entered the barn. The door was broken down, the walls were bent, straw was scattered all over the dirt floor, and rope ends were strewn about. Near the end wall, a pole as tall as a man was dug into the dirt. There were two iron loops for sticking the hands into, and on their ends were chains to tighten them. Lower down there were also two loops with chains for the feet. In the rays of the sunset the pole appeared red, as though covered with something thick that looked dried. The last rays of sunlight played on the pole through the gaps in the walls, and the tree branches looked like drops of dripping blood. Pity and horror pressed on my heart, and feelings of revenge clenched the palms of my hands into fists.

"Come here, I'll show you some more," Uncle called to me. "We can't stay here too long. If somebody sees us hanging about, they'll suspect that we're looking for something to steal." As he talked, Uncle was kicking straw from a piece of log. "Look," he said, "here's a block of wood into which they'd put the ones who had done something wrong." He finished kicking the straw from the wood block; there were maybe several feet of it. In the middle of the block two holes had been cut through lengthwise; the block was split in half. On one end there was a hinge, on the other end was a plate with a lock that held tight. Opening half the block along the hinge, Uncle explained; "There," he said, "they would seat the person on the ground, put one foot into one hole, the other into the block's second hole, put the other end of the block back, lock it and you just sit there with your legs sticking out. You can't move at all, you can't even move your legs. Sometimes the man would sit there in the stocks for several days so that he didn't run away from his punishment until he was indicted, while they investigated his guilt. There was no way you could drag away a block of wood like that. There used to be more tools lying around here," Uncle continued, poking around. "Some triple leather belts that looked like chicken feet hammered onto some wooden sticks were kept here. They were called disciplines. They lashed people with those contraptions. At the first lash of the discipline, the tortured person's skin would burst. Soon he would be swimming in blood, but they'd beat him as many times as had been ordered, while one of the masters counted the lashes. This kind of whipping took away half the victim's vitality or even all of it for the rest of his life."

Uncle kicked around in the straw, but he couldn't find the discipline. He surmised: "Probably the shepherds got in at some time and carried them off to destroy them." Going outside, Uncle related some more details, but all I could think of was how distressed we were by Abromas and Fokas at our estate, but here even worse horrors were taking place.

Uncle laughed: "Once I too had to sit for more than half a day in the block because of Bogušas. You see, one night somebody had cut down the birch tree that grew right on the boundary between our place and the estate. In the morning," he recounted, "I was still in bed, the steward and his men came rushing in, yanked me out of bed, dragged me to this barn, and put me in the stocks. I was terrified, since I was still so young, having left my master right after my father's death. Mother ran over shrieking, while I was sobbing because we didn't know why I was being punished. But when they told us it was for the cutting down the birch on the boundary, I laughed with relief. Leaving me in the stocks, they tore back, searching everywhere–the eaves and the tents, looking high and low for the cut-down birch and traces of the culprit's footprints. But the birch had been thick with many branches, so you couldn't hide it just anywhere. Not finding even a branch of the tree, they returned home and let me go. In any case, they couldn't punish me or whip me. You see, I belonged to royal land. If I'd been the master's valet, or someone else's serf, they could have gotten away with beating me or punishing me some other way. Releasing me, the master told me to be on the lookout for whoever cut down the birch. If I tracked him down and let him know who it was, he'd give me three rubles.

"All right, all right! I told them, but when I was alone, I thought to myself: You'll never see the day when I serve as your spy, you executioner. In fact, if I find out who did it, I'll warn them and help them hide." Uncle was chuckling as he told the story, "But my arms and legs sure shook," he admitted.

(Laurynas's tale in his own words ends.)

Julija Marries Laurynas

So, remembering all the hardships and injustices of the poor serfs, Mister Laurynas told his stories, telling of his own pain at the same time. Most often he complained that no one felt for him, no one had ever loved him then or loved him even now. It was not enough that his life was bitter and that, from his young days, hard work and slavery were his lot, but besides that, the emptiness of his heart oppressed him. He couldn't find anyone to hear him out, and he couldn't find comfort anywhere.

With such persuasive talk he won not only my sympathy but also my pity. I wanted to comfort him. He understood where my sympathies lay, and thus he tried to get together with me as much as he could to converse further. It didn't take long for us to start planning our wedding. But he kept lamenting that since my parents were of the gentry, they would not let me marry a peasant.

I was determined not to let anything stand in the way of my marrying him. Not only that, I agreed to marry him just because he was a peasant and was wronged by fate.

It seemed to me that it was a noble deed on my part to marry such an unhappy man.

When the masters found out, they forbade it and tried to talk me out of it, stressing: "He's a peasant and poor, with no education. You'll be lost with him."

The master even wanted to let him go but couldn't find a pretext to do so. These warnings served to attach me all the more to him.

Together, we attended the great feast day at Žemaičių Kalvarija. My parents and sisters also came. I showed off my fiancé to them. Everybody liked his appearance, but on learning that he was a peasant, Mama cried profusely. She'd never had a peasant in her family. And here her first son-in-law wanted to wheedle himself into the family, and he happened to be a peasant. She didn't want to give me permission to marry him, even begging me to give him up.

My father had the opposite opinion, not caring at all about his being a peasant as long as he was a good man and wasn't a drunkard. He thought he was used to serving on the estates, so he could earn bread for his family. Father agreed, and I didn't pay heed to mama's pleas to give him up.

We got married within a few months, on September 20, 1865. The wedding took place in Plungė because my parents held the party there, as they lived in that parish.

We served on the manor over the winter until St. George's, but from April 23, 1866, we struck out on our own.

Hardships Begin

Over the winter I kept asking, even begging, my husband to look for service on some other estate, but he wanted nothing to do with it. Finally, at my final request, he tried to look for work at the Oginskises by the forest. He went on his horse, a beautiful bay. He stayed at the village of Rietavas, where he ran into some woodsman of the Oginskises at the inn. He asked him how best to approach the master and how to find out about going into service there.

"My dear man, if you want to lose your bay horse," he advised, "then come serve here, because you can't go riding around like a master. But if you want to keep the horse and not lose it, then cross yourself and get away from Oginskis's estates and his service."

Thus frightened off, my husband no longer looked for anything. He got on his horse and came riding home, getting nothing for his efforts.

After that, he no longer looked for service, declaring: "I've had enough of having a master over my head. I'm better off plowing and harrowing, digging the good rich black soil and being master over myself."

My father had bought several dozen hectares of land with some dilapidated buildings, where he allowed us to farm temporarily. Since his father had already died, my husband received an animal of each kind and bread from his mother and brother, until we could get some of our own.

This is where my difficult life and all my worries began.

The biggest hardship was that I had to get up so early. At the manor I used to sleep until seven, sometimes even later. On my own place, I had to get up at four at the latest. My heart would quake getting out of bed. I started to doze off even while milking the cows. We bought a goose with some goslings; they'd start to gaggle—you'd have to let them out early. The piglets squealed. And breakfast had to be started. You'd have to think of what to make: there were no potatoes, beets, or cabbage. Just flour, grain, a little bit of bacon and milk. All the food we had was a little grain to make porridge. You'd have to bake bread and knead dough—it was such hard work. Bring in the wood, start the fire—I couldn't gauge the temperature, so the bread would burn. Other times it wasn't baked enough—all this made the husband grumble. The same with the cooking: first the food didn't have enough salt, then it had too much, or it was burnt. I poured the milk into the porridge and it made a mess. We used up the buttermilk. I couldn't manage to salvage even a bit of cream for a speck of butter.

The cows gave very little milk because the pastures were poor. Moreover, there was nothing to feed the cattle at home.

Since there was no grain for feed, the piglets lost weight. The flour had to be saved for bread. The grass for the pigs had to be gathered from the waysides. Nettles cut my hands, but the grass had to be cut in spite of my poor hands. On top of that, water from the well had to be carried uphill.

The cabin had no floor, so when you swept it, dust swirled around like a windmill. The windows were so caked with mud, you couldn't even scrape them clean. The clothes got worn, so you had to wash and scrub them the best way you could.

One job followed another, and I couldn't make up my mind where to start first. We wanted to hire a girl, but you couldn't get one in the spring–they were all taken by Christmas. He got only a boy for the outdoor work and a young shepherd for the animals. The housework and taking care of everyone was left to me alone–to work yourself to death. If something was not done, supper or lunch was late, then you'd hear about it right away: "Look how lazy our housekeeper is. Maybe she dozed off somewhere?"

All spring I ran around with my tongue hanging out. I got so exhausted from so much work, I couldn't drag my feet anymore. To hell with my dedication! What use was it for anybody, especially for me? The only answer was tears. And even those I had to hide because my husband got angry whenever he saw them.

"What's the use of bawling for no reason at all? You just have to keep working and not be lazy. The more we work, the more we'll have."

Work, work, it seemed there was endless work waiting to be done in the house, but there was nothing to show for what you had done.

My folks lost their place. The old count died, so the son became the master. As they say: new trees call for new woodcutters. That's the way it was here–the young masters took up farming their own way, exchanging all the old servants for new ones. Since my folks were among the old ones, they had to give up their place to the newcomers.

Toward fall they moved back onto their own land. There was nowhere for us all to turn around: the cottage had only one room, and the entry was the size of a pocket. There were four of us; and then the old folks and two sisters; four people got added on. They stuffed their things into the granary, but there was nowhere to put the bed for sleeping. Mama was old and ill, and the winter was cold. It was four versts to the church, and she wanted to go every Sunday–better yet, every day. So they took a few rooms in town, and Mama and her daughters went to live there, close to the church over the winter because we ran out of space at our house. My little daughter took over the corner, because someone so little needed a good space and warmth.

In the spring Mama and her daughters returned, and Father himself took over managing the farm on his own land. We were forced to go out into the wide world. We rented large and small farms for short or long periods, and often for just one year.

Almost every spring, piling our belongings into wagons and leading the animals, we would move to a new place, hoping to find greater comfort and better luck. But we didn't find mountains of flour anywhere–everywhere it was the same troubles, similar hardships. Either the potatoes rotted, or the rye disappeared, or sometimes the summer hay didn't grow, or it went to seed after mowing. At other times the pastures were poor or there wasn't much feed. Some animal keeled over or one of the little ones wasted away. We were always short; we couldn't seem to make ends meet.

My husband thought I was a terrible housekeeper, and that was why there were so many losses. It seemed to me that he didn't know how to farm, and that was why we couldn't get rich. But putting us together–we were both exactly the same, not knowing how to do anything. We were impractical and were not used to hard work. We tortured ourselves and lived in poverty like rats drowning in buttermilk. We scolded each other and got angry over any little thing—the hen drowned, the gosling got caught by a crow, the piglet died.

"What kind of housekeeper are you? You don't look after anything," my husband shouted at me. "It's because of you that everything is going to pot."

"But you're such a good manager, you can take care of everything... you can scare away the crows."

Years of Poverty

Whatever the loss or misfortune, I was left with blame and tears. Besides that, God was so good—He blessed us and kept blessing us because every two years or year and a half, a little one fell into our lap. And each one was met with my salty tears.

Then my husband would console me saying: "What are you going to do, Mama! God gave it to us; you're not going to throw it away. We'll suffer and care for it, we'll raise it somehow."

It was all right for him to be calm, while I tortured myself, night and day, listening to the squealing. Could anyone have enough patience to listen to it all? No doubt about it, my husband was handsome, blue-eyed, with curly blond hair and beloved by me, but sometimes he aggravated me so much that I didn't even want to look at him.

Added to all the hardships, worries, and dissatisfaction was longing. You couldn't know anything about the outside world–nothing except gossip, women's blathering, useless details, arguments, and jokes. All we heard about were the daily incidents at home or at the neighbor's. No newspapers, no news from anyone or anything farther away.

Finally, there weren't any books to read besides the prayer book. It was tedious and dull to waste away among the humdrum of everyday work and child-rearing. Tied down and locked up with the children, day after day. It was work and worry without any relief. The same trifles burdened one to death. If only you could just rid yourself of them, you'd jump up and run away wherever your feet carried you.

While the children were small, it was torment to be alone with them by myself. Sometimes I had a hired girl, sometimes not. If we ended up with a smaller place to rent, there wasn't enough space to hire anybody, so we tried to do all the work ourselves. If we were lucky enough to get a bigger place, we hired a girl and a boy.

As the children grew, they had to herd the animals according to their ability, the pigs, the geese. In the summer everyone was busy with their work, so there wasn't any time left over to teach the children even how to read.

My oldest sister pitched in. Since she had established herself at the hostel in Varniai, she took in my children over the winter and taught them to read, how to say their prayers, and learn the Ten Commandments. She took them to confession and brought them home again in the summer. So in the winters, she taught my children religious things because she didn't trust me and scolded me that I taught them only how to read and write and neglected their religious training.

We taught the children in Polish, as my sister couldn't get any books in Lithuanian, only prayer books. We thought that having learned Polish, afterwards they could read in Lithuanian.

Yet another concern for me was the children's clothing. While they were small, old rags sufficed, but when they grew up a little, they'd have to go out or to church. It seemed you needed everything, because it was embarrassing to send the kids out in tatters. The boys refused to go out looking like beggars, but the girls especially were ashamed to be seen in rags. There was no money to buy each one of them new clothes. I couldn't weave and spin homemade ones all by myself. So I tormented myself, mending outgrown clothes from the bigger ones and fixing them up for the littler ones. I sewed clothing for the children from my old clothes. So I lived in poverty, year after year, until the girls grew up a little and were able to spin and weave for themselves.

They finally brought my hands some relief.

Another source of distress ate at my heart. In the summertime the girls were at work or taking care of the animals. During the winter they had to spin and weave, so there was not a moment left for schooling. All they knew was what they learned from the prayer books taught by their aunt when they were small. If one of them found the interest, in the evenings or on holy days, she'd take a pencil or a feather and scratch away a bit, at least once in a while. And encouraged to learn writing, another one of the three girls said: "Why do I need to learn to write? It's not as if I'm going to earn my bread by writing. I can read from a book, and that's enough."

My husband agreed with my daughter, but as for me, it was a dagger in my heart.

Mama passed away in 1874, when my children were still small. My younger sister got married, then my father took the son-in-law onto his own land and took it upon himself to pay our legal portions. But my brother-in-law had no luck with the farm either. Over a period of several years, he barely managed to pay me back my portion of three hundred rubles, but the older ones who were single didn't even get that amount.

Father, too, passed away three years after Mama's death, unable to pay his sisters' portions. My brother-in-law gave up half his land to them, but it was mostly bog and peat rather than arable land. The oldest sister, as I mentioned, was in the hostel in Varniai, and the second one went out on her own, in service in Petersburg and, relative to the times, earned good money.

She had taken my oldest son, Kaziukas, to be baptized and for some reason got it into her head to send him into the priesthood. Having come home for a family gathering, she rented an apartment at some old medical assistant's who promised to watch the child. When he'd come home from school, they'd teach him some more at home. She paid them ten rubles a month to be taught for two years. The child barely made it through grade school, and so his dream of priesthood ended. Afterwards he worked as our hired hand.

From the very start, my husband didn't love his son. He would beat and whip him for the smallest transgression. If I took his side, then it became my fault: I'm raising unruly children, I'm teaching them to disobey their father. Father acted like a despot even when our son had grown up. The man was stubborn, and he wouldn't stop arguing and scolding. The two of them fighting just tore at my heart. When the time came for Kazys to enter the army, he took off for America in 1891, and we never heard from him again.

At first he wrote a few letters and sent some ten-dollar bills to pay off the debt, which he'd borrowed for his journey. After that, not a word, nor any message as to whether he was dead or alive, not even to this day.

Earlier, as I mentioned, we made a living renting other people's land, as sharecroppers. In 1884, my husband's brother invited us to come and live with him. His land was large, so he had to hire workers, and his wife was an old woman, some twenty years older than her husband.

In feudal times, the same lady who had taken my husband onto her estate told Laurynas's brother to marry an old maid whose own brother was rich and died a bachelor. On the farm you need a worker, just as a single girl needs a husband. The lady herself was in charge of assigning who had to marry the girl and farm on her land. The lady considered releasing my husband from the estate if he wanted to marry her. But on seeing the miss, Laurynas crossed himself and ran away. And so since his oldest brother was still left, the lady forced him to marry the old maid, threatening that if he didn't obey, she would send him to be a recruit.

Having married an old maid, the young man lived on and waited for her to die so that then he could marry a young wife. But while he was waiting, he himself got old. He got tired of taking care of everything. He had no children, of course, so he invited us to come help him, saying: "Your children are almost grown already, you can hire a farm hand and farm the land."

We moved there and worked the land: plowing, harrowing, sowing, threshing, cutting the meadows with a scythe. We gave Laurynas's brother half of all the harvested grain and feed. He lived the way he'd always lived, only he didn't have to hire workers, and we had enough bread. Our family was smaller now. There was some left over to sell from our half of the farm.

We lived at the brother's for six years. During that time we married off one daughter right there in the village. Our son, as I related, went off to America, and our family shrank in size.

The old lady, our sister-in-law, took ill. Expecting her to die soon, the brother let us go. We went to the village of Užvenčiai to farm the land once again.

Not long after, the old sister-in-law passed away. After burying his wife, the brother started to run around the countryside to all the young girls to find one to marry. He was looking for a young one, and she had to be pretty and rich. Although his land had good soil and was large, the brother was over sixty years old and no one wanted an old man like that. Finally, right before Lent he latched onto his next-door neighbor—a young girl. Coerced into it by her mother's brothers and sisters, she married him. As she herself said, she wasn't marrying the old geezer but his land and wealth. Before the wedding she demanded that he give her six hundred rubles from his land and confirm the documents at the notary's.

During the wedding the old man realized his disappointment—all his life he had so desired a young wife and her love, but here his bride didn't even want to look at her husband cross-eyed. She just danced and reveled with the young people and openly told everyone that she didn't love her husband and wouldn't love him. She had wed him for his land and wealth.

"An old man like that is probably not going to live long. Later I'm going to marry a young one, even if he takes the land away from me and makes me leave the farm, he'll still have to pay the six hundred he's signed off on from the land, and with that I can marry into even better land than his."

Exactly a week after the wedding, the old man died suddenly. In the evening he was well, but that night he got sick. He didn't let anyone know. In the morning only the neighbors found out that he was already gone. Without exception everyone thought that the bride had poisoned him.

The police started to bother them, not letting them bury the deceased. Officials came, and the doctors cut up the deceased and examined his parts. They put all his insides into glass jars and took them with them. They arrested the bride and took her away. The farm was left empty, so we moved back at once.

My husband had two more brothers: one lived on the land their father had left, the other one had married a widow and lived on an excellent farm. The two of them clung to the dead brother's inheritance. It wasn't enough that they auctioned off all his possessions; they didn't even leave us the land. They took their case to court, hired lawyers, wasted money, and ripped away two thirds of the land from us, leaving us farming on twenty hectares; that is, they divided the dead brother's land into three parts. All three had to pay the deceased's wife the six hundred rubles, which had been signed over before the wedding. The wife spent about half a year in jail and came back scot-free.

Who can describe all the details of that unpleasantness, the heartache we had to endure through that lawsuit? On our own backs we experienced people's greed, their lack of mercy, and the disgrace of relations who wished to tear the last bite of bread from your teeth, though they already had more than enough of every-thing themselves. My husband even fell ill from all the distress.

I felt pity for the dead old man, who just wanted so much to live with a young wife. I was sorry for her, too, her stupid talk–"the old geezer won't live long, soon there will be a change." Because of that she caused people to wonder whether she had put an end to the old man. Whether she did or not, only God knows.

My Longing to Read

As I mentioned earlier, I always longed to read, but there was always a shortage of books for me. Wherever I could get some, I borrowed them to read, but most often I got only religious books that my sister would get from the priests or bought zealous ones for herself–sticking me with all kinds of "heavens" and "hells."

When we moved to the brother's, I became acquainted with the neighboring gentlemen. They took an interest in me: how I came to speak Polish so well. I used this to get Polish books to read. We didn't worry about Lithuanian writing. Lithuanian writings were prohibited, and that was that. In addition, I taught my children to read and write in Polish.

One of our neighbor's sons was at the Šiauliai gymnasium. When we went there, he was still only in his first year. When he came home for the summer or holidays, he always played and ran around with my kids. Looking at the children, pain would pierce my heart: "Why can't I send my child to the gymnasium?"

As Poviliukas was going back to Šiauliai, one person asked him to buy this, another that, giving him money, and I also asked him to lend me some books to read.

Several times he brought back a couple of books, and after I read them, he took them back again. All he could get were Polish books.

A rumor started making the rounds that in Prussia, they were publishing Lithuanian writing, but if they caught them bringing them to our part of the country, the Russkies punished them fiercely.

During their sermons the priests started to frighten people away from the forbidden works. It was not enough that it was a sin to transfer and distribute them or sell the godless works, but it was a greater sin to read them because they were written by atheists, Germans, and non-Catholics. It was not enough to lose your soul with these kinds of readings, you could incur the government's punishment—jail or deportation to concentration camps.

Such curiosity came over me—somehow, somewhere to at least get to see those works. But no such luck, you couldn't even ask about them.

"Do you want to get caught yourself and get others in trouble?" were people's first reproach. "Well then, keep still." One time, Poviliukas came home for Christmas. The very same evening he came running over to us. He looked so happy, jumping up and down, saying: "Auntie! You won't believe what kind of treat I brought?" Pulling a book out of his shirt, he showed me. "Look, you never saw one like this yet."

Tearing it out of his hands, I looked, and even my eyes dimmed. "The newspaper Aušra in book form, the whole year's copies, sewn together."

"*Žemaitiškai* Lowland Lithuanian!" I shouted in surprise. I leafed through it, reading it, and couldn't believe my eyes. My hands were shaking.

PHOTOS OF ŽEMAITĖ IN LITHUANIA
AND IN THE UNITED STATES

Žemaitė in Panevežys in 1909

Džiuginėnai manor where Žemaitė lived
from 1864-1865

Žemaitė with her granddaughter, Elzė Veikšaitė in Vilnius, 1913

House in Vilnius in Lauryno Stuokos-Gucevičiaus Street where Žemaitė lived and worked; it is now a restaurant called The Green House

Žemaitė with her son Antanas Žymantas
in Chicago ca. 1918

Žemaitė after one of her lectures in the United States
receiving flowers

Žemaitė with her friends and patrons, Dr. Andrius Bulota and his wife
Aleksandra in Chicago, 1916

Žemaitė with Aleksandra Bulotienė
by Niagara Falls, 1916

Žemaitė in Cleveland

The Injustices Done to Village Girls

Speeches by Žemaite at the First
Lithuanian Women's Congress, 1907

The First Day's Speech

I'd like to say a few words about the injustices village women have to endure.

A girl with poor parents is often hired out to serve outside her home before the age of ten in order to bring up children or to herd animals. No one worries about her after that: the parents are relieved that the girl is earning her own bread, and the housekeeper just makes sure that the girl does as much work as possible, pushing her to her limits. For the rest of her life, the girl is left to support herself and make material and moral decisions on her own.

The daughters of farmers who are better off must earn their own bread from an early age, too. Together with the boys, they herd geese, pigs, and cattle and help the mother around the house more than the boys ever do: they sweep, peel potatoes, prepare the feed for the pigs and feed them, milk the cows, and they bring up the younger children at the same time.

Grown young women work in the fields alongside the young men. They not only use the scythe but also do the other jobs, like plowing and harrowing, as seen in the Lowlands (Žemaitija). Some jobs that the girls have to do are harder than those the boys do—such as tying the rye after it's cut with long scythes or pulling flax. Around the house they also do more work: they spin, they weave, sew and mend for the family, wash the laundry, and bake bread. In the daytime, after the men have gone to the forest, they often take care of the animals. Even the parents—especially the mothers—acknowledge that it's the girls who bear the bulk of farm work at home.

A wealthy farmer, let's say, one who has about thirty tenths of land, sets a part of it aside for the daughter: several cattle, a horse, a few of the smaller animals, some of the implements and grain, and money according to his means. If she marries someone with a lot of land, she gets more, but if she marries into less land, they give her less.

If a groom happens to come along with very good land, but he's in debt up to his ears, then he says: "Sir, give me several hundred rubles to pay off my debts, then I'll marry your daughter."

If the land suits the father, then they bargain over the daughter's dowry. However, if the father doesn't give enough, the debts remain, so that's not good; he has to give enough to cover the entire debt. He gathers all the kopecks he's saved up and borrows more so he can free his daughter. The character of the groom doesn't matter at all; whether he suits the daughter is of even less concern.

If the girl cries and says she doesn't want to marry that fellow, the father declares: "If you don't obey, you can go into service for someone else. You won't get a kopeck out of me. I won't give so much as a thimble for your disobedience."

The mother is often on her daughter's side, but who's going to listen to a stupid old woman's chattering: do women know anything? The helpless girl has to listen to what the father says. Not only that, but the groom doesn't show up for the wedding until the father counts out the money they've bargained for, down to the last penny. Stuffing the money into his pocket, he gets married. The girl, who has seen the groom only a few times, leaves her parents' home with the man. She is forced to live with him and adjust to his character. Having been a drunk before, he drinks away his wife's dowry after he gets married. The wife can't save the dowry, which has been handed over to him. Without it he wouldn't have married her in the first place.

The wife is forbidden to meddle in the husband's business: he goes to the market, he runs around the county, any kind of business is for him. He rides or goes out almost every day, and you, girl, toil at home, care for the fields, look to the animals, take care of the children, eat your bread, of which there's none, and if you mutter against your drunken husband, you'll be left with bruises from his blows. There's no one to complain to, no one to comfort you. "Why didn't you raise your voice against someone who is a brute?"

When he's drunk away all the possessions, he will rush off to America at the first opportunity and it'll be up to you, the wife, to care for the children and the indebted land. Usually, it's the girls whose parents have forced them to marry for good land that have such luck.

God forbid a farmer's daughter should fall in love with some poor boy, even the most decent fellow. When she marries him, she doesn't get a penny for her dowry. After working on the farm for decades without pay, her father throws her out with just the clothes on her back. Often when a daughter marries someone quite wealthy, she'll get a few hundred more for her dowry. If another daughter of the same parents marries some fellow with no land or only a little, she gets only a few rubles or some scrawny cow.

An unmarried girl works for her father to old age and never gets paid. When the father dies or gets old, he hands over his land and all his possessions to the son. The portion intended for the daughter is doled out to her by the brother, but only upon her marriage.

She has to continue to work for the brother in the same way, and often he doesn't want to pay her either. He tells her that she'll get her portion from him when she gets married. If the girl doesn't like working for free or doesn't get along with her sister-in-law, she is left with nothing.

There is no way to complain, since everything has been done according to custom: once the parents die, the son gets everything, and if the daughter doesn't marry, she loses her portion of the dowry. As for a son, when he wrongs his father, he is driven from the land and receives nothing. Yet when the father dies, the son lays claim to the land and gets his portion back. But a girl does not have the right to ask for her part. If the father left her nothing, then the brothers won't give her anything either.

Nor does the mother have the right to assign portions to her children. As long as her husband is alive, he alone is in charge of the children and without asking his wife, disposes of the family wealth like a despot. Often to get back at her, he deliberately does not do what she wants, just to show her that he can do as he pleases.

If the mother becomes widowed, she raises all the children equally, and when they are grown, the sons take the land, portion it out among themselves, or take payment from each other for their share. As for the girls, if the mother didn't marry the daughters off or didn't save at least a few rubles for them while she was in charge of the land, then the sons don't care about giving them anything from the land. If the girls marry at some point, they might throw in a scrawny cow for them, but if they don't marry, then they have to work for their brother, and if they don't want to, then it's off to serve some stranger.

An unmarried girl works at her father's, then at her brother's her whole life. The brother's children grow up, she gets old, her health deteriorates, and no one can stand her. They consider her a worthless mouth to feed. As long as the brother is alive, she gets by somehow, but if he dies, hurry and pack your beggars' bags and go set the dogs to barking. Who can she complain to? Everyone will say, "What's the wrong in that? If she can't do the work anymore, then she gets no bread. Is anyone going to feed her for free? She should have married—she would have gotten her portion."

Hired girls also are scorned and wronged by all the men. Their pay, compared to the boys', is half—supposedly they do less work.

After a hard day's work, the hired man comes home to find everything on the table, and because he's tired, he rests. But for the hired girl who's been running around the house, there is no time for even a minute's rest. In the morning she gets up earlier, in the evening she goes to bed later. She cooks and bakes, sees to the pigs and cows, and takes care of all the chores around the house. Moreover, during the busy times, after doing the chores, she has to run out to the fields. But it's the pastime of men to talk and say that women don't do any work; it's they alone who work.

Women are cheated out of their fair share at every opportunity. For instance: if an inheritance is passed down from some childless uncle, only the males get the inheritance. They don't share it with the womenfolk–it's not the custom.

So the girls, terrified of making the dogs bark as they go begging at the end of their lives, have only one option–to get married. Even though they have to work harder and raise their children alone in hardship, once they get married, at least they get some of their portion. When the children grow up, if they're decent, they'll feed their mother. The girls are wronged everywhere and at every step, but the greatest injustice is that they don't get an education equal to that of the boys. There's nothing to be said about poor people whose children are servants, but even a somewhat wealthy father sends his sons to the lower grades and sometimes even to the gymnasium, but he takes no care about educating his daughters. "Why spend the money, they don't need it. They'll just get married and all that education will be wasted. The boy will join the army or go to America, so he has to learn how to write a letter by himself. But the girl–she won't get a clerk's place; so you just have to teach her prayers, in order to mumble over a prayer book a little, and that's enough." That's how the village farmers put it. We hear that in the noble class, the fathers or brothers act much more justly with the girls as far as education and the dowry goes. But the village girls, in a word, are their fathers' slaves, their husbands' slaves, and finally their sons' slaves, as well. This slavery goes on for generations, from mothers to daughters, and no one cares to free themselves from the men's domination.

Women of the intelligentsia who understand the sorry state of village women should and must find some way to equalize village women's rights, especially with regard to education.

The Second Day's Speech

Yesterday I was attacking the men, blaming them for everything, and you, sisters, publicly agreed with me, complaining that men drink and beat us.

Your strong words and grievances pierced my heart; I thought about it and took a hard look at how much our hides are in physical danger. I'd like to briefly tell you the conclusion I've come to.

Could it be that we cooperate in this? It is said: "remove the beam from thine own eye and only then search for the mote in thy brother's eye." So let's take a look at how we ourselves behave with regard to our beloved whiskey.

When we have any gathering or hold a funeral or a baptism, we invite the relatives, and the first thing we all do is set the tables with bottles, large and small, and we women start in urging the guests to partake. If someone doesn't want to drink, we command them and carry on: "Are you angry, don't you love me? This isn't poison, you won't die–it's God's gift, drink, drink, bottoms up!" In this fashion we beg our guests and make it a point of honor to make them drunk out of their minds. All excited, we ourselves sit around the table and sing: "Let's drink all we can and not leave a drop for any man!"

This is what we do: when a child comes along who can barely reach the table with his nose, right away we give him a small glass of sweet liqueur. The child swigs it down to the last drop, of course, while we women laugh and rejoice at having introduced poison to the child, perhaps for the rest of his life.

And so from childhood we accustom our children to drinking. When they grow up to be shepherds, standing by the state liquor store, they toss the small bottles back and pour them down their throats. As they get used to drinking but can't afford it, they start snitching some from their fathers. Even though the mothers are aware that this is going on, they often treat it lightly. "Boys will be boys, what do you expect!" It's not enough that they get drunk by the liquor store, but they stuff their pockets full of the demon bottles. Then they take off for the evening dances, making merry and accosting some sweet girls, forcing them to glug it down. What consequences often result from that, each one of us knows all too well.

Intoxicated by the whiskey, the unfortunate girl sinks down into the filth of immorality. We women, suspecting such a girl, especially some poor young hired girl, we, dear neighbors, when we meet over the fence, whisper to one another, point fingers at her, and snicker: "Look at that one she's already fallen—she was unlucky, the poor soul, she shouldn't have slept around, now she shouldn't put on airs, you see, finally she got caught!"

The poor girl remains in our eyes as the worst kind of slut. We all look down on her, point fingers at her, and lash out at her with our tongues. No one consoles her, no one takes her in, no one says a heartfelt word to her. You'd think it was her fault alone.

Beaten down by cruel words and swimming in tears, the girl doesn't have enough strength to suffer the women's finger pointing. She's left to seek relief on her own; often she ends up under the ground. Finally, when the girl's infant grows up, how do we treat him? When a child like that gets into a little trouble, we are quick to say: "Whoever heard of a bastard being honest?" And the kind of names a child like that hears are embarrassing to pronounce even in public. How is the poor thing to blame, why does he have to suffer and carry a heavy cross all his life? For what? What is the reason?

Right away we point at the mother: "It's her fault, it's because of her." Why don't we point our fingers at our sons, the seducers? Why don't we question which one of them is more to blame? Turning his cap over his ear, the alleged seducer mocks: "My cap is my cap for all that, and she got what she wanted." Everyone laughs and agrees with him. Not only the men, but we are just as much to blame, especially if this kind of wiseass is a rich farmer's son. Then not only does the father stick up for him, but the mother all the more so. Even if she suspects her son is to blame, she goes after anyone who reproaches her dear son's doings with all her might. Swearing, she argues: "She's lying, the slut is lying! She wants to latch onto a rich fellow, let her bring witnesses to prove that he is really to blame, let her bring them!" Tell me, does anyone at any time hold up a candle to this kind of behavior?

The way it looks to me, and maybe some of you gathered here will also agree, is that all the immoralities and misfortunes flow from that tasty whiskey; that friend of ours is most to blame. Let's we, women, agree and take it firmly on ourselves to get rid of that wretched stench. Let's not drink any ourselves, let's not buy it, nor hand it out at weddings or baptisms or funerals. Let's throw the bottles away from our tables; let's get rid of that cursed fashion. Let's not be afraid, even if our husbands like to take a nip, they won't be angry if the few pence that would be spent on whiskey at some party remain in our pockets. But often when celebrating, especially at weddings, we spend dozens of rubles just on whiskey.

Dear mothers, it would be better, when raising your children, to protect them from smoking tobacco and drinking whiskey the same way we would guard them from fire. After all, those children are small today, but tomorrow they will grow up, the day after tomorrow they will marry, and once again they will torture their women by drinking and beating them. If we don't raise our children differently and don't give up whiskey, the next generation will cry over it the same way we do now.

Our sisters from the intelligentsia are reading papers here about child-rearing, about education and schools. We can use their advice; but I, your sister, also a farmwife, beg of you: Listen to me, toss away those damned bottles so we can't even hear their clanging, nor see them!

That way our heads will stay lighter, and our pockets will remain heavier.

PETRAS KURMELIS

One morning as dawn was breaking, a dense fog blanketed the entire earth so thickly that the rays of the rising sun could not break through. Above the fog, shining right there in the skies, the bright sun sparkled on the morning clouds, transforming them into fluffy white gauze. The fog hung in the air. At the slightest breeze, tree branches swayed, scattering large drops of water from their leaves laden with so much moisture. Without warning a strong wind arose, driving and dispersing some of the fog on high. But the low, damp fog hugged the bone-dry surface of the earth stubbornly and drenched the ground with its thick dew. The mists spread high, turned into clouds, and fanned out throughout the skies. The sun's rays blazed through breaking clouds, which in turn were covered by new creations. Thick walls of cloud mingled, jostled each other while fleeing across the heavens, but when any bold ones ventured near the sun's orb, they grew pale and thin. At first, without any rays the lone sun stood bare, appearing white and somewhat list-less, even sleepy. Slowly beaming through the fog, it rose higher, parting the clouds to bravely breathe a golden warmth on the glistening earth. Bathing in the cool dew, all heaven and earth shone radiantly.

People rejoiced at the beautiful morning of the Feast of the Assumption. Wherever you turned or looked, you could see it was a holy day. There wasn't a soul in the fields, but the roads and paths were filled with people coming in droves: on foot, on horseback, and in wagons. Passing one another, they hurried toward the church. As if holding a broom in her hand, each woman carried a bunch of flowers made up of all kinds of blooming grasses gathered from her garden and wildflowers from the fields. Almost all the older women's bouquets contained a fully opened thistle. Now the churchyard and the town were crowded. The almshouse yard and the churchyard wall were full of wagons, and people kept arriving along the roads. Not a soul remained in the yards and farms–everyone had streamed into church. At last the wagons dwindled, but space for where to put them also got scarce. A last one drove up and stopped by the churchyard. The wagon was brand new and handsome, pulled by a solid gray mare: in it were a husband and his wife with a couple of children on her lap. The woman descended, lifted the children out, and brushed the straw off their little clothes, straightening them. She wound the bunch of flowers with the thistle poking out into a handkerchief, held a book in the other hand, and walked to the church; holding onto the edges of her skirt, the children alongside. Left alone, the man tended and fed the mare.

"Well, well! Doesn't uncle have a nice wagon!" said a youngish man, approaching. "Spanking brand new, straight from the shop," he said, bending down to take a look. "Did you buy it, or did you have it made?"

"Don't you recognize Petras Kurmelis's handiwork?" replied the first man.

"How am I supposed to know? And who did the ironwork then?"

"Why, he himself. If he takes on a job to make something, he makes everything from start to finish and binds it all together. The only thing you have to do is get in and away you go."

"If someone's handy, they're handy!" praised Zolys, touching it. "After all, he's my close relative. Why, his mother is a Zolaite. But since he got rich, we don't see much of him anymore–of course, I'm not rich..."

"Oh, that's not true!" Gorys defended him. "He doesn't put on airs. If he doesn't speak to someone, it's because he doesn't have the time to waste at that moment. He's made a stack of cupboards, chests, sleds, and wagons for himself. You couldn't touch them for less than a couple of hundred rubles."

"Relative or not, he's a really smart and hardworking young man. Only now that his mother's become so frail, he's run into trouble: he's going to be left without a housekeeper. He doesn't really have one now. The old woman rarely gets out of bed. They say the doctor has given up on her."

"So why did he wait so long to get married? He could have had a housekeeper! Now he has to rush around to get one. Uncle, why don't you set him up with someone? You live right there, close by. It's not the time to go running around when the chickens are already hatched."

"Heck!" Gorys waved his hand, "I tried to match him up a couple of times, but he's always dragging his feet when it comes to marriage. Doesn't matter who you pick for him. Obviously, there were some decent ones in the bunch, but there was no pleasing him. If it's not one thing, it's another that doesn't suit him, and he won't bother to go calling. I don't know what he's thinking. Here's his bay: see, here he comes on horseback. Bring the horse up to my wagon–let it have some feed!"

Petras Kurmelis

Something flashed in Zolys's head; he muttered to himself: "I know what he's looking for: I can guess."

"The fellow's not getting any younger, and now he's not of a mind to wed," said Zolys, tying up his horse. "It's always like that. If you don't marry when you're young, it's well-nigh impossible to get around to it when you're older."

"Look at that bay, now there's a horse built like a brick wall!"

"What do you mean? Look at all his animals! It's a treat for your eyes to see them. He's got no end of good luck. That family just prospers: they wean their calves and keep them by their side. Their horses don't even look like workhorses; even their piglets look like they've been bathed in milk. Who knows if it's the mother's doing or if Petras will be so successful on his own? The way it is now, life is just a breeze for them. Of course, you need to take good care of things, too."

When mass started, all the people from the waysides made their way into the church. After the sermon they were hot and weary; they hurried and shoved each other on their way outside, looking for refreshment in the shade. Petras Kurmelis also came barreling out of the church, wiping the sweat off his brow. He was a mature man, tall and stout, with a slight hump on his back. His rough hands were as hard as iron, completely black from years of hard work. He was born with a dark complexion. His hair and whiskers were black, but he looked even swarthier from working in the sun. His blue eyes were a little sunken and wrinkled already, revealing that he was past the first bloom of youth. His outdated clothing was too big and hung on him, making him look even older. His coat was of brown boiled wool, his pants and vest of plaid homespun, his knee-high boots were large and heavy. A scarf was tightly wrapped around his neck. In his hand he held his cap, brim part up. He walked with big, lumbering steps, as if he had trouble lifting his feet. As he was approaching, Zolys pulled him aside to the wall and began talking:

"Petras, I heard the bad news about your dear mother being ill."

"It is quite bad," Petras sighed. "Very bad, but what are you going to do. You can't escape God's will."

"You poor fellow, you'll have to get married. God forbid your mother should die, what are you going to do alone without a mistress? You're better off picking yourself a rich bride ahead of time, one with several hundred rubles to her name, then it would make it worth your while," Zolys spoke sincerely. "Even if you choose one with nothing, I know you'll survive. But you'll have to treat the wife like a wife: you can't expect her to do the work of a hired maid. Pick a rich one, then at least you'll have the advantage of having enough to maintain her. At the moment you have enough to get by, but in time, who knows, a very rainy day may come. And in the meantime the interest will come in handy, too."

Petras was so pleased with Zolys's advice, his eyes even lit up. "That's true, Uncle, it's true what you say," replied Petras. "I've thought about that myself. But who has the money in this day and age? Everybody's poor, they're in debt up to their necks. You won't find an extra kopeck in anybody's pocket."

"But their daughters are dressed up to the nines, anyway," added the uncle.

"I need to get married quickly, otherwise I don't know how I'll manage."

"If you listen to me," said Zolys, "I'll probably be able to find you a wife. Even though she's not very graceful, but you'll get a stack of money."

Petras Kurmelis

"My good fellow, where would you find someone like that?" asked Petras.

"Why, our forester Kupstys has some moldy old bills. He's gathered quite a pile giving away the master's forest! The logs and cords of wood have all ended up in his pocket. And he doesn't spend a kopeck anywhere. He doesn't even let his girl get dressed up, doesn't even buy food. One fellow gives him a half-bushel of something; another comes up with a small lot of land in return for wood. Everyone angles to remain unnoticed while helping himself to the wood, and the forester has no objection to filling his own pockets. Kupstys is clever–he doesn't let word get around. But he told me once: 'If it worked out decently for my Marcikė somewhere, I'd scrape together up to five hundred.' And the sons get such good salaries at the manor. I'm sure they'd pass their sister several ten-ruble bills. If you want, I'll make the match right away: now there's a girl. Though she doesn't have much going for her and has no possessions, she's well-off when it comes to money, a really good catch. There's many a fellow chomping at the bit to get her, and she'll be a prize for you, too."

Petras remembered seeing Marcikė when he was looking for his horses: he accidentally came upon her rolling in the berries in the woods. He remembered that she was a fat, sturdy, red-faced girl, and that she was wearing a very dirty shirt. "That's not so bad, we'll see what happens later."

"He'll give you the money up front, before the wedding, in secret, of course," continued Zolys. "He won't require a note or anything–he keeps out of the master's way. If he stays a forester another few years, he'll collect twice as much. Afterwards you'll take care of the old folks at your place, and all the inheritance will be yours. Won't that work out well for you?"

Petras was mulling all this over as Zolys went on quietly: "And with the woods—what a chopping feast you'd have! Kupstys doesn't play high and mighty with others, just think what he'd do for his own son-in-law—you could just keep taking, as much as your horses can carry: you'd have lumber for the rest of your days. You'd even have some left for your children." He went on in a hushed tone. "It's not a sin to steal from the woods: the master didn't water them. God grew trees for all of us. As long as nobody catches or punishes you, might as well cut down as much as you can."

Petras really liked Zolys's talk. The matchmaker whispered in his ear without stopping until vespers were over, praising his good catch. Petras dreamed about the rubles and about the wood he would cut down for free. Afterwards, while he was crossing the village, as luck would have it, the girls kept getting underfoot. Some of them laughed, teasing him: "Petras, let's head for home!"

But Petras walked along with a stern face because he wasn't in the habit of carrying on with the girls. By the tavern he accidentally came upon Zolys with Kupstys. Zolys was taking Kupstys for a beer, but he refused to leave Petras behind. Although Petras tried to get out of it, he had to obey his uncle. Though Petras limited himself to one mug, Zolys got them to agree to the match. Petras promised to accompany his uncle to Kupstys's house that very evening.

Whether driving, riding, or on foot, the men took their time, lingering here and there. The women took off for home first. Just as in the morning they had headed for church, now that everything was over, they walked home in groups. Since the sun had just passed noon, there was still time, so the girls knew they didn't need to hurry to get away. Gathering in twos or threes, they went off laughing. They reached one group; on the way they caught up to even more girls, and soon they had formed into a large gathering. Chattering and making a din, they talked about what they'd seen in church or in the village.

"Did you see how Petras Kurmelis was decked out today?" said one. "I bet he's about to get married."

"What kind of decked out is that!" laughed another. "Any time I see him, he's always wearing the same brown coat and striped vest."

"And no doubt his winter cap?"

"Of course, and his felt boots! Ha, ha, ha!" they all laughed.

"Go on and laugh," said the oldest one, "but the heart of each one of you would go pitter patter if she could only throw herself at him."

"There's no point in pitter-pattering or throwing yourself: he's not for us, girls."

"For us or not for us, but, girls, do you know something, I wouldn't marry him. How those Kurmelises have gotten under my skin! Never mind his riches, I'd be better off marrying the poorest guy I could find!"

"You worked for them? Then you know them well."

"They really got on my nerves: they're forever grumbling. The mother's that way and so is Petras. You can't do anything to suit them nor do any work the right way: it's never good enough, never done properly, so there's no pleasing them!"

"Petras seems so stuck in his ways, yet you see how he wants to have everything prim and proper."

"God help us, how proper! Everything has to be swept and dusted. Every morning you have to clean as if they're expecting guests. If they don't like something, they'll grumble like a beggar who's spilled his last beans. God forbid a girl should end up with one like him."

"There's nothing wrong with someone like him. Just give me Kurmelis with his homestead, you'd see: I'd make all the corners shine like glass and keep him as fit as a fiddle."

"Don't worry, you'd still have your share of trouble with him: now he's all dressed, then he's dirty again, you wouldn't have enough white shirts for him. Whether he washes up or not, he stays as black as soot. You think you can clean up someone like that? As far as the spotless corners are concerned, that's more the mother's doing. She won't allow a straw or a speck of dust anywhere. Or if it's a dish, it will always be in the wrong place. You'll never put it in the right spot to suit her. Petras got used to it from his mother—you won't be able to please him either, no matter what you do. There's no end to it, sister. With the cooking, the eating, or the dishes, it's always something—you'll never get it right. He finds fault no matter what, he's sure to grumble! The heck with them! I've had enough of their finicky ways!"

"They didn't get on my nerves or anything at all," said a pretty girl who was just catching up to them. "It's almost a year now, and I haven't heard a nasty word from either of them. If you just do everything the way you're supposed to, nobody complains. I could live there forever. The mother is very kind to me. Today, after I had gone over everything, she let me go to church. She stayed home alone. Of course, you have to know your place and come back on time. Let's get a move on, shall we?"

"It wouldn't bother me either; it would be as comfortable as warm wool."

"Oh really? With that miser? He shakes and quivers over a bite of bread or a handful of flour. And just try getting a kopeck out of him. He's just the type to be 'warm wool' for you. They're always suspicious. They think the hired girls are always stealing, always eating everything in sight! They keep their keys in their pockets; you'd think that everyone is just out to steal from them. It's mostly the mother: she's a miser, she'd press wax out of the slops if she could. She's always watching to make sure the girls don't take a bite! Poking around like such a busybody, she's managed to sit down on her tail more than once."

"Girls," interjected another, "after all, what's a mistress for? It's her job to watch over the hired help, to conserve the bread and the rich butter. That's why you can't please everybody, sometimes you have to keep the help in line. The mother can be a model for all mistresses."

"Saving and hoarding her goods all her life, she's quarreled with all the girls and what came of it? She can't take it with her in her coffin. The next one to come along won't be saving anything."

"But if the next one to come along follows in her footsteps, then everything will be just fine."

"Who knows, Petras will look for a big dowry and a girl with hundreds of rubles. Any way you slice it, girls, she won't take care of the house like the old mother did."

"Can't you entice Kurmelis somehow, Janė? If I were in your place, at his side all the time, he'd be mine in no time flat."

Janė smiled shyly and fell into deep thought for a while, then the two girls began whispering quietly.

"Oh, yes," said a third girl: "No doubt about it, whoever ends up in Kurmelis's hands will fall into a pot of gold, that's for sure! If only I were rich, I'd be first in line."

"What do you mean, he's not for you or for me?" laughed yet another one. "I'd pull his boots off, wash his face, give him food and a kiss."

"Ha, ha, ha!" they all laughed. "Even such a swarthy, dark one?"

"That's enough of competing over Petras: he's not for us, no, not for us! You'll see: he'll bring home some sweet little thing. She won't worry about his age or his swarthiness."

As the girls arrived at their farms and each one started off to her dwelling, their talk had to come to an end.

On the way home, Petras stopped at his pasture, removed the saddle from his horse, and let it go join the other horses. Then he went home carrying the saddle. It was a feast for his and anyone's eyes to see the house that stood before him. Why wouldn't you rejoice–the least little thing was in order: it seemed that all the corners just shone. The buildings were ship-shape, some newly roofed; the garden was surrounded by a fence made of spruce branches, the yard had been cleanly swept, the cottage had new boards on the walls, the chimney stood straight up on the roof, and the shutters were whitewashed. No implement could be seen thrown down, nor any rag spread on the fence. Petras took the saddle to the granary but found it locked. He put the saddle on the footstool by the door and stood in the yard admiring the apple trees in the orchard. They were laden with fruit, one side completely red, which made him wonder if they really were apples. Gazing around one more time, he petted the dog and went inside.

The cottage was bright with a high ceiling, the benches and tables had been carefully scrubbed till they were white; the dirt floor had been swept, the walls whitewashed. Everything was

Petras Kurmelis

bare except for a few pictures and a crucifix on the end wall.
There wasn't a piece of clothing out, nor any rag showing, no
dish hidden in the corners. The floor under the benches had been
cleaned. The air was fresh because the scent of mignonettes from
the garden was wafting through an open window in the cottage.

His mother, still dressed, was resting in bed, looking as if she
had just laid down and gone to sleep. Closing the door quietly,
Petras took off his coat and hung it on the rafter. Slowly he sat
on the bench in front of the bed, leaned his arm on the table,
and sat looking at his dear mother. She was pale and almost blue,
her eyes sunken and shut. Snuggled into the white pillow, she
lay there curled up with her white arm covered with blue veins
stretched out at her side, as if she were dead. Her legs sticking
out from under her clothing were also white. She was breathing
heavily, moaning out loud at times. Afraid of waking her, Petras
sat quietly and mused to himself:

"How much those little hands have worked, how many kopecks have they saved! And those feet! As far as I can remember,
they've never stopped for a moment. She's left traces of her blood
on all the paths. Now she's going to leave everything and everyone behind. Whether I like it or not, I'll have to put someone
else in her place. You can't do without a woman. They know how
to save every kopeck and turn it into something. It seems that
men like me work all the time, too. I don't snooze, but there's
never any money. I try so hard not to spend any, but everywhere
you turn—several rubles are already gone. If I could just put a
couple of hundred away with interest! Zolys has it right: 'She'll
be a prize for you, too.' Just think, the principal will always be
preserved. And lumber is horribly expensive. Before you can sell
something you've made, you first have to pay for the wood. But if

you got it for free, you could just keep working. At least it would be a new kopeck–one could savor it. Mother is adamantly against stealing from the woods. Who can blame her, when Father died doing just that? Why did he have to steal so much?"

Sensing that Petras had come home, the hired girl brought in the dinner, and after placing it on the table, left the room. While eating, Petras kept looking at his mother and continued to muse: "How would she feel seeing another in her place. She's been telling you to get married for such a long time, and now you can't wait. I won't be able to handle it alone at all. Uncle hit the nail on the head, but how to find the courage to tell her!"

Without moving, Mother opened her eyes, took a look around, and closed them again, saying: "If you want some milk, here's the pantry key. Tell Janikė to bring it or better yet, go along with the girl. If she's left on her own, she'll treat herself. Don't let the cat in, be sure to put the lid back on, otherwise a rat can fall inside."

After coughing for a while, she lay quietly again. Petras resumed thinking: "You have to know all the reserves and keep them from the girls, the cats, and the rats! You have to conserve the milk. I'll be satisfied with just beets. Janikė is clever, I won't let her into the pantry. I know, I can't let any of them into the granary: there's wool, flax, skeins, no order anywhere. God, if she should die soon, how would I carry on here with everything? The doctor cost several rubles, too, but he was no help at all, she keeps getting worse. Even lying in bed, she still attends to everything, but when she closes her eyes for the last time, who will look out for everything? I have to get married. If I married another over her living body, I'd be a rotten child! Maybe she'll get a little better yet? There's still time for that..." Suddenly Petras started to feel strange somehow; the beets had no flavor; he couldn't

Petras Kurmelis

swallow the bread. He picked up the key and, carrying his dish, went to get some milk. Entering the pantry, he couldn't remember the last time he'd been there. He looked around as if he were in an unfamiliar room. A row of pots was set on the dirt floor, all covered in white. A white scarf protected the butter dish. A shelf with cheeses was at one end; on the grindstone were pots with grain, a small dish with lard, under the ceiling hung a pole with kielbasa sausages and a few sides of bacon. Standing up, he looked around: he had no idea from which pot to pour himself some milk or how to prepare his beets.

Running in, Janikė cried out: "Who's opening and shutting the pantry door—is it the dog?"

The girl was pure, young, dressed modestly as befitted a holy day: her apron and shirt were lily-white, her waist bound by a thick belt, her yellow hair gracefully braided, and her eyes as blue as blueberries shone cheerfully. She also displayed two rows of small, close-set teeth. A virtuous girl as sweet as a strawberry.

"You want some milk?" she asked, laughing. "Give me your plate, I'll get it, I know how you like it."

Taking the spoon, she scooped some milk from the bottom of one pot, then some cream from the top of another. She kept pouring and stirring the milk. She placed the dish into Petras's hands, saying: "Wait a moment here, sir, I'll get some feed for the chickens." She put the cloth back over the pots, took a dish with her while running around, and poured some grain into it. She took another dish to collect flour for the ducks, then, spinning around, she hurried to chase the cat out, and finally locked the pantry. Returning the key, she looked straight into Petras's eyes and smiled at him mischievously. Petras was astonished at Janė, as if he were seeing her for the first time.

Maybe it was the Sunday attire or her direct glance or her alluring smile that sank so deeply into his mind that made Janikė's image remain before him after he returned to the cottage and was eating. He wanted to see her again–he kept looking to the door, but, alas, she didn't come in.

The sun had already moved well past noon. Petras started to worry about his trip to Kupstyses, because he knew that his uncle was waiting for him, but here was Mother, who didn't show any interest in discussing the matter of his courtship. Having eaten, he marked time, putting on his coat, setting up his cane, glancing at the bed every minute. Suddenly Mother was seized with a coughing fit, and, unable to say anything, she pointed toward the open window. Jumping up, Petras shut it. When her coughing subsided, Petras started to tell his mother what he'd heard from Uncle Zolys today–though not everything–and where he was planning to go. Raising her hand, Mother said: "As you wish, my child. You're not a young man anymore, you know best and it's all the same to me: I don't think I'll be around much longer. Maybe I won't get on the daughter-in-law's nerves. A girl whose parents are poor, one who's seen hardship can be hardworking and affectionate. Go have a look at this girl just in case, after that you can decide what to do."

He was on his way out when his mother called him back again, saying: "Tell Janikė to watch the orchard: I saw Juzukas pick up an apple before he jumped over the fence."

"Never mind the apple!" Petras just waved his hand.

Going out into the yard, he saw the saddle on the footstool and went back for the key. He hadn't had time to unlock the granary, when Janikė suddenly appeared again.

"It's a good thing, sir, that you came by way of the granary," she cooed: "I'll get what I need. Maybe you won't be back home so soon. Mother is lying down."

Once more, smiling at him oddly, she looked him straight in the eyes, then, suddenly spinning around, she gathered grain for the piglets, flour for the sows, more flour for supper. She whirled around, working so quickly that Petras's heart couldn't help but rejoice.

"How she remembers everything!" he admired. "If only someone so capable would care for Mother until her end, and me for the rest of my life."

A flood of sweetness welled up in his heart. The desire to embrace Janikė came over him. He wanted to say to her: "Care for me and love me until death… and I will love you always."

Just as he was about to reach for her, suddenly the idea popped into his head: "Well, there's no shortage of ones like her. Zolys knows better: 'With the hundreds of rubles at least you'll have enough money to maintain a wife."

Locking the door, he said sternly: "Don't be late with the supper, tomorrow is not a holiday. Jonas should go to bed. I'll take care of the horses myself. Here, take the key in."

Taking the key, Janikė looked him in the eyes again as though taunting him and burst out laughing. Petras turned away, spat on the ground, and walked off, shaking his head, all the while thinking: "Probably she knows or suspects where I'm going. Women have a good sense and especially one who's so smart. But she's beautiful, too. There's no need to roam around looking: she'd be good. She's devilishly quick. Mother says: 'Go look around just in case…' In the meantime nobody's going to catch that one, she'll still be here when I get home."

Even though he tried, there was no way he could turn his thoughts anywhere but to Janikė's eyes, which shone bright blue in front of him, nor could he stop her gay laughter from ringing in his ears. Again he spat.

"What if I didn't go?" the thought came to him. "I promised Kupstys. Uncle Zolys will be angry that I lied to him. I'll go see how it turns out. Later, they can't force the girl on me. If she doesn't suit me, we can just shake hands and leave. This one is the same as any other. She'll be just fine. A girl is a girl, but the rubles will come in handy." When he heard an anxious voice calling, Petras gave a start: "Why are you so late?" Zolys was waiting for him halfway. They went the rest of the way together, talking about the hundreds of rubles, the accrued interest, how he'd cut the lumber for free, until gradually all the talk blotted Janikė's image from his mind.

Kupstyses' cottage looked like a regular pigsty: low, dark, smoky–but to make matters worse, it wasn't the least bit clean. The few small, old windows were moldy, dotted by flies–obviously they were never wiped. There were cobwebs on the ceilings that hung so low they almost brushed over one's nose; the sweepings from the floor had just been pushed aside under the benches, the bed was messy and full of dust. Countless rags and dishes littered the room along the walls. The table was covered in potato peelings. Not being used to this, Petras wrinkled his nose, but he remembered the old saying that gold glitters even in ashes. "That's not so bad," he thought, "we'll see how it turns out, later." The Kupstyses descended on the guests, but it was mostly the wife clacking like a woodpecker. She bent over backward to serve them treats and to entertain them. Sensing that Marcelė was around somewhere,

Zolys found her and brought her inside. Petras was taken aback; this wasn't some little Marcelė, but a whole big armful of Marcė! She was a big, tall girl, a real fatso; she must have gained weight very recently, because even her clothes were skintight. She barely fit in her blouse, it was about to explode, the sleeves were almost up to her elbows, and her arms looked as tight as sausages. Her hair was messy, the top of her head barely combed. Her skirt had also grown so short that it didn't cover her bare, dirty legs, and often you would even get a glimpse of her haunches.

Zolys tried to talk to Marcelė, to say hello, but she only hung her head, scowling and smirking.

"Don't bother her," said the mother. "The child is timid, since so few people come our way. Marcė's not used to strangers; she's shyer around men. Why, she doesn't even dare open her mouth."

Petras didn't look at the girl closely, since he had more than enough to talk about with her father regarding the farm, the price of wheat, the woodmen's pay, his own handiwork, and so on.

"Well, all right!" shouted Kupstys. "You do all the work and I'll provide the lumber. Come tomorrow around cock's crow, I'll fix up a whole wagon of the finest lumber, as dry as a bone; no matter how you decide to use it, it'll do. And if you want some from trees that are still standing, you can choose any you like. For a good man I can deliver them without taking a kopeck."

Bringing Marcė closer to the table, Zolys kept winking at Petras to talk to the girl. The only thing that came to his mind was to ask: "What is it you're working on now?"

"Don't you know, sir?" the mother interrupted. "Why, a woman's work, there's nothing to show for it. Though our homestead isn't so big, the work's the same: she'll fly around about the chores and the animals like a butterfly. We just got rid of the loom yesterday. There was a bit or two that needed weaving. I can't walk anymore, Father is in the woods, all the work is on her alone."

In the meantime, taking Zolys aside, the father promised him a cord of wood if he'd just match them up somehow.

Toward evening Kupstys saw his guests off. The mother and Marcė, who were left in the cottage, were arguing: "You crazy woman, you pig!" scolded the mother. "You don't understand anything. Look at how much luck is coming your way! What kind of burden is it to you? A homestead with everything in it–you think you'll ever have to worry about work or hardship? You'll sit there like a lady and boss the girls around."

"You can go yourself, if that swarthy old man suits you!" Marcė mumbled now and then. "The heck with his riches and homestead! You won't pack me off to that lout, don't even think of it! As if I couldn't get a younger one!"

Returning, the father overheard Marcė's talk and set to scolding her, too: "You rascal, you pig! So you think you can make fun of such a fine man! You're not worth one of his shoes. If he'll only take you, you should kiss his hands and feet, and just go with him!"

"If you want to, you can go move in with him yourself!" Marcė yelled angrily. "But you can't force me to go after him and that's it! I'm telling you straight!"

"You're still talking nonsense? I'll whip you on the backside in a second! Wasn't it enough making hay in the woods without doing any work! When you end up in a husband's hands, he'll beat your hide, you'll start getting down to work all right, screaming!"

"Stuff it up your nose! You think you can scare me with a beating! I'd rather go and hang myself!"

Saying this, Marcė turned on her heels and went straight to the woods. Watching out the window, the mother warned the father: "Why frighten the child like that? You could make her sick. There she goes into the woods. Suppose you find her swinging from a branch?"

"Don't worry, she won't be swinging. Pranukas will get her down! He's loafing about the woods, of course."

"Ha, ha, ha!" laughed the mother.

The father continued: "God save us from the foolishness of that kid! He's always hanging around here with his horses; and that girl of ours, isn't she a devil? As soon as she hears his whistle, you just turn around and she's gone. I would have sent Pranukas packing a long time ago, but I just keep quiet, controlling myself. Of course, I have to avoid him like any dog from the manor. He could report me to the master anytime. Maybe some husband will capture her, then that good-for-nothing will be left standing with his mouth wide open."

"Just don't frighten her so terribly!" said the mother. "The child is right in saying that 'you won't make me go by force.' It's better to convince her gently and lure Kurmelis in with that lumber."

"You don't have to give me lessons on that–I can handle it my own way!" The father waved his hand. "Even if I frightened Marcė at the beginning, it won't hurt her. After all, it's up to you to talk her into it the way you know best!"

Marcė went along the beaten path through the thickets, avoiding the branches; frowning, she hurried along. Suddenly someone jumped in front of her and blocked her way.

"My tasty little strawberry, I've been waiting for you for such a long time!" a young man said, catching her by the hand. "Why are you so late, maybe you've brought me some cheese?"

Making a face, Marcė could scarcely get the words out: "I was on my way to hang myself…"

"Are you mad?" laughed the young man in astonishment. "Why would you want to climb so high? What happened? Did father whip you or something?"

"He's planning to whip me and beat me. He's making me get married. I'm not going to obey him. It makes me sad to part from you, but I'm better off cutting my throat."

"Who's intending to marry you?"

"Why, that old geezer Petras Kurmelis."

"Really? And you're still getting on your high horse? Then you don't have any more sense than a fool! If I was in your shoes, I'd skip along to him."

"And you, Pranelis, can talk like that? You give me up to someone else so easily? So you were lying when you said you loved me?"

"I love you and I will always love you, especially this evening." Saying this, he spun Marcė around until both of them fell down under the willows. "That husband of yours isn't going to separate us! I wouldn't let you go to some fellow who is poor, of course! But to someone so rich–you're free to go! I couldn't take you away from your happiness, could I?"

"What kind of happiness is that," cried Marcė, "to be a slave to someone as old as that!"

"It's not like you're some hopeless ninny. You'll deceive that old man of yours at every turn. You'll lead him around by the nose like he's some calf. That husband will dig in the dirt, and his lady will feast her eyes on the young men." They laughed and sniggered together. "It's easy to make a fool of him. You'll see how I make up to him; I'll be his best friend, and yours, too. Just get the money from the devil, and make sure you keep it by you!"

As they whispered to each other, Marcikė's laughter became more merry. She no longer had thoughts of cutting her throat or hanging herself; instead, she rolled around on the ground with Pranukas and stayed in the woods until sunset.

Petras also wandered down the paths in the same woods, but in a totally different direction. The sun was down almost at the edge of the sky but still shone clearly, penetrating all the corners of the landscape, as if it hadn't enjoyed earth's beauty all day long. The clouds, which were transparent and white, rosy on top and golden on the bottom, surrounded the sun in smaller and larger patches and slowly escorted it downhill. High above, the sky was wonderfully blue. Opposite the sun in the east, the sun's brother—the pale moon—stared in fright. Glancing around, it jumped up, rejoicing that it was its turn to replace the sun. The clouds hovering around the moon were white; some of them were brave enough to dare to cover the moon's face.

The wind in the woods soughed lightly, swinging the hanging spruce branches gently, rocking them like infants put down to sleep for the night. Already glistening in gold, the leaves of the branching birches shimmered against the sun and floated to the ground, quivering. In the shade a redheaded boletus mushrooms stood tiptoe on one foot, herding the yellow chanterelles to keep them from separating. But the boletus couldn't rein in the red pine mushrooms and the milk-caps, which were scattered all over the birch grove. Close by, another one of its brothers was sticking its pale head through the moss. Next to it a toadstool's little head glimmered as red as its neighbor. In the thick spruce grove a curly lingonberry patch lay with its red berry clusters hiding among the thick leaves. On occasion the air was quiet in the woods and there was no wind, but one could always hear a mysterious murmur, like some incomprehensible speech or a strange song. For some it may have been joyful, others may have found it sorrowful or just natural, but it reached the deepest chords of everyone's heart.

Petras went along the paths, oblivious to the beauty of the forest because various ideas and images churned in his head: Janikė and Marcė, his homestead, and the Kupstyses' cottage all stood before his eyes. "Ah," he thought to himself, "let Janikė be stuck in such a rotten cottage, soon her neat and tidy ways would break down and she'd stop smiling. And that other one, Marcė, is different, of course. But in a friendlier place she'd become gentler. Certainly she's not delicate, so she can do the work... We'll see how it turns out, later. That Zolys has a devilish tongue; he can walk circles around you if you're not on your guard. 'Four hundred rubles,' he says. Those Kupstyses sure are sweet people. Then he says, 'I'll provide the lumber, just cut yourself as much as you want, you won't have to pay a kopeck for it.' Easy to say, 'cut it for yourself.' But if you had to buy it, just imagine how much it would cost."

Absorbed in looking at a tree trunk, he exclaimed: "Oh my, what a slender one!" Lumbering toward it, Petras managed to step on a red-flecked toadstool and crush a bunch of chanterelles. Approaching a small oak, he measured it with the palm of his hand and tried to shake it. Leaning his head back, he looked up at the top, estimating the length of the beam it would make.

Petras Kurmelis

"That's a healthy one, sturdy like iron! The master would not be satisfied with a three ruble note for it–far from it!"

He saw another oak, which was bent. Without taking his eyes off it, he calculated its height and circumference with such concentration that it seemed he could see right through its sapwood and core. He marveled: "One like that would make a fine sleigh, a very fine one, indeed!"

A skittish rabbit jumped out of the thicket. The dog ran after it, squealing as far as he could follow. Frightened of the dog, a squirrel fluffed its tail and, quick as lightning, jumped into a tree. Flying from one treetop to another, a crow cawed right over the dog's head. Petras didn't see or hear anything, he just let his eyes sweep from one tree to the next, calculating each one's color, price, size, and sturdiness. While sizing up the trees and enjoying himself, he trampled over many a berry, crushed many a mushroom. As he was crossing the woods, the sun sank with only a trace of shine. The gold from the surrounding clouds disappeared, their rosiness retreated, until finally the clouds turned gray. Twinkling shyly, the stars above flashed here and there. As time went by, the round moon shone more brightly, shoving the pale clouds to the side. Along the woods the bog covered itself in white mist. Beyond the hill from the chimneys of Kurmelis's farm, a column of gray smoke spewed to the heights.

Coming out of the woods, Petras passed straight through the stumps in the direction where the chainsaws were resounding–down, down he descended until he was enveloped in a dense fog. Reaching home in the evening, he related what he'd heard and seen to his mother. At the end of his talk, he concluded: "Whether the girl is rather plain or very beautiful, it's all the same to me. The important thing is to get the money. Frankly, I didn't pay much attention to the girl, I only saw her from a distance. She looks like she's healthy and not at all delicate."

"You did well, my child, it's a good thing you didn't get too close to her," the mother praised him. "To make love and caress one another–that's a wicked sin. So the priests tell us. You'll manage the lovemaking after the wedding."

Every chance they had, the Kupstyses kept trying to talk Marcikė into showing more affection for Petras. Sometimes the father would coerce his daughter, while the mother tried to sway her by spoiling her: she tried humoring her, gave her the best food, let her sleep late. If the mother sent her to do any work, Marcikė would cut her off as if with an ax: "Stuff it up your nose! Can't you do it yourself? I'm being married off and I should go to work too–I won't do it." With nothing to do, Marcė rolled around by the waysides like a cow. When she got bored, she'd take off for the woods to pick berries. More often she wandered over to the estate stable in search of the groom. Then she wouldn't come home until it was pitch dark. Sitting together under a bush, the two of them made fun of Marcė's future husband.

Petras's wedding was postponed because his mother passed away. Left alone, Petras found it hard to manage, since he didn't trust anyone, so he locked everything up and carried the keys in his pocket. Half the day would go by before the hired girls could manage to get some butter or flour. Often because this took so long, they couldn't prepare meals or feed the animals on time. There was no order left in Petras's life: the hired hands didn't get along anymore, arguing all the time. The worst was Janikė, who became as obstinate as a goat, fighting with everyone, yelling, and being impudent to Petras at every turn. It was clear that a mistress was absolutely essential. Petras understood his dilemma. Therefore, he was the one to make Zolys nail down the agreement with the Kupstys girl. Besides, he had already hauled out several wagons of lumber, so now what Petras wanted more than anything was to get his hands on the money from Marcė's dowry.

As soon as they arrived at the cottage, Zolys, with his skillful tongue, talked the in-laws into putting the money down there and then. Kupstys didn't try to wriggle out of it: he put three ten-ruble notes on the table for Petras. At first Marcelė kept her mouth shut, gaping like a grown calf taken to market, but when she saw her father handing the money over, she understood that this was no joke and started bawling out loud. Anxious to get the cord of wood promised him, Zolys consoled Marcė every way he could think of. Cornering her in the entry, he sincerely tried to persuade her:

"Marcelė, my lovely little dove, what are you afraid of? No doubt Kurmelis is no spring chicken, he's worth a whole lot more than some poor young fellow. What a homestead he has! You won't want for anything–unless it's pigeon's milk. Every girl in the neighborhood is going to be so jealous of you!"

"So true, so true!" interjected the mother as she passed by.

Zolys whispered until the wrinkles on Marcė's forehead faded; afterwards she spoke to Petras more kindly. They decided to announce the marriage banns in church on Sunday. His mood improving by the minute, Petras became elated. Marcelė warmed up to him so much that she even kissed his hand.

"A pleasant girl!" he assured himself. "Although they only gave a small part of the money so far, that doesn't matter, we'll see how it turns out, later."

Since it was so soon after the burial, Petras didn't want to have a wedding, but Marcė started carrying on once more with her big mouth, yelling and refusing to marry Petras. But why shouldn't there be a wedding? Petras couldn't decide what to do. If he didn't have one, it would be better for him: first of all, it was so soon after his mother's death, it wouldn't do to make merry; second, there wouldn't be any expenses. "But," he debated with himself with the phrase old folks like to use: 'if your wife you don't obey, dry bread you'll eat every day.' What are you going to do with young people, they want to celebrate on their last free days, and so that's that. We'll have to have at least a small wedding."

The cottage was cramped at the Kupstyses, so they settled on holding only the girls' shower at the bride's and the big wedding at the groom's. There was no one at Kurmelis's to arrange things, so throughout the entire week, Kupstienė took charge of all the organizing in his homestead, paying for the wedding details from his account, the way she saw fit. She invited all her relatives and hired the musicians. At the beginning of the wedding, during the girls' night, the Kupstyses took Petras to the granary to hand over the promised dowry. Searching through her chest, the mother unrolled her scarves, untied all the knots, handed over the money to the father, who in turn spread out the bank notes for Petras–first several red ones, then blue, green, yellow. They laid them down, put them in a pile, but still they couldn't come up with even a hundred rubles. Once more the mother went through the chest, untying more knots, but she still wasn't able to find a hundred.

"Well, children!" the father turned to his sons, "You contribute, too."

"I'll give ten rubles!" shouted the older one.

"I'll give the same!" announced the second one.

"Only we don't have it on us right now. On Sunday, dear brother-in-law, on Sunday we'll give it to you for sure. Now that you have the money in hand, it's as good as having your wife. God bless you, may you live happily! Here's to your health!"

The brothers drank, ate heartily, kissed everyone, danced away, and made merry.

Seizing the money, Petras pondered: "It seems like a big pile, but actually the total is rather small. Zolys told me: 'Four hundred, four...' The brothers promised more, but, of course, they're lying—I should toss it to the dogs, obviously they are cheating me! If it wasn't for the lumber... Zolys brought it over himself, he talked me into it, and if the forester gets angry at me, he could alert the master and show him that I stole the wood. I'd catch it like the devil then, there's no good way to get out of this. Well, as long as there's a mistress, there'll be someone to watch over things. If I go back on my word, who's going to return what I've spent? Beer, cakes, vodka—I paid for all of it and it cost a bundle, all right. Look how much meat they've consumed! It would all go to waste! There's no way I can live alone any longer. If I throw this one over, where will I find someone else so quickly? Janikė can't even put together ten rubles. Given even a hundred for interest, that's not so bad, as they say: add a bit and subtract a bit."

The groom calculated in one corner; the bride sobbed in another. In the meantime, the estate workers showed up for the wedding. The musicians revved up the music, the dancers whirled more wildly. Then, in the end, the bride wiped away her tears and danced like a madwoman the whole night through.

As autumn approached, the sun rose later each morning and went to bed earlier each evening. At midday heavy mists blocked the light, as if jealous of the sun for allowing its rays to spread warmth on the earth. Driven by the wind from one edge of the heavens, the clouds rose, blustered, flew, and turned into rain in the middle of the journey, then settled down on the other edge of the horizon. One cloud rushed in, but just as quickly the wind swept that one off. The sun barely peeked out, but immediately the wind drove another cloud down the same path, which in turn released its rain with a rumble. Each cloud kept wetting the warm summer soil with its rain, making the earth thick with mud, subduing its vibrant green.

Gone were the swaying wheat and the fragrant grasses. The meadows were shaved, the fields lay bare and brown, the woods appeared sorrowful, only the gardens remained green; barely a few of the vegetables survived the cold rain and winds.

Everywhere the womenfolk were toiling in the gardens, dragging baskets and mesh sieves on their backs and storing cabbages and beets under the eaves to keep them from rotting. No one touched the gardens at the Kurmelises: they were all still hauling in the potatoes. When he thought of the amount of work yet to be done, the hair on Petras's head stood on end: his neighbors had already tidied up their gardens, but not even the potatoes had been brought in at his house. "I wonder what's happening this year?" Petras thought to himself. "The work moves so slowly! The trouble is, no one's trying to hurry in the least. One young man is dithering away his time in the barn; it doesn't seem to matter whether one or two women pour the potatoes into sacks, in the evening there's always work left to do. The girls lollygag around in the potato fields, singing without a care. There's no one to tell them to keep at the work. Why should they hurry? My mistress acts like a houseguest; she doesn't see anything. It's been five weeks; you'd think she'd be rested up after the wedding. I have other work to attend to, but then I catch the help roasting potatoes in the barn. No doubt they don't eat them plain; probably they heap the butter on as well."

Petras looked up at the sun and went inside. A dog with milk on its snout rushed out in front of him. Right away Petras noticed a pot of milk turned over on the hearth, a kettle on its side, buckets in the middle of the entry, moldy pans, an uncovered butter churn with butter clumps on the bottom; grimy buckets lined up along the wall; bowls sticky with dough, and the sieve tossed on the ground. Petras only reflected: "My, oh my! We'll see how everything turns out, later…"

In the cottage the breakfast dishes were scattered on the table, the dirt floor was not swept, potato peelings were trampled underfoot, the bed unmade. Opening the door to the guest room, he found his mistress sprawled out on the bed. Going up to her and embracing her, he woke her gently: "My dearest Marcė, aren't you rested up yet, what's going to happen? You must know that we're drowning in chores; you have to get up for a change."

"You want me to take over your work?" snorted the wife.

"You don't have to take it over, just keep your eye on it at least. Not only don't you go outside to cheer up the hired hands, but you're not taking care of anything indoors either: a pan is spilled in the hearth, a bear would break its head in the pantry, the cats have the run of the house. Why didn't you lock the pantry? The girls are roasting potatoes in the barn. You know they don't eat them plain; they stuff themselves with butter from the pantry. Why can't you take charge of the granary key?"

"Stick your keys up your nose!" she growled at him.

"Well, at least clean the cottage," continued Petras. "Just look at it, it's like a pigsty. It's lunchtime and you haven't even cleared off the table: the hands will come in to eat. How sloppy can you get?"

"Stuff it up your nose!" muttered the wife. "Why did you send the girls out to work, if they haven't cleaned up? Did you bring me in as a hired girl? Don't even think of it!"

Hearing her rough talk, Petras jumped back. Shaking his head, he thought: "Oh my, oh my, we'll have to see how everything turns out, later."

In the meantime, the hands came in for dinner. They laughed uproariously in the entry. Rushing inside, Janikė shouted: "O Holy Virgin Mary! Oh my goodness, such a mess everywhere! Even the table hasn't been cleared–that's enough! Barbė, light the fire, let's hustle, the master will come home, he'll grumble again like he did this morning. Here, you carry the dishes away, while the dinner heats up, I'll start cleaning the cottage however I can manage."

"But what are we going to eat?" Barbė yelled out from the entry. "Some creature ate all the grain, and the kettle is turned over on its side–that's the work of the pigs. Puddles of milk all over–such a waste. Just this morning the master said, 'The mistress will take care of it herself.' Well, this is how she took care of it. We don't know where he's gotten to. The smithy is locked."

"Hurry with the dinner, get busy!" urged the hungry young men, rushing in. "Is this the time to sweep? Tomorrow it'll rain, then you'll get your sweeping done."

Watching from the guest room window, Petras was as silent as the earth. The workers' words fell on him like rocks. Marcė turned onto her other side and complained, sighing: "O Jesus, how my head aches!"

Spurred on by his wife's words, which were as sharp as a knife, Petras charged into the house, ordering the hands: "Don't shout when my mistress is sick. Pour yourselves some milk or get something else for dinner."

Putting on his cap, he hurried out to the smithy, remembering an urgent job he'd promised to do for a neighbor. He couldn't even think of eating. The hired hands stayed on: one was hammering, another was trimming some wood. They carried on with their work, laughing at the mistress's illness. One of them said: "She's as healthy as a horse!"

Another added one better: "You thought it was bad when your wife died; well, believe me, it was much worse when mine got better."

Returning inside to get the tool he'd forgotten, Petras overheard their jokes and once again turned red with embarrassment. In the smithy, he immersed himself in work, hammering and flogging forcefully, breaking out in a sweat. He wasn't hungry in the least, but for some reason he felt weak. After an hour or so, Gorys suddenly appeared, shouting: "There's my man! I heard the clanging, so of course I realized that you had picked up my job. I'll at least pump the bellows for you, because tomorrow I really need the wheel. I can never find you home, so I brought you a taste of our slaughter here." Saying this, he pulled out a piece of meat and some kielbasa from his coat, all neatly wrapped in a white kerchief. "Have a bite of the fresh meat, dear Petras," he coaxed, "It will give you strength."

Petras glanced at the tasty morsels–the meat certainly smelled good.

"I should take Gorys inside to find some bread," he considered, "but who knows if they've cleaned up yet? How can I take him into such a pigsty? I'd be better off to go get the bread myself."

Bending down, Gorys pulled out a piece of white bread and a flask worth ten kopecks.

"Put your hammer down," he said. "Wet your whistle. Take a swig straight from the flask, then you can have a bite."

Petras threw down his cap, relaxed a bit, crossed himself, then took a swig. Since Gorys was egging him on, he downed a second. There was barely a drop left in the flask. Without any persuasion he ate the meat and the bread and piece by piece he polished it off. Smacking his lips, he crossed himself and thanked Gorys. He felt somewhat stronger. All the unpleasantness fell away, he forgot all his pains and resumed his work in better shape.

"Have you got a job that you've promised to do for someone?" asked Gorys, smoking.

"Yes" he replied, "I've promised a double sleigh for our parish priest. I just don't know when I'm going to get to it with the never-ending house chores. I can't seem to get around to my own work."

"Why do you care about the housework? The potatoes and the gardens are coming to an end. That's nothing: the women can clean them up by themselves. I used to see your deceased mother bringing in the beets like a cat dragging in a mouse. Of course, this mistress of yours is no match for the likes of her. But when she gets going, she'll blow the gardens away with the girls, you'll see."

"If only that were true," Petras thought to himself.

"What kind of price did you agree on with the parish priest?" continued Gorys.

"The job has to be all done–so you can just sit down in the sleigh and go, all my own material, fifty."

"Goodness! A pile of money! You can give up your farm duties for that. Now you've got it good: your wife's young, she'll see to everything–you can just keep making money hand over fist."

Petras sighed. Then he finished Gorys's job. His neighbor paid and left. Petras got ready to pick up something else. He decided to look around the house first, just in case. He thought he heard the wife walking around the yard. The piglets were squealing. He noticed that the trough had been washed, so it must be that they hadn't been fed since morning. Crossing the yard, he saw the granary was open; he looked inside and saw a wandering pig setting up housekeeping around the bins. He chased it out and went into the cottage–everything was the same as it was this morning; except that the dishes had been cleared from the table and left dirty in a corner of the entry; the spoons were scattered on the floor facing every which way. Casting a glance into the guest room, he found the bed empty, no sign of the wife. He cheered up, thinking that she had gone to speed up the potato diggers. He proceeded to the barn, where he found the grain shoveled into a pile. The chickens and the pigs were still trampling on it in ever wider circles. Lying on the chaff, the little shepherd was fast asleep. As he chased the animals away and grumbled at the kid, Petras could hear the diggers from afar: they were laughing in the garden and throwing potatoes at each other.

Coming up to them, he cried out: "Aren't you going to stop fooling around? There's still loads of potatoes left, and you're not hurrying up in the least."

"There's six more days after Sunday!" laughed the girls.

"And where's the mistress? Isn't she here?" asked Petras.

"Why, she set off across the field a little while ago, probably to her parents," piped up a child, pointing to the woods.

"Why didn't you feed the piglets?" Petras asked the girls. "The troughs are empty, looks like you haven't attended to them since morning?"

"You think we can get to everything!" the girls countered.

"First, we're supposed to hurry with the potatoes, now you're yelling about the pigs, where's the time to prepare the slops? Besides, there's no flour, so they squeal and won't eat–is that our fault? Cook dinner, make breakfast, come in from the barn, it's time to milk the cows; there's no time left to strain the milk, we're run ragged, how can we do it all?"

Petras didn't stick around to hear the end; he walked along with his eyes fixed on the ground. Standing by his workbench, he reminisced: "Mother was everywhere: she took care of the animals. The hired hands kept at it. We didn't strain ourselves in the least, everything got done quickly. She liked to say: 'Dear child, don't worry, just do your own work.' And now who will keep things running smoothly? Unless she comes around? Well, we'll see how it turns out, later… But what if Marcė doesn't change? What if she goes back to the parents', or maybe she won't ever stop sleeping?"

Pain pierced Petras's heart and overwhelmed him; he spat on the ground.

"Gorys has already butchered a pig, while ours are still thin like slivers. Last year's meat is all gone. It's not surprising: first the burial, then the wedding. Gorys's whiskey is so potent. It won't hurt to buy some and keep it on hand: take a shot whenever my heart aches."

*

The sun grew faint around Christmas, winter set in fast and hard. The soil froze solid as horn. Rivers and ponds turned to ice, and afterwards a down of snow covered everything. The days were quiet and windless, the biting cold stung everyone even if it was sunny. And the nights–why even ask? The stars in the sky shimmered and shone, while the snow just squeaked and squealed underfoot. The roads packed down like shiny glass; no matter where they were headed, no one dared take any shortcuts.

Throughout the woods people bustled about and scurried to work. Kurmelis wasn't to be caught napping either. One bright, cold morning he drove off to an unknown place. Both he and the horse, frosted in white, returned nearly at twilight. The young men were loitering around the barn, but the women stayed inside, of course. The girls were nearly finished with peeling the beets in the corner, while the mistress, her hands idle, sat by the warm fireplace. Next to the wall a rock weighed down a barrel, while another one was being filled with beets. Entering the cottage in a rage, Petras wrinkled his nose and no sooner had he shaken off the snow than he started to grumble: "What have you turned the cottage into, you slovenly little pigs! Look at all the mud and snow tracked inside; the dirt trampled on the floor! The air reeks with the stench of sauerkraut. Couldn't you peel and pickle at the other end of the house? This cottage has never seen the likes of such havoc!"

"It's all your fault anyway! But you still keep on snarling!" the wife retorted harshly. "You've put your sleigh at the other end of the house–where are we supposed to go? If you don't like the smell, then turn your nose the other way."

Gritting his teeth, Petras sat at the table and looked around for a knife to cut his bread. Not one of the women made any sign of moving.

"Give me my dinner," demanded Petras, crossing himself.

"There isn't anything left to make it with," answered Janikė, as she glanced at the mistress.

"Why didn't you leave some beets?" hissed Marcė, "You think I carry them around in my pocket? You can get your dinner yourself."

"It's clear to me nothing's going to happen here. I have to look for my dinner myself."

Petras left the room, recalling that he still had some liquor for when he got upset. Going into the other end of the house, he took a flask from the corner shelf and examined it in front of the window. He took one shot, then another, and put it down again. Afterwards he cut himself some raw bacon in the pantry, taking it inside and eating it with some bread.

Getting up, Janikė brought in a frypan.

"Give it here," she said, "I'll fry it up right now, there's a fire going."

Running out with the bacon, she brought it back lickety-split, all sizzling and smelling of onions. She put the frypan on a board in front of the master.

Rolling her eyes, Marcė reddened and glared at Janikė sullenly. Barbė started scolding Janikė: "If you keep running around and dallying somewhere, we won't be finishing tonight. You'd think there wasn't anyone else to fry it up besides you? She sits there on her behind doing nothing, that is, unless her head starts aching again!"

Enjoying his meal, Petras's face turned red as he gradually warmed up. Getting up his courage, he started talking: "I bought some trees, we have to cut them up before the road freezes over. Tomorrow the young men will go out to chop them down. Mistress, see to some warmer clothing for the young men: take care of the felt boots and mittens and mend them—that's enough of sitting on your hands doing nothing!"

"They got along without me up to now, they'll manage tomorrow. Do you want me to put their pants on them, too?" retorted the wife.

"Nobody asked you to dress them," said Petras more sternly, "but the clothing has to be sorted, mended, and handed out—that's what a mistress is for. Why did you come here, if you didn't want to take over somebody else's place? Aren't you ashamed to be so young and so lazy? My mother was old and gray, and you remember how she worked; you saw the way she buzzed around as busy as a bee—you'd have to hang on to her skirt hems to keep up with her."

The hired girls bent over, stifling their giggles. Rolling her eyes, Marcė grumbled angrily and snorted out loud:

"What do you want from me? Aren't you tired of scolding me at every step? You're forever bringing up that old biddy of yours! Did I offer myself to you? You didn't want me, just my money! You'd think you're my boss, you're always complaining about my work as if I were some kind of hired girl," she mumbled, put on her sheepskin, tied her scarf on, and banged the door on her way out.

"Since she's so angry, at least she'll bring the clothes for the men," thought Petras. "I should go help her find them. We'll see how everything turns out, later."

"Where are the mittens you wore last year?" he asked the girls.

"They're hanging on the rack, on a little pole. The felt boots and the woolen pants are there too, everything we need," Janikė explained.

Going outside, Petras noticed the closed granary door." Where did she disappear to?" he wondered. On the way to his workbench, he drank up his last shot. Forgetting about the clothing, he started working on the sleigh, planing and decorating it. He put down his work only after dark. In the evening, when the hired hands gathered inside, he related how much forest he'd bought and where it was located. Then he remembered the clothing. He started looking around for his mistress. Searching high and low, he found her fallen onto the guest room bed. Lighting the lantern, he was forced to look for warmer clothing for the men himself.

Worry on top of worry, it wasn't Christmas yet, but come Christmas, there would be more worries still. That's the way it was for Kurmelis: though there was upheaval before Christmas, it wasn't too bad as long as the regular hired hands were still around. They came to the end of their work year, waiting for Christmas, still looking after the animals and doing the chores. When Christmas arrived, Petras hired them for another year, but since his wife hadn't said a word to them—not a one agreed to stay on. Petras could scarcely persuade Janikė to remain for a week until he could find someone else. Thus all the regulars scattered and went their own ways. From then on Petras didn't even have time to look at his workbench, let alone get anything done. As if the household chores weren't enough, he had to go looking for hired help.

One evening Petras came home hot and angry for some reason or other. Of course, he'd had no dinner and, as expected, supper wasn't even started. Janikė had spent the day with the feeding and the chores, so she was late returning. Having made herself some eggs, the mistress was rolling around in bed as the sun was setting. Seeing how things stood, Petras could no longer control his temper and began scolding his wife in earnest: "Don't you understand, Marcė? I've suffered enough already, this is the last straw, I'm going to whip you! You've got to pick up some kind of work! If you don't want to work, then at least go and do the hiring, so I won't have to waste my time. You're about as much use to me as a billy goat–neither fat, nor hair. You just lie there days on end, is that fair? The hell with it, if you were a pig, I could at least butcher you! Why, you're just a blight on my farmstead–I can't even find hired hands. Go, hire some girls!" he thundered more furiously. "Get to it! The women are not my business. If you don't hire some–you'll have to do all the work yourself. Let's see how you laze around when Janikė leaves."

"Stuff it up your nose with that Janikė of yours!" Marcė snarled in a low voice, still lying down. "You've hired help without me before, and that's the way you can keep on doing it now. What do I care, if you don't get any help! Stuff it up your ass, why don't you?"

"Looks like I'm not making any headway getting you off your butt," continued Petras. "I'm bringing your father over tomorrow: let him see which one of us is to blame, how you don't carry your weight around here–then he'll put welts on your back!"

Standing alone outside after supper, Petras thought to himself: "My life is such a waste of time, it hasn't moved forward at all! I can't do any work. I don't make any money. Tired of waiting any longer, the parish priest bought himself a sleigh: there go my fifty rubles! The last one hundred went out to paying salaries–I always used to cover the salaries. Mother, dear mother! I lost you and ever since everything is going down the drain. All she does is cut me down, the devil take her! If you say anything, or even go to the outhouse, she just growls under her nose like some bear. Who can tell why she's so miserable? She's always frowning and filthy, you'll never catch her being civil to anyone. It seems no one admits to gossiping, but the rumors fly like bees. Anytime you talk to someone, they tell you straight out: 'How come your wife doesn't do any work at all, she eats by herself, the hired hands just get plain porridge, the girls have to do all the work.' Maybe she'll start working for once, when she's the only one left? We'll see how it all turns out, later."

Waking up at cock's crow next morning, Petras was astonished: the wife was already up, she and Janikė were both fixing breakfast. Also jumping out of bed at sunrise, Petras went out to care for the animals. He barely managed to finish the feeding, when along came Kupstienė. Goodness, how she took to lashing Petras with her tongue, rebuking him relentlessly: "You heartless creature, you monster! You took so much money from us, look how you gobbled up our child! You make her work! Finally you let the hired girls go! Why did you marry Marcelė? Why did you come begging to us, when you had a girl of your own at home? You just wanted her money! My child was like a bird in a cage with us, she never had to put her hands in cold water, while you force her to work! Is it her job to feed the pigs, and milk the cows? What are your hired hands for? What kind of master are you anyway–you haven't bothered to do any hiring up to now? You'd better find some decent girls, instead of keeping that whore. You keep your wife in the place of a dog, I'll show you!"

One after the other, her words struck Petras like blows from an ax. At first Petras didn't know how to react, then he didn't know what to say or even how to open his mouth. Finally he got up his courage:

"Let her hire some help herself," he stuttered. "Let her get whatever kind she likes. That's what I want, I just want her to make an effort to do it herself."

"You want her to ride around?" The mother shouted over him. "Can a woman take such cold? Decent husbands don't treat their wives this way! She doesn't even have the status of a shepherdess here with you: you're always full of reproaches, always persecuting her. You can't control your tongue, you lecher. There's no place for the child here in her own home with all these girls around."

"What girls are you talking about? How are they in the way?" Petras tried to stay calm. "Don't you know mistresses work everywhere?"

Meanwhile dressed in traveling clothes, Janikė appeared and announced: "Goodbye, mistress, and you, master! So you don't have to go to the trouble of reproaching me and convincing her to see me in a better light, I am leaving of my own accord. I didn't milk the cows this morning, nor did I feed the pigs—housekeepers, it's up to you now! Goodbye!"

"W..w..wait," Petras couldn't get a word out because he couldn't make up his mind whether he should stop her or let her go.

"See, there's your sweet one, your nimble one," shouted the mother, "she showed you her behind! She proved what kind of master you are, too! If I'd had any idea about this, you would have never set foot in my house!" the mother berated Petras almost in tears. "You gobbled up my child, used up her dowry—and the little one is forced to work so hard all the time!"

"What goods, what dowry?" asked Petras, managing to come to his senses.

"Didn't you take the money?" she screeched, reminding him of the facts. "And didn't you take all that lumber? Does that count for nothing? All those nights you got as much as you wanted for free. Isn't that the truth? Don't you know you can spend time locked up? Stop persecuting our child, or we'll show you where thieves belong!"

Petras felt as if he had been hit on the head with a club; darkness shimmered before his eyes. "And who is the greater thief—the one who accepts shady giving or the one who gives stolen goods?" Petras asked, as if he had just woken up.

The mother acted as if he had thrown mud in her eyes; grimacing she replied: "If everything's fine, then no one needs to know anything about it, but if something's not right, then it's all no good. You'd be better off keeping your wife where a wife belongs and keeping mum about everything—you know what you are."

Totally beaten down, Petras couldn't respond with anything, so he fled out the door. Once more at his workbench, he remembered the medicine he'd brought home for his aching heart. Pulling out the flask, he took a few swigs. He grew a bit more composed. With his elbow on the table, waiting for breakfast, he considered: "The mother came and chased the last girl away, left us with no one... That may be all right. Let's see how the wife gets along by herself; I won't say anything, no matter how messy the house gets. She thinks I'm chasing after the hired girls. Like I'd even so much as looked in their direction! I don't have the least cause to feel embarrassed. Who can stand up to a woman? Marcė wasn't too lazy to go and fetch her mother at the crack of dawn. 'Is it fair for her to work so hard?' she has the nerve to ask. Of course not for someone as lazy as she is; all that my wife knows how to do is eat and sleep—that devil Zolys turned my head! Janikė is a hundred times better!"

In despair Petras downed another swig.

Spring followed quickly on the heels of a hard, severe winter. As long as the cold held, things were at a standstill, but with spring's spreading warmth, nature sprang to life overnight. Right before your eyes waters rose, ice cracked, melted into froth, and floated downstream. As snow slipped down into eddies, trees clothed themselves in budding brightly colored leaves, the ground covered itself with sprouting green grasses. The sun's rays sparkled merrily now, the breeze blew more warmly. If perchance some small cloud wandered over from the east and splashed thick drops on the ground as if pouring sweet milk over it, then the freshly watered grass rose to double its height. Shaking the dew from the newborn leaves in the woods, the wind carried the sweet scent of spring in all directions. Shining brightly, the sun evaporated the nearby clouds with its warmth, seeming to laugh as it rejoiced at the beauty of its world. All waking birds wallowed in the sun's warmth, each one singing its joyful notes. Not only did the woods reverberate with chirping and whistling choruses, but the earth's insects announced themselves in their own unique voices. Warm evening mists refreshed everything, from the earth's plants to the minutest beings. Mother nature teemed with life: whispering and fluttering, all manner of creatures flew through the air. Foaming in whirlpools, streams gurgled and flowed downstream. Meadows ruffled up with green rushes; fields torn by plowshares turned a rich black. Although country folk found their greatest enrichment in a cornucopia of beauty, they were happiest at seeing that their animals, which had eaten nothing but dry fodder all winter, were now chewing soft young grass to revive them.

Everyone was making merry–people as much as animals and birds. Only poor Kurmelis felt no joy. The whole winter dragged by in worries for him. Because he hadn't managed to craft anything, he had no profit from the free lumber that had brought him much happiness the year before. He roped in hired hands like stray calves: if he found somebody from somewhere and hired him, that one would stay only a few days. No sooner would Petras bring another one back–and he would be gone, too. He wasted time looking, and besides that, plenty of misfortunes befell him at home: the calves died, the piglets froze, cows burst their udders–another cow hanged herself on the fence. Petras was even afraid to ride the horses, which had lost so much weight that they were barely as heavy as crows. There was precious little feed left in the barns. Wherever he stepped, Petras was beside himself: among the debris in the granaries and the cottage–a bear would lose its head. His wife hadn't changed at all: she ate for five, slept for three, and even when she wasn't sleeping, she rolled around in bed as much as she wanted. Summoned to work, Marcė muttered under her breath, and if she ever heard a harsh word from her husband, she'd fly out right away to bring her mother over. Kupstienė would browbeat Petras, accusing him of ever new glaring faults, berating and cursing him as her Marcelė's good-for-nothing husband. Incapable of quarreling with her, Petras would give in and slink away to help himself to a shot for his aching heart.

After taking the horses to the woods to graze one morning, he went to check on them toward evening. Looking for them

Petras Kurmelis

about all the thickets, he overheard something like voices or sobs nearby: he stopped to listen–someone was talking. He crept closer, and hiding in the thicket, he heard a female voice exclaiming: "Why didn't you talk that way then? But no! It's clear now that all of you conspired against me like devils: 'Lucky for you, what good fortune! You'll be loved, you'll be the mistress, you'll do whatever you want to do!' Where are your sugary tongues now, when every hour I'm swimming in tears?" she sniveled, as she spoke. "And worst of all, you were the one to use me the most. May your tongue rot in your mouth!"

"How did I use you?" asked a male voice. "Why are you blaming me? You have bread, you have a good husband–work, get to work, don't be so lazy, and you'll see how everything will be just fine."

Not following the conversation very well, Petras looked down to see who was arguing. When he saw that it was his wife with the manor groom Pranukas, he jumped backwards. Holding back a sharp sigh, with a quivering heart, he pressed up to a tree; his ears catching the words flung out in front of him.

"So that's how you've turned against me now, is it? Back then you knew how to sweet-talk me!" shouted Marcė. "You were quick to declare: 'who will separate us? I love you and will always love you! Your husband won't do anything to us!' And now? You hide from me and are ashamed to show yourself to me! Liar... You used me! If you didn't love me, why did you deceive me, why did you lie to me?"

"If I had rejected you myself, and stopped you from getting married, then you would have cause to complain. Well, let's leave it the way you say, it all came about because of my tongue... The fact is you married into a better place, you married a good man–

what kind of misfortune is that? Just be a decent person yourself, learn to love your husband. You have every reason to love him. Besides, I had no place to put you."

"It's true what you say, what kind of misfortune is that?" sobbed Marcė. "But I can't get used to him, I can't make my heart do it, I can't even look at him, I can't love him. Forget his riches and farmstead! I wish I'd never laid eyes on him. He keeps saying: 'Be good and get to work!' It's all very well for you to talk. You don't know how hard it is to be with a person you hate! Everything is unpleasant, there's nowhere to calm your heart. I looked for you all through the woods in the fall–you kept hiding all the time. Then all winter long I waited for you to appear–you didn't show your face. I came upon you accidentally today, and this is how you console me! You rotten liar, this is not what you promised!"

"Sure, I made promises until I got rid of you. And didn't I tell you clearly after the wedding: 'Goodbye, Petras's wife, this is the last time I'm seeing you. I wish you well!' Now you have everything... There's nothing to whine about: you have more than enough of everything, all you need to do now is simply love your husband."

"You have more than enough of everything, learn how to love..." Marcė repeated. "Yes, it's true, I have more than enough of bread and porridge. But did my husband give me love? Did he ask me even once: do I love him? How can I love him, when there was never any talk of love between us? No, he doesn't love me! I can't forget you, Pranas: you're in my heart and in my head. I feel that I remain in your heart, too. We can still get together, we can talk affectionately like old times, can't we? After all, that's what you promised."

"Well, devil take it, there's a woman's thinking for you!" retorted Pranukas. "Would I wear a cap on my head, if that was all the brain I had? As if there weren't any girls left in the world? Get lost, go milk the cows!" he added and picking up his whistle, he started in on the song:

Spring fields everywhere in blossoms abound
But there's many more pretty girls to be found...

Blushing, Marcė jumped up, spitting in his direction, mumbling under her breath, and disappearing into the woods. Singing and whistling, Pranukas circled his horses.

For a long time afterwards Petras stood rooted to the spot: staring wide-eyed in front of him, he couldn't focus on anything. "So he put her in her place and took away all her hope," he surmised. "Maybe she'll come back to her senses? Maybe she'll stop all her nonsense? We'll see how it all turns out, later..."

He wanted to calm down, to forget all he'd heard, but he couldn't, because Marcė's words rang over and over in his ears: "I can't look at him nor force my heart. He gave me bread and porridge, but he didn't give me love! Did he ever ask if I could love him or not? It's so hard to be with someone you hate," It's true, it's hard, his heart also agreed. "You didn't ask her about love, you didn't ask even once!" his conscience glared at him. "You didn't look for love nor did you give it, you don't love her!" confirmed his heart. "Such a slovenly good-for-nothing—who could love her?" argued his mind. "Forget his riches! Nothing is pleasing!" "That's the honest truth." He thought to himself. "It would have been better if I'd never laid eyes on that lumber!" shuddered Petras. "Now I understand why she's always so sullen... You see, she loved another. But why didn't she tell me? She's more to blame than I am. No, the scoundrel is more to blame. He lied, he deceived her, and then he was happy to be rid of her. He, Pranukas, is the guilty one!" Petras heard Pranukas's whistle, which seemed to be whining and chiding him, "You didn't ask her, you didn't. You're the most to blame!"

Mother nature was making merry, as if she were laughing, and enjoying the beauties of spring. The expansive sky was clear blue. The sun shone and warmed all things equally with affection. All the clouds scudded eastward, only to be shored up by a bright, multicolored rainbow. Subsiding, the breeze scarcely caused the fresh, yellow leaves to quiver. Petras didn't take note of any of it; oppressed as though under a heavy rock, he closed his eyes and sighed. The full blame for his misfortunes lays on him. Pain stabbed his heart, Marcė's reproaches spun in his head, he had no ground to stand on. It seemed as if the sky and the mountains were falling on him, too; as if the whole world, even the birds, as common folk say, were accusing him. The speckled thrush in the fir tree over his head was chirping clearly: "Don't blame anyone, don't blame anyone! You're to blame, you're to blame!" Whistling, the yellow-beaked starling confirmed, "It's true, it's true, it's true!" The loud hoopoe deep in the woods carried on, "you-you-you, you-you-you!" The woodpecker contributed to the chorus, "Yourself, yourself, yourself, yourself, yourself!" On the edge of the valley the tiny nightingale chattered, "Oh yes, oh yes, you yourself, you yourself, more to blame, more to blame!" Flying by, even the crow cawed, "For sure, for sure, for sure!" Truly angry, the blue pigeon cooed, "Beat Kurmelis, beat the toad, on the back...on the back!" The speckled finch poked fun at him too: "Marcelė's hundreds–clink, clink, clink, clink, clink!" Soaring on high, the

Petras Kurmelis

fidgety swallow gave Petras a tongue-lashing: "Poor thing, poor thing! Never touched, never loved, don't expect love!" Quivering up high, the plowman's friend, the skylark, continued, "you said, you said, it's all the same to me, it's all the same to me, as long as she's rich, as long as she's rich. Riches she has, she has, luck she hasn't, luck she hasn't. It's not all the same, see, not all the same." Fluffing its feathers, the black grouse forcefully advised, "Sell the bad wife, buy a good wife. Sell the bad wife, buy a good wife." And the water hen wading in the fen chattered, "He'll be bald, he'll be bald!" Lastly, that poor little insect, the gnat, hummed into his ear, "Bro', bro', you went for a ruble, you went for a ruble!"

Petras's ears rang with pain while all of them accused him. He stared at the sun, which seemed to wink: "There was love, child. There was a search for love, there was asking, there was asking for permission, there was a time for love!" Petras listened for what other babbling was down the hill. Winding in the valley, gurgling over the rocks, the brook chattered, "Complain or not, a wife's not a sleeve, you can't turn her inside out. Lucky Petras, she's a good wife."

Petras couldn't escape from any of it. He wrestled with his hot head so it wouldn't catch fire; he clutched at his aching heart so it wouldn't burst. He turned his back to the rainbow, where he imagined he saw Janikė's bright face, her yellow braids, her arms spread wide, her blue eyes beckoning, "Come, come! I'll take you in, I'll comfort you…" He was about to stretch out his arms, about to nestle up to her, but from the menacing cloud Marcelė's grim face came between them. Scowling at him, she appeared to be mouthing the words: "How many times did you ask me–will I be able to love you, or will I not? Love is what I need, love!" "She wants love," he reflected, "I'll give her love, I will–I'll love her with all my heart…" Out of nowhere the oriole whistled straight into his ear, "You lie, you wretched thing, you lie!" Acute pain pierced Petras's heart, he sighed out loud, "Mother of mine, mother! Why didn't you tell me to look for love?" A frog croaked from the ditch, "I told you so, I told you so, I told you so!"

As he was reproached by everyone, persecuted by all, Petras's pain turned into anger. His teeth chattering, he raised his hand, "The finger to you, you rotten old toads, the finger to all of you!" he bellowed and stumbled to the other end of his house without looking back. There, he got his beloved whiskey down from the shelf and chugged it down, down until there wasn't a drop left in the flask.

All country folk hope fervently for beautiful weather during the Feast Day of Saints–Simas and Judas, the first spring fair, but they just had to wait and see what comes of it this year! It rained cats and dogs the day before, pouring down all day over the fields and meadows, splashing puddles on the sides and muddying the road. Nevertheless, clear patches could be seen farther above the rain. The little stars twinkled so happily before dawn, and the evening star appeared to be laughing. The blue-eyed dawn dispersed its white light. The morning awoke like an eye emerging from beneath sleepy lashes: first you saw the whites, then, as it opened more, you could see the pupil. Quivering like a teary eye, the lazy sun shone shyly. Hundreds, even thousands of shining sunbeams were reflected in each puddle, in every bubble, and in each tiny dewdrop. The entire earth was ablaze in gold and pearls. Rejoicing, each person was planning to leave earlier because each one had myriad errands to run. Country folk acknowledged: "A beautiful dawn has broken, so there'll be a good fair." The goslings were grown, so were the chicks; the onions and carrots were ready, but there were no women left at home. Like a brood hen with her goods stuffed around her, each one sat at the back of her wagon. At the front the husband lashed the mares with his whip and strode across the mud, splashing his way toward town. If you want to make a kopeck, then you'll have to give up the last bite going into your mouth.

It may still have been early, but the town was already over-flowing with people. The men waded and splashed through the mud, while the wives quarreled with the Jewish women, making the piglets squeal and the hens cackle. Around noon the sun hid itself somewhere. Although not a cloud was in sight, the rain appeared from who knows where, starting with fine drops, then steadily increasing, finally bursting out into a heavy downpour. Getting soaked and moving on quickly, the buyers offered the women less and less each time around. Discouraged, the men headed for the taverns; the women sold their wares at half price because they were tired of standing in the rain.

The beauty of the fair dissipated: this one sold his wares, that one not; one bought something, another didn't; hurried by their women, the frustrated men, cursing, got ready to travel home-ward. By mid-afternoon the town was already emptying. Hanging their heads, the horses stood listlessly harnessed to their wagons; those who had managed to get away from their wives only by leaving them home saddled others. Men have more im-portant errands to attend to.

"So what, let the horse wait, it's not going to weep at your grave!" the men declared, keeping each other from leaving. "Not even the devil can get home in this weather! Maybe it'll stop raining."

"It's true, no one can go home now."

Agreeing with one another thus, they thronged and shoved in the taverns. If they found some bench by the wall, they planted themselves and sat in a row in a room as thick with smoke as the mouth of an oven. The talk mixed with the clang of flasks and glasses and competed with the shouts of those partly or completely drunk. The sober ones smoked their pipes in the corners and spat. Kurmelis stood in this end of the tavern among the men, who were pushing and shoving on the dirt floor, which was thoroughly muddy. It was gray and dark from the smoke, making your head spin from the stench and the humidity. With his boots muddy halfway up to his knees, his clothes steaming and dripping, his cap pushed back, Kurmelis staggered drunk among the throng. Watching him, two smokers by the fire were discussing: "Well, Petras is already nice and drunk. He's completely out of hand with the drinking. As long as his mother restrained him, he was a decent man at least, but look at him now! He's going to the dogs, all his wealth is going to disappear down his throat…"

"No doubt about it," said the second one. "The man who's handy has a wide gullet, too. I saw him selling some beautifully made chests."

"What a man he used to be! Who could have guessed that he'd end up like this?"

"You know, after his mother's death, the mistress changed," laughed the second one.

"How true, everything's changed, now there's not a cow or a piece of bread left."

"Hey, Berkis, get me a pint!" shouted Kurmelis, waving to him with one hand and holding Zolys by the collar with the other. "You're going to drink, my matchmaker, you rotten festering toad, you're going to drink! To hell with you!" he threatened,

Petras Kurmelis

clenching his teeth, and raising his fist as if measuring where to punch him in the face.

In the corner the men glanced at one another and started laughing: "Aha, he's going to treat his matchmaker for the good wife he got him."

"Is the matchmaker to blame if he let himself go?" retorted the other one.

Zolys tried to get away, saying he had no time, but Kurmelis wouldn't let him go, shouting: "You're going to drink, you bastard! Are you worried about my money? I sold two chests...I'm going to drink up the profit! Oh yes, you bet! To the devil with it... you're going to drink!"

Holding up a flask with a bagel stuck on it and a shot glass in his other hand, Berkis was making his way to the men at the table closer to the fire. Kurmelis was dragging Zolys backward; Kurmelis and Zolys and the two neighbors gossiping about him all ended up in the same corner.

"Ah-ha," shouted Kurmelis, slurring his words. "And the two of you are loafing about here?"

"Hey, Berkis, give me a flask for two gold pieces... Hop to it or I'll break your bones!" G-r-r-r-r, he ground his teeth. "All of you drink, you rotten toads! The hell with it... Cheers, match-maker!... Sss–so-o... a drink to my neighbor Gorys!"

"Thank you, thank you," said Gorys, on being greeted. "But first you have to treat your matchmaker..."

"Do you, sir, consider me no good?" declared Zolys. "From my hands Kurmelis has a wife like a round onion, three years have passed. Now he has a chubby son. Take note, even today I matched another couple. I really know what I'm doing; they've already finished the prayers, and on Sunday they'll announce the banns."

"Is that right?" marveled Gorys. "Whom have you matched up?"

"Drink, the hell with it!" shouted Kurmelis once more. "The money's still burning a hole in my pocket."

"I matched up Pranukas Stapučiukas with Janikė Kadaitė. Year before last she served at this one's here," Zolys pointed to Kurmelis. "While taking care of the horses at the manor, Stapučiukas impressed the master. Now he's getting the forester's job." Turning to Kurmelis, Zolys revealed: "Your poor in-laws will lose their place–they've been carrying on too heedlessly…"

The whites of his eyes popping out, Kurmelis listened to this sour melody. Picking up a full glass, he poured it over his teeth, started coughing as he choked, even his skin turned pale. Coughing and spitting, he rolled out the door. Smacking into a wall, he made a fist in the wind, mumbling something or other. His sight grew dim, his throat felt like it was being strangled, his ears rang loudly, everything was mixed up in his head–he felt as though all his forest lumber was falling on him, he couldn't turn his stiff tongue over, only his teeth kept grinding away.

"I didn't go inside and I won't, and I won't let you go there, either. Let's wait a little bit. If he doesn't come out, we'll leave," a familiar female voice echoed in Kurmelis's ears.

Turning in their direction, he forced his heavy eyelashes open so that he could see where the voice was coming from. First he focused on the muddy boots, the hems, the apron's lace, the black gloves, the wool shawl, and then finally the white kerchief… "Oh, the bright face… the same! The same dear blue eyes!"

"Jan… Janė," he tried to speak with his frozen tongue. First he coughed, then spat, and finally sighing, he asked: "Janė, is, is it true? Zolys… the s.o.b. is lying," he tried to say, but his tongue wouldn't obey him.

Falling silent for a moment, his eyes half-closed, he looked to see why no one was answering him. Bending over the shoulder of a young man, Janikė was whispering something in his ear. Clenching his teeth, Kurmelis spat and groping along the wall, he started talking to Janikė: "Jane,... don't you know me... They say you're getting married. Married? Why, I'm not drunk... let's talk.. I'll..."

"How would I not recognize you, Uncle?" replied Janikė and kissed his hand. "Though I see you rarely now, we haven't changed so much that we wouldn't know each other."

"They say you're getting married, and Zolys is the match-maker?"

"Yes, I'm getting married. We've already announced the banns. Here's my young man," Janike pointed to Pranukas who stood beside her.

Kurmelis felt as if someone had poured cold water down his back. He fixed his frozen eyes on Pranukas who turned his back to him:

"Oh, he's very familiar!" recalled Kurmelis. "All he needs is a whistle in his teeth..." He clearly remembered the words he'd heard. "Be honest, love your husband and everything will be all right!"

Coming even closer to Janikė, Kurmelis asked her in a low voice: "And do you really love him?"

Janikė laughed, but Pranukas wouldn't let her utter another word. Seizing her by the hand, he urged her: "Let's go, it looks like we'll miss meeting the matchmaker."

Saying this, he led Janikė off and disappeared into the crowd. Kurmelis gazed all around, but they were gone. "Zolys, that good-for-nothing." he wanted to curse, but he could only manage to clench his teeth. People passing by were pushing him, he leaned back against the wall, but they were still shoving. With his head down he crept farther along the wall, his eyes fixed on the ground. He felt some kind of weight pressing down on his chest pushing him to the ground; a black curtain slipped over his eyes; his arms and legs became paralyzed. Kurmelis forgot Zolys, the whiskey buddies; he forgot his horses and the wagon. A mixture of images swirled in his head: Jané's blue eyes, Marcé in her dirty shirt, his sour-faced child… Marcé's clear voice rang in his ears: "I can't force my heart, I can't even look at him." Finally a whistling medley of tunes, fast whirling dances made his head spin.

Until they'd emptied their flasks, Kurmelis's buddies in the tavern thought no further about him. When the whiskey came to an end, they began to miss him. Waiting for him, they put down enough money for a half bottle. In the meantime, dawn started to appear.

"Where did our Petras go?" they asked each other.

"If he's got any money left, he's drinking somewhere else, don't you know?"

Zolys laughed again about missing his young couple. And so all of them, cracking jokes, crept out of the tavern. Outside a fine rain was falling, but it was heavy enough so that water splashed down from the eaves in streams. Roaring, the wind blew away the rain and the gray clouds. It also chased off anyone left from the fair. Everyone headed for home, splashing through the mud. The men searched high and low for Kurmelis outside. They noticed his horses still in the marketplace; confused, their heads hanging down, they stood in the rain. While the neighbors walked around their saddled horses, Zolys was the quicker one–he waded over, unfastened his horses and drove over to the tavern.

"Where did that Petras go to?" they questioned, all missing him. "Dawn is already breaking. He's dead drunk–how's he going to get home?"

Gorys wandered around behind the tavern, and almost stepped on Petras.

"Here's that good-for-nothing!" he cried. "He's fallen down behind the manure pile."

They all rushed over and started to rouse Petras, lifting him from the ground. Coming to, Kurmelis looked around with his pale eyes. The whistling still rang in his ears. The loud ding-dong of the church bell, summoning to prayer, added to the din. Petras stood up and gazed around: all the waysides looked gray, the earth and the sky as well. The rain and the wind roared, causing Kurmelis to tremble from the cold. He woke up, sobered up a little, fixed his belt and cap; neither his gloves nor the whip from his wagon were in his coat any longer.

"Let's go inside," said Petras. "Maybe I can at least find my whip, the devil's already taken my gloves. We'll take another shot for the aggravation and the cold."

Zolys was ready, but Gorys wouldn't let Petras go: he grabbed any old whip and forced him to get into his wagon. As darkness fell, fumbling, one after the other they set off for home. As he left, Petras still spewed his venom at Zolys. The riders got off to a faster start, while Kurmelis curled up in the middle of his wagon; the horses dragging along in the middle of the road.

"What's my hurry? Who's waiting for me? Unless it's the dog?" considered Kurmelis. "I sold two chests for seven rubles. They slipped down my throat. Not even a bagel for Kazelis. Oh well, he's still so little, he doesn't know the difference. If only she'd scold me sometimes like other women nag their husbands:

'Are you man or devil, why do you drink so much? Why did you drink up all the money?' But this one doesn't: it's all the same to her, she wouldn't care if you lost the last shirt off your back. It's true–nothing makes her happy, she doesn't even love the child, she has no heart... Ech, that damn Zolys!"

Before his eyes he saw Janikė with Pranukas and the Kupstyses' dilapidated cottage.

"They'll dust it, dry out the dirt floor, and wash the windows... If only I could change places! I'd give up all my belongings, the whole of my homestead; I'd go into the woods, to that rotten cottage to be with Janė, bringing only Kazelis. And Pranukas could come in my place. More than likely Marcė would change, too, since she loves him anyway. Wedlock: till death do us part–brrr!..."
He shuddered. "They say they switch wives or husbands in other countries. If only they'd trade me for some gypsy! Even that dark one wouldn't be like her... The way I'd cherish her and love her!"

The wind whistled sharply into his ear: "Not the love of your heart, no, not!"

"He who's hit rock bottom no longer searches for anything... Aren't they fortunate? After they're wed, they'll both be happy."

Zolys appeared before his eyes again.

"Such bad luck–I didn't meet up with him earlier: I would have gone on treating him, and plying him with whiskey, until he dropped down dead drunk," he schemed, clenching his teeth. "Why did Zolys pair them? Maybe it wasn't him? They could have already loved one another..." Once again he ground his teeth.

The horses came to a halt. Barking and squealing, Cimbalis bounded up to him. Petras straightened: it was dark like a hole in hell. He rolled out of the wagon, all frozen, shaking from the cold. Fumbling, he unharnessed the horses and then let them into the stable. Throwing the horse-collar on the ground by the wag-on, he made his way inside. The cottage was warm; it just smelled unpleasantly sour. Petras's hands were stiff with cold; no matter how many matches he struck, they all went out or fell from his fingers. Marcė was snoring in bed. Somehow or other he lit the lantern. There was a dish on the table with something in it.

"That's my supper," he realized. "Potatoes and cold gravy... If only I could get a small dish of something warm... brrr!" his whole body shook.

The child stirred in the cradle and whimpered. Petras bent down, wanting to hold the child and kiss him, but the stench was so bad that he jumped up and had to back away.

"Marcė, Marcė!" he shouted out loud, waking up his wife, "The child is soiled, get up and clean him up."

Turning over on her other side, Marcė mumbled: "If he's not crying, leave him alone."

Petras sat down on the bench; he warmed up a little, and then felt like dozing off. Taking off his cloak, he covered his head with it and fell over on the bench with his sheepskin on it. After he lay down, he kept shouting: "Marcė, Marcė, mother! Did you hear the news? Listen, are you sleeping?"

His wife grunted.

"Your folks lost their place–the master let them go. Instead of them he's putting Pranukas, his groom, and that one's marrying Janikė who worked for us. They've already announced the banns."

Slurring his last words, Petras fell asleep. Marcė listened to his first words still dozing, but the last bit of news struck her like lightning: she sat up in bed, gazed around with sleepy eyes, falling over only to cozy down again, turning over on one side and then on the other, but sleep eluded her entirely. Petras was snoring. Marcė got up, cleaned up the child, laid him down, and rocked him for a while. Sitting on the bed, she rested her chin on her hand: she smiled once, then tears rolled down her cheeks. Sighing once more, she lay down and then quickly got up again; smiling and wiping away her tears in turn. Calming down somewhat, she mulled the news over and over in her mind until cock's crow, but sleep didn't return. The clock struck three. Marcė jumped up, sighed, glanced over at Petras, and went out to rouse the hired hands. The girls came into the cottage and sat down to spin. Kazelis let out a cry. Picking him up from the cradle, she dressed him in a white shirt, kissed him, pressed him to her bosom, and kissed him again, all while her copious tears dripped onto the child's face. Rocking the child, she put him back in bed and lay down next to him. The child fell asleep, then Marcė jumped up again, telling the girl to clean the table, start the fire, and heat up breakfast. The hired girls glanced at each other and giggled, wondering, "What's the big news that makes our mistress into such a housekeeper?" Sitting on the bed, Marcė rested. Myriad images and memories flooded her head. Zolys loomed before her.

"That horrible devil, why did he pair those two?" she thought, cursing. "May his tongue rot away for talking me into it!"

Pranukas appeared before her again. She could almost hear his words, "You'll have more than enough of everything, you'll be the mistress."

"The rotten bastard," she wailed. "Let him see the great plenty I have now—in no time Petras will drink it all away."

She glanced at her husband once more.

"Piece of rot!" she exclaimed to herself. "He doesn't tell me how much money he's squirreled away somewhere, nor how much he drank, not like other women's husbands who tell their wives everything."

The child cried out. Hugging and kissing him, she said aloud:

"Kazelis, my little one! Your father is going to drink everything away, he's such a drunkard, always soused. Although he hides everything from me, I can still see our lives going downhill. By the time you grow up, there won't be anything left."

Fixing her eyes on her husband, she mused to herself: "Lying on the bare bench, eating nothing all day–he'll get up and go off to work or to the smithy again. I wonder how many rubles flowed down his throat yesterday."

THE DAUGHTER-IN-LAW

"There's no way around it, Ma, we'll have to get Jonukas hitched. He'll have to find a girl with a cushy dowry. That way we can pretty much pay off our debts. The way it is now, we can hardly stick our noses outside, especially at the tavern. Those leeches surround us. One wants his interest, the other his hay or the crop he's owed, yet another keeps pestering me like the devil, 'when do you think you'll be giving it back?' You'd swear they didn't have anything else to talk about."

"So why do you hang around the taverns?" the wife reproached him.

"They'll come up to you in town, too. Doesn't matter how sick you are of it. Even on an empty stomach, you have to treat them to a pint. It wouldn't be so bad if that were the end of it. Add on one more round, then another, and before you know it, they've put away several flagons. And when they get drunk, watch out—they're real wolves, ready to tear you into bits for those damned debts. I'm going to give up the homestead. Let the boy take it over, let him pay up, I'm washing my hands of it."

"Yeah, yeah, that's all we need! Give everything away, then the young one will push us around! I'm not giving it up, I'm not letting him have it as long as I'm alive," the wife yelled, growing more furious. "I'm not handing over the ladle to any daughter-in-law, oh no! I don't want a mistress over my head. I won't take a single bite from a daughter-in-law's hands. That's not going to happen, I'm not going to go along with it!"

"Na, na, na, rattle away like a Jewish peddler's creaky wagon! Go ahead, don't give it up, just stay here and gawk when the creditors auction it off, then you'll get busted in the teeth! As if a daughter-in-law's going break your neck! Keep that tongue of yours from wagging, and everything will turn out just fine!"

"The daughter-in-law will put up with my tongue, whether she likes it or not," growled the wife, "but the spigot's going to be turned off for you now, you won't have any more money for swill. Who got us into these debts anyway? You've poured most of your livelihood down your gullet. Would it hurt you to live like a decent fellow? Anyone can see how Maušas got rich, while you only went downhill. And to top it off, you're going to put a daughter-in-law on my neck. Just wait, you'll find out!"

"Oh, just be quiet!" spat the husband. "I'll plow you in the chops, if you don't stop! It's going to be the way I say. Jonukas will get married. He'll get some cash and we'll live off the fat."

"I'm not giving it up any other way," the mother kept shouting. "I'll keep house while the daughter-in-law works someplace else. She'll bring home her own dough."

"I'm telling Jonukas to ask Mateušas to be his matchmaker. Both of them can go to Driežas's Kotrė. No telling what she's like, but the money's as good as in our hands. They're giving us four hundred rubles. You can't snivel at that kind of dowry. Though my homestead's a bit run down, the soil is damn good. Driežas has nothing to complain about. And then there's sonny, isn't he a catch? Tall and handsome, that's our Jonukas. The girl's sure to fall for the likes of him."

"Blast it, who on earth have you picked now! That dark-haired, big-nosed one, that good-for-nothing, that idler," the wife rose up shouting. "She's spoiled rotten, all prettied up, gussied up, all crackling in her starched linens. She'll be walking with her nose in the air. If it isn't enough that she decks herself out for church, but she stays in the house all dolled up like a prissy missy, too. She'll go out raking hay in a white blouse, her scarf and her apron fancied up with an iron, with her peaches-and-cream complexion! Is someone the likes of her ever going to make a decent housewife? Nah, the real scoop is that she just wanders around outside and around the house, rake in hand. Heard tell she never does any work, just a little sweeping, a little scrubbing. Then she sits at the loom, or picks at some embroidery, nothing but trifling stuff. Never any real work–phooey! I'm not putting up with someone so useless! At my house there's no need for any fancy stuff! What I need is a workhorse just like me!"

"Now, ma, what nonsense are you jabbering about? Who do you think is doing the work, then? After all, Driežas doesn't hire any other help. Kotrikė carries the load all by herself. The father's a stickler, forces her to work like a horse."

"What are you arguing with me for? As if I don't know anything. A girl's work isn't equal to real work. Look at their place, their whole house is swept and dusted, both indoors and in the yard. There's not a straw, nor any sweepings around. The beds are made, all white. That little trickster Kotrikė spends all her time on that. If I were her mother, would I let her carry on with such foolishness? I'd give her what for, so she'd be doing something that's work! Her father pays no mind to what's going on.

He just keeps making money hand over fist. Dressing up that dark-haired scarecrow of his with hundreds of rubles. He's going to stick her to somebody yet, cheating some decent fellow who doesn't suspect anything."

"No one's going to put one over on us," assured the father. "As long as they hand over the money, there will be no need to examine the girl. You're not going to churn butter from her looks. As long as she brings us the money, there's no need for anything else."

"And what about you? Wouldn't you know how to throw money around even without a daughter-in-law? Look at you, your homestead's worth more than that Driežas's, but you're still as poor as a church mouse with all that damn boozing!"

"Well, it isn't your pocket I'm drinking from, is it?" the husband shouted. "It's none of your business! It wasn't yours I drank. It's my land, my homestead, everything's mine, I have the right. I can drink it all away if I want. So what are you going to do to stop me? The more you blather away and try to prevent me, the crazier I'm going to drink! You ought to know that your barking won't stop anything. You ought to be quiet, if you don't want to get punched on your mug!"

"That's all you know: 'smack on your mug, punch you in the teeth!' It's because I'm telling you what you don't want to hear, and that's the truth. If that's all that Jonukas is going to amount to and that's all he's going to listen to his wife, then he's better off herding pigs some more years than getting married off."

"That's all we need—for him to listen to a wife! That's not going to happen! He'd be a real calf minding her. You think a woman has enough brains to rule over a man? If she starts to babble, sock her in the teeth with your fist, so she has to lick herself off."

The wife rushed out the door, jabbering; fast on her heels, Jonukas, the Vingis's only child, crept in, just about the time the father was bragging, "Tall and handsome he is, that's our Jonukas!" His appearance was tall all right, but he was stout, too; he had enormous shoulders, a pot belly, slightly stooped because of his height, his hands tarred like a sled's crossbeams, his legs as crooked as old fence sticks, mouth gaping as big as a basket, nose like a good-sized cucumber, eyes with dark circles like a mole's; a huge head, topped with a disheveled, gray mop, hunched forward, a thick neck stuck onto his trunk, his forehead shoved upward and a cap turned sideways. His lower lip hanging open revealed large yellowed teeth with saliva dripping down freely. His cheap felt overcoat, crumpled and wrinkled, bristling with straw and twigs, was a sight to behold. His shirt and pants would have been happy to be called white. They were muddied so thick that a dog couldn't bite through them, with rips and tears in them, they looked as if they hadn't been laundered for a year. His filthy feet stuck barefoot into his clogs, he crossed the dirt floor, stretched, yawned, threw another glance at the little clock, sat down on a bench at the other end of the cottage, and stretching his legs in front of him onto the floor, he started picking at his stained pipe while checking his pockets for tobacco.

"Where have you been?" asked the father.

"Sleeping. I lay down after breakfast, and I've been hitting the sack ever since!" he yawned.

"Did you look to the horses?"

"Yeah, yeah, sure! The horses aren't my business on a holy day! Yeah, Pa, what are you going to do, if you don't look after them?"

"The horses aren't going anywhere I reckon?" the father flicked his hand, "Well, did you stuff up the stove in the barn at least?"

"Yeah, yeah, what do you think! It's always my job! So why did you leave it empty up to now?"

"Well, that isn't any trouble, the rye will dry by tomorrow," said the father, waving his hand again.

"God be praised! Not sleeping for a change?" the mother said in surprise, as she stepped inside. "Folks finished up and came home a long time ago, and you still haven't had your dinner. You'll have to go hungry because of all that sleeping of yours."

"Yeah, yeah, what do you think! Why are you surprised, when you didn't bother waking me!"

"How can anyone wake the likes of you? Didn't I call you? But you're sleeping soundly like a fat pig, no one could wake you in time even with a trumpet blasting in your ear. You're like some boulder, you big lump! Look at those swollen eyes—you've turned into a useless sluggard, sleeping all the time, is that good for someone so young? You'd be better off going to church and going berrying afterwards, like other folks' kids. Like those ones over there, singing, amusing themselves, while you're turning into some sour pickle."

"Yeah, yeah, that's for sure! I've heard plenty of those sermons of yours already," the dear son growled back.

"The young one's right on the money," snorted the father. "Forget the sermon, just put dinner on the table, on the double."

Jonukas slid behind the table, and while taking a loaf of bread from the corner of the bench, he cut himself a couple of thick slices. The mother shuffled in with a bowl of buttermilk the size of a lake and threw in a handful of coarse salt. The son looked around for a spoon. He looked in the drawer, on the windowsill, then on the floor. Seeing it under the bench, he picked it up, brushed the dirt off with his fingers, and smacked it into his bowl. Biting off big chunks of bread, he started to slurp the clabbered milk while his huge ears went up and down as he chewed. Smoking his pipe, the father started in again:

"Jonukas, are you getting married or aren't you? Find yourself some girl who's rich, or I won't be able to pay off those damn debts. I can't get rid of those devil creditors, who give me no end of grief."

"Yeah, yeah, sure! Who got us into debt in the first place? Why is it up to me to pay them off? And what's more, show me a girl that's loaded with cash."

"Just hop to it quickly, and I'll show you where to get one. Go grab hold of Driežas's daughter, and you'll see how many rubles they'll spread out for you!"

"Yeah, yeah, that's for sure! Why don't you go grab Kotrė for yourself? She's dark as can be. Her eyes look like June bugs, and besides she's old, a whole lot older than me."

Overhearing Jonukas's whining, his mother barged in brightly, "See, aren't I right? I told you Kotrė's no good for our Jonukas. Why, she looks like a Jewess or a gypsy, or the devil knows what? When she got old, they couldn't marry her off, so you can be sure she's not much of a catch. Don't take her; we don't need the likes of her. There's plenty of decent girls around!"

"Jonukas, don't listen to Ma. She's lying, she's used to talking nonsense! Just you listen to me, do what I tell you, and if you don't, I'm driving the two of you with mother out. I'm renting out the land until I can pay off the loans, and you and Ma can go wherever you please."

"Yeah, yeah, for sure! Get going yourself, start being a beggar, but I'm not giving up the land!" The mother shouted over the son's ranting: "Nothing doing. As soon as you get hold of the rent, you'll get it into your head to go drinking. Once you're dead drunk, the debt stays a debt. You're not going to rent the land, not over my dead body! Look at him, wanting to get everything for himself! Haven't I poured all of my health into this piece of land? Go ahead and rent it, just try, but see if I let any outsiders into my home."

"Shut your yammering mouth!" the father cried out. "In a second you're going to get it in the chops! Such a big lady to give orders here. You're better off feeding the pigs. It's going to be the way I want."

Turning to the son, he cajoled him, "Treat Mateušas to something, take him to Driežas's and get an agreement going, and don't dilly-dally around, because when you announce the banns, they'll come over to look at the farm. That's when we'll settle on the dowry."

"Yeah, yeah, sure! They say Kotrė doesn't even want to get married off."

"What kind of nonsense is that? As if it's going to be up to her! As long as the father agrees, he'll give a share to her and won't give a darn about what she wants. He'll make her go."

Things turned out the way the father said. Jonukas and Mateušas paid a visit to Driežas. After they were treated to drinks, the matchmaker sweet-talked and bargained on Jonukas's behalf. He knew how to make the best use of his tongue. It was his job to praise and convince others, thus they kept Driežas salivating. The young suitor stretched and yawned, but before too long he agreed on the dowry.

Kotrė cried buckets of tears. The mother tried to console her gently, while the father scolded her angrily. If she was going to be stubborn and disobey him when she was being handed something good, he would send her away and not give her anything at all!

When Driežas went to inspect the Vingises' farm, he found everything neglected and run down, but he agreed anyway and even added more than he'd promised to the matchmaker's dowry. He exclaimed, "The soil is rich, the meadows can be sheared like sheep, the gardens abundant. The buildings, well, we can easily fix those. We'll all get together and build new ones. There's not much to worry about. We won't have to pay anyone off their share. No one will come and take away a cow when they can't pay their debts. I'll set up my sweet Kotrė like a little hen sitting on her eggs."

Some of the neighbors criticized Kotrė; others reproached Jonukas. And then there were those who tried to scare her off with the parents. The rest just shrugged their shoulders.

During the three weeks that the banns were being announced, wherever Kotrė went, she couldn't see her way through her tears. Jonukas didn't suit her in the least. The mother pitied her, but she didn't have the will to go against her husband's wishes. The father, however, didn't even bother to listen to anyone; all he could talk about was Jonukas's land, the good homestead. He tried to convince Kotrė that she would live like a lady and get rich. He promised he'd help to fix up the place. As for her husband, she'd get used to him. He assured her, "You'll wake up the sleepyhead, you'll spur the lazybones on. Jonukas is still young, he'll learn to love you, and he'll listen to whatever you tell him to do."

The few weeks before Kotrė's marriage rolled by like a heavy creaking wheel as she made plans for the wedding and worked on the farm. After the wedding, she returned with her husband to his parents' house. The dowry wagon tried to make haste, but it lagged behind, because it was so laden down that the lathered horses could barely drag it along. There were two wardrobes and two chests as if stuffed with rocks, and there was no end to the bundles, bedding, and clothes. The wedding guests hauled them out of the sagging wagon and dragged everything into the leaning granary with its broken-down doors.

In the yard the guests splashed and waded through mud up to their knees. Kotrė shivered with horror at the sight, but a part of her was already casting an eye on the yard–cleaning out the manure, pouring gravel and pebbles on the paths. It would be almost like home, except that the fences were hopelessly broken down.

The husband led Kotrė inside. The parents as well as the wedding guests and musicians hurried into the entry to greet the daughter-in-law.

Kotrė fell at the parents' feet, kissed their hands, then gave each one of them a long and very delicately woven piece of linen. The mother invited the bride and groom to the table, set out food and drink for them, and urged them to partake. Looking at them, she rejoiced and voiced her amazement: "Who would have thought that sweet Kotrė would end up my daughter-in-law! When my Jonukas was going to be baptized, she was big enough to open the gate. Why, she was a grown little shepherdess even back then. What are you going to do; this must be God's will. You gave us a lot of gifts; thanks be for that. The linen is so fine, it looks like it's woven by a real weaver, I can tell."

Kotrė swallowed her first mouthful of refreshments, which were mixed with a dose of bitter peppers–her new mother's stinging words.

The father was soused, his nose quite blue. He ran helter-skelter around the room, pretending to take care of everything, while often clenching his fists. In a wheezing voice he croaked: "It's going to be the way I say!" Then, lighting a smelly pipe, he slumped down on the other side of the daughter-in-law. Getting close to her, he muttered:

"My land is like gold, my homestead's overflowing with the best of everything, you'll roll around like a kidney sizzling in fat, you'll be fed good, all you have to do is obey me. Your dowry is measly, your inheritance doesn't amount to much! Jonukas would have gotten more somewhere else, anybody can see how tall and handsome he is, and smart as a whip. They found all kinds of fault with you, but nothing stopped him. There must be plenty of good fortune in those cards of yours. Let's drink to that."

The father filled his glass and toasted her: To your health!

The stench from the father's pipe and his whiskey breath made Kotrė almost sick to her stomach. Turning to her husband, she saw his mouth hanging open, saliva dribbling down, as he dozed soundly! Chills ran up and down Kotrė's spine; despair overwhelmed her when she realized that this was the kind of family she had married into until her dying day. It dawned on her clearly that she had only one real dad and only one beloved mom who belonged to her, who truly loved her, but who nevertheless mercilessly gave her away into a stranger's hands. Quickly she decided that she couldn't call her new parents dad and mom, but papa and mama, according to Polish custom.

The bride and groom sat imprisoned at the table long into the night. Kotrė grew quite dizzy from the smoke and stench and was reeling from the mother's hurtful insults, the father's ramblings, and the guests' bawdy jokes. Slipping away from the table and its unaccustomed food and drink, she somehow made it to her bed in the dark, her head bursting with pain and fever. Kotrė fell across the bed and buried her face in the pillow, which very

The Daughter-in-Law

soon became soaked with her flowing tears. She sobbed until sleep calmed her tired head.

She didn't rest long, however, since the door creaking from the wind disturbed her sleep. She awoke frozen and trembling from cold; she became aware of where she was only gradually. Groping around in the strange place, she barely managed to shut the door. Then, catching hold of some covers, she stayed curled up until dawn. Alas, sleep escaped her as images of her wedding day shimmered before her eyes; various bits of conversation rang in her ears. As her head cleared, she recalled the events of the previous day. She remembered that with their blessing, she was separated from her parents and handed over to another family, and that at the priest's behest she was married to this husband until death would part them.

She sighed, crossed herself, and rubbed her eyes.

"Could I be dreaming? Oh Jesus, holy mother Mary, it's true! But where is he? It's the first night after the wedding and he's not here! The roosters are already crowing, dawn is near, and soon the musicians will show up to wake us. What's going to happen? The bed is not made, the groom is hiding somewhere, the bride is still in her wedding dress from the day before, they'll think she must have been drunk. Probably the others are still drinking and dancing. But it's dead quiet, nothing to be heard. What is my dear mom up to? It's my first night in a strange place away from her. Now I'll be calling this my home. How will I get used to it? What will they make me do here?!"

These and other thoughts raced through Kotrė's mind. Often hot tears fought their way into her eyes, but she made herself swallow them. She told herself that crying wouldn't help. She'd have to arm herself with humility, patience, and perseverance against her new family's persecution. Woefully she now felt that there was no one on her side; everyone was critical, judging her every step and word.

As dawn was breaking, Kotrė jumped up, straightened her things, made the bed, got dressed, left the door to the granary ajar, and went inside the house.

Not a soul was in sight, not a peep to be heard. The wedding guests were fast asleep. As a result the animals took the opportunity to snuffle around in the corners. The calves and sheep mucked around in the yard. In the entry, the pigs clattered the pots and pans and squealed when the slops spilled. The cottage door had been lifted off its hinges and placed on the opposite wall. It seemed the mischief-makers were bent on playing tricks to freeze the old folks out of house and home. Inside, the father had fallen across his bed and was snoring away. Tired of fighting with the pigs, the dog was gnawing on a bone. The mother's feet were stuck under the stove, and her head rested on the fireplace. Wrapped in her sheepskin coat, she was sleeping sweetly in the ashes as if they were down pillows. Cuddled around the crumbling fireplace, the piglets were grunting, begging the housekeeper in vain for breakfast, but she was dead to the world. Hopping up on the table, the rooster urged his hens to peck at the crumbs, but they were too busy fighting with the cats by the overturned milk pots. The shy goslings flocked together next to the threshold, cocking their little heads as they gawked at the musicians stretched out on the benches. But when the men groaned once in their snoring, the goslings took fright and hissed. On the dirt floor the mud was almost as bad as in the yard, and in the entry–what's left to say, you couldn't even wade through it.

Seeing the disorder, Kotrė got chills down her spine, and her hair stood on end. Even so, she didn't give up. She sent all the animals packing. With difficulty she set the door back on its hinges, stuffed the broken windows with rags to keep the wind from blowing, and picked up the dishes and put them back on the corner shelf. Seizing the twig broom and the dustpan, she got busy cleaning and drying the floor as best she could. She happened to glance at the ceiling: nothing but cobwebs. At the sight of them, she couldn't help herself and ran the broom over the beam a few times. Waking up, the mother raised her head, looked around with half-open eyes, and piped up:

"Well, heaven help us! What's this, a new housekeeper! Are you going back to your old ways? Sweeping? We don't need that around here! If you don't wade through the muck, you won't get any bread. Besides this is no way to behave today! Getting up before the guests come to get you up and greet you? Maybe you don't have any linens to gift the musicians with? So, I see you left your husband by himself, and rushed back to clean up. Who asked you to do that anyway?"

Kotrė smiled sadly at the mother's greeting and replied gently:

"Forgive me, Mama, for getting up so early, but I couldn't help it. You see, I got terribly cold and I couldn't stay in bed. I went looking for warmth and for my husband, because I didn't know where he disappeared. And then, when I looked around, he was nowhere to be found. I didn't find any warmth either. I discovered the door had been removed, making it cold, wet, and windy everywhere. But you, too, scarcely slept, like me you've had no rest. Now I want to clean things up a bit. Then we can start the stove and all get nice and warm."

"Who's to blame for that?" mumbled the mother. "Last night you rushed off to bed by yourself, and that sleepyhead's fallen down somewhere and is snoring away. Don't scatter that sand so thick: it's gonna fly something awful once they start the dancing."

"Fly from this muck?" laughed Kotrė. "Mama, you'd be better off saying they'll trample the mud even deeper."

"I see you know how to talk back!" the father burst in growling as he crawled out of bed. "Your first morning and already you're putting us down! Ma will keep house here as she's done all along without any help from a lady the likes of you."

Without grabbing a bite to eat, Kotrė rushed outside. From the sitting room end of the cottage she heard someone snoring, fast asleep like a log. Opening the door slightly, she was amazed to see her husband sleeping in bed like a pig in straw, next to the shepherd. Jonas had pressed his bedmate to the wall, who in turn had pushed Jonas back with his lace-up bast shoes, dirty to the knees. The shepherd had muddied Jonas's back and the whole side of his wedding clothes, which Kotrė had sewn herself from beautiful and expensive homespun cloth. She was heartbroken not so much over the wrecked clothing as she was frustrated because it was impossible to wake her husband. She shouted, shoved him, pulled at him, almost in tears, but he kept on sleeping, snoring as loudly as a dozen men. Hearing Kotrė's pleading voice, the mother rushed into the room, glanced around, and took everything in at once.

"You act like you're so quick and able," she said to the daughter-in-law, "but you're ready to bawl over nothing. You don't know how to do it. Watch this!"

Grabbing the shepherd boy by the hair, she tossed him out of bed onto the dirt floor, shouting: "You little scoundrel! Take

The Daughter-in-Law

your shoes off when you get in bed next time! And you there, missy, don't stand there shoving Jonukas around. When he's had enough sleep, he'll get up. Now's not the time to blubber! Last night wasn't the time to lock yourself in the granary, was it?"

Seeing the mother's rough behavior, Kotrė was taken aback. She didn't even hear the end of her ranting because she felt so sorry for the shepherd, who was crying out in pain and trembling with fright.

In the meantime, the mother fetched the musicians. They grabbed their music, playing marches in honor of the newlyweds. But even though they played as loudly and as noisily as they could to greet the newlyweds, there wasn't any way they could wake Jonas. It seemed he only wanted to accompany them with his snoring.

Kotrė brought out the rolls of linen as gifts for the musicians and spread her fine tablecloths out on the table. The wedding guests roused themselves from the straw; the neighbors gathered together, laughing and poking fun at each other's lodging for the night.

Kotrė loaded the tables with the cakes and farmer's cheeses that she'd brought, set out the flagons, invited the guests and the parents to partake of the feast. Catching sight of the whiskey, the father didn't need any urging. The mother continued to resist like a stubborn goat, but finally, after downing a few shot glasses, she became very talkative. Over and over, she related the same story to each person, how last night the daughter-in-law hid from her husband, ran off to bed, and locked herself inside the granary, then refused to let anyone in. Poor Jonukas knocked and pounded on the door but couldn't beg his way in to lie down beside her. Worn out from the exertion, he was still in the house, sleeping. The women laughed, made a great ruckus, and swore out loud.

Some smirked, others just nodded their heads, but not a one said a single word in Kotrė's defense.

The time went by quickly as the guests mingled and danced. Unexpectedly, the bride's family came in, clanking and rattling—her brothers, relatives, and the matchmaker with his wife. Kotrė's face brightened when her people showed up. She invited them in and treated them to the best she had to offer. Since the father was soused already, he shouted and argued, waving his hands, praised his land, which was like a golden apple, and bragged about his tall and handsome son, "that's our Jonukas." He then raged that he had gotten a poor daughter-in-law who wasn't worthy of his son. The matchmaker, quite riled up by now, argued back, defending himself and poking fun at the foundation of the father's house, which the dogs could run through, and his leaking roof covered only by the sky, and his doorless and windowless palace. At first it was in fun, but then they really got into abusing each other, making rude gestures, and finally almost got into a fight. Banging his fists on the table, the father kept shouting:

"This here's my manor, my property, and there's no room for uninvited guests! If you don't like it, then get out! It's going to be the way I say!" The quarrel embarrassed the whole party, and, like cornered mice, each one looked around, trying to figure out how to get away quickly. The wedding guests from Kotrė's side left noisily; one after the other the neighbors scurried out, too.

Pretending to be drunk, the mother curled up in bed, as if she didn't notice a thing. Frightened out of her wits, Kotrė trembled in a corner. Consumed by his fury, the father didn't even see that only a few guests remained. He started to pick on the musicians, intimidate the daughter-in-law, and attack the mother, threatening to give them all a good hiding. As luck would have it, hearing

The Daughter-in-Law

the father howling around the house, Jonas finally stirred from his sleep. As he opened the door, he was already booming: "Yeah, yeah, sure! That's all we need! Enough's been coming out of your mouth already! Instead of making a ruckus when you're drunk, you'd be better off lying down!"

"Yep, that's for sure! There's no one the likes of you, just lying there sleeping and snoring day and night!" said the father, suddenly backing off. "Anyway, with me in charge, you don't have any worries. Once you've slept and eaten your fill, you got it into your head to get hitched. Then you dragged up such a pauper for a mistress to sit on my land. Don't be counting on it, I'm not going to let you get away with it, because the way I say, that's how it's going to be!" Again he stamped his foot hard into the mud.

"Yeah, yeah, sure! Who's afraid of you here? It wasn't my idea to get married! Only reason you forced a wife on me was because you needed the money, you couldn't get out of your debts. Now you're putting on airs, after you got the Jewish moneylenders off your back, because of me!"

"As if I needed the money! Well get it straight, you paid off the land for yourself! That's why, sonny, you have to learn how to be clever like a fox! If you want to do well in life, follow in my footsteps. Beat down those women. If you don't do it, then they'll lead you around by the nose."

Kotrė's brother, who was still making a racket, cried out from the middle of the room, "So long, Dad! Thanks for telling me the truth about Jonas's marriage! And as for you, brother-in-law, make sure you take good care of your wife because if you don't, you'll answer for her happiness. After all, you took the four hundred rubles and her dowry!"

Saying this menacingly, he snapped his deer-foot-handled whip in the direction of Jonukas's nose.

"Yeah, yeah, you think I'm going to shake in my boots because of you?"

As life creeps along, so death follows the same way. That's how it turned out for Driežas's Kotrė: her wedding set the course for her future happiness. She couldn't please her in-laws in anything. No matter what Kotrė did, she was always blamed; whether she walked or sat, talked or held her tongue, laughed or cried, worked or slacked off–it was never any good. The father never called her anything but slut or beggar, constantly reminding her that Jonukas was worthy of someone better. The mother, who told lies at every turn, denounced her daughter-in-law in front of the men, and gloated that on account of her tongue, she had directed the father's curses away from herself onto Kotrė, who bore the brunt of his wrath.

Spring had arrived. After yesterday's rain the skies had brightened. The sun heated up, refreshing and warming the ground, freeing it from the prison of a cold, hard winter. How the earth had suffered, constricted by the cold, weighed down by numerous snowfalls, distanced from the sun, frozen and numb for such a long time. Today it was as if nature was laughing happily, reawakened and warmed by the long-lost blazing that caused the dear earth to steam as it released the last frost from its depths. Surpassing the sun's rays, the light wind puffed warmly, hurrying to dry earth's muddy surface. Here and there the snow was still hiding, lying white under the fences, but taking fright at the sun's brightness, it was retreating, disappearing, turning into slush, warming and melting, changing into water. Finally it was washing out meandering pathways for itself and flooding downhill to the creek, foaming in its haste. The woods ruffled up and turned gray with buds abundant everywhere. Each little bird sang its song with a different voice, as if worshiping spring's dawning. The tapping of the black grouse, the skylark's warbling, the frogs' croaking, the insects' whining–all voices united into an echo that spread through the air, creating an incomprehensible buzzing, wonderfully tender to the heart and pleasing to the ear. The leader of a large flock, a hefty gander returned from the south screeching; it knew the way well, and behind it followed a large flock, divided into two long rows that flew due north noisily. The white swans whizzed above the pine trees, waving their wings heavily, honking loudly, looking for a spot to land. Somewhere beyond the woods one heard the cranes croaking. There were endless throngs of ducks swooping in, quacking, splashing in the meadows; now they rose in flocks like clouds and ran around helter-skelter. The long-legged stork walked around the fields as if on stilts, gathering straw, filling his beak, then rising to his nest. Once there, he put his head back and clattered; waving his wings, he defended himself from his enemies circling around. The sparrows feeding on hemp seed chirped happily around the stork's nest. The wagtail, jumping around by the pond, flipped its tail.

On the Kutvailiškiai farm the lush rye field appeared to be clothed in a green wool shawl. Anyone alive and well moved and bustled around the orchard; each one showed their delight in a special way, rejoicing in a joyous spring at last. Taking turns, the spotted pigeons flew in unison from one roof to another. The red rooster, leading a flock of hens out to the wood chip pile, crowed loudly, shaking its rosy cockscomb. A dapple-gray goose, standing on one leg near the entry, crooked its head while listening to see if its goslings were twittering in the pen. Jumping up on a log, the tabby cat puffed up its fur, raised its tail in front of Rutkiukas the dog, while the latter, running around in a circle, barked, yelped, and whined at times.

The sun had hatched flocks of little children on the cottage's foundation. Frozen and dirty, they played with damp sand; the older ones were already barefoot. They rode around the road in circles, their noses and legs red, chattering happily with each other:

"Mommy's going to dye a whole bunch of eggs tomorrow, a big pot, heaping full! And did your hens lay a ton of eggs? We're going to have fun playing with them on Easter."

"She's going to dye ours 'wed,' I'm not going to hit 'yers', I'm going to 'woll' mine."

"And I'm going to take 'yers' and break it–pop!"

"I'm going to tell my mommy on you," the little one chirruped back, whimpering.

The men were out on the wood chip pile wearing their winter caps and their patched woolen gloves, but they threw their sheepskin coats on top of the fence while trimming stakes in their shirtsleeves. Another man, hitching his mare to the wooden plow, tried to work the garden. Already with their water buckets, the little girls were waiting for the chance to throw cold water at the plowman, to make sure his mare will grow fatter. Elsewhere, the master was raking up a storm, tidying the small yard, and cleaning up around the animals. When the sheep wandered in from outdoors, he counted the lambs, pointing with his finger raised to his nose. On a different plot of land, next to a pile of logs near the newly built covered threshing barn, a group of men was busy, making a racket. A gray-haired man drove a bunch of pigs out of the rye, then, whip in hand, he approached the men and lit into them:

"Are you crazy letting the pigs destroy the rye like that! You'd think the devil got into you. Ah well, that's springtime! There isn't so much laziness on the whole earth as with humankind. Whatever God gives us, we cast the bread aside ourselves. I'm telling you: if you don't take care of your own pigs, remember, don't come whining to me, if one of them doesn't come home. Otherwise, if I have to shoo it home, I'll pen your pig up, so whoever it belongs to won't get it back without paying me a ru- ble. I can see that there's no getting along with all of you. I have to treat you like devils when you get into the rye. You'll have to shout for Jesus and Mary–the damage those pigs do!"

"Thank you, thank you, Uncle, for once somebody is speaking up! It's true, it's really sloppy of us to neglect things the way we do."

"Too bad I don't have any dogs; the devils would get a pig or two."

Another man whose pig was also in the bunch just had to add: "I happened to spot one of yours in the rye yesterday, too."

"Look at that, pick on me, why don't you?" the old man was quick to defend himself. "Isn't it the devil who makes you do it? We all have to watch out, or none of us will get any bread."

That's how the men locked horns in the fields while the wom- en buzzed around indoors. In the cottages, they cleaned, raised clouds of dust, washed the ceilings, brushed the walls, changed the bedding; in the kitchen they kneaded dough or set out the cakes they had already baked. Another woman carried bowls of flour from the granary to the house. In every corner the women were busily whirling around: preparing to bake, washing meat, making fresh cheese, whipping butter, slicing bacon. In every house the chimney smoked from the fired-up oven, sending var- ious mouth-watering smells wafting throughout the village. Sent from one homemaker to another, the young women ran as fast as their legs could carry them, hurrying to get their work done this evening in order to have less work left for the morrow, so they could leave for Easter earlier.

But there was one homemaker, poor thing, who had no success at all because her cakes didn't rise. She ran frantically around the village with a cup looking to borrow some yeast, asking in one yard, then in another, but they were out of it everywhere.

"I have to hurry to the end cottage where they made beer during Lent, maybe I'll find some there?" she mumbled to herself.

Finding Jurgienė churning butter, she hugged her and pleaded:

"Dear Jurgienė, my little pigeon, give me at least a pinch of yeast. Father bought such expensive flour. I'll catch it from him when my cakes fall."

"But I have so little left, they all kept helping themselves to some. Why don't you go over to the Vingises'? I saw Kotrė just now bringing home a whole jar from her mother's. She's sure to have some left."

"I was there, that poor soul! I walked in on such a row, there's such strife going on there!"

"I bet they've ganged up on Kotrė?"

"They're all quarreling like dogs, sister. Lord help us, it turns out that Kotrė has quite a tongue on her. They're abusing each other left and right, that's the trouble!"

"Oh, so that's the way it is, she's starting in herself. Kotrė's not going to put up with it."

"Well, who could hold out with those people? Kotrė's tried humbling herself, but she's suffered enough. After all, I'm over there day and night, and I see everything. In the beginning, at her homecoming, she tried to win the parents over, always serving them kindly and pleasantly. She rushed around them, she would have carried them around in her arms, if she could have. Nothing helped, they laid into her then, and they're still laying into her now. She's had enough of it already, now she's sick and tired of it, and she's talking back like an ax hammering a rock. Kotrė's no slouch herself, oh no."

"They met their match. Bravo! It's about time for the Vingises to get it, they deserve it, goodness knows! For all the tongue-lashings the old witch gave me, the way we fought the late parents in court, Vingis himself being a witness for their side. It would be so good if the daughter-in-law would split their forehead in two! I'll tell you how to teach her to do it!"

"You don't know the poor soul! After all, it was because of me that Kotrė started quarreling with them. I talked her into it myself. At first the mother never stopped scolding her, the father in turn swore and cracked his whip. And Kotrė's stubborn, too: it used to be she'd yell and scream out of anger, but she never swore. I'd ask her: cat got your tongue? You brought such a big dowry, you paid off their homestead, and now you let them beat you down, it isn't right! So that's when she started abusing them. Now she doesn't hold back a word. What a wicked tongue Kotrė has, that's the trouble!"

"Well, what does that husband of hers say then?"

"Is there any way you can call that blockhead a man? He's not a man, but a monster, rotten through and through, without a head or a heart either. No matter how much trouble Kotrė takes with him: kissing him, caressing him, getting him to talk, petting him, trying as hard as she can to awaken feelings of love in his heart, to turn him into a man–nothing helps! All he can say is 'Yeah, yeah, sure!' and that's it. That one's a lazy good-for-nothing. It's an awful fix. All he knows is fighting with his old man."

"Well, what do you know! They can beat down the parents together."

"If only that spineless so-and-so doesn't turn against her! He doesn't give a hoot about his wife. When the father starts scolding him, he just tries to weasel out of work. On the other hand, Kotrė is such a frantic worker, she goes to it like a crazy woman. Work just melts in her hands. The old woman Vingienė is hardly over the hill, but she won't bring her daughter-in-law as much as a drink of water while she's slaving away. Look at the way she's cleaned up the yard, even that run-down cottage doesn't look the same. Who would have stuck their nose inside before? Now it's as dry and clean like everybody else's shanty. That's why the mother's snorting like a bull because Kotrė's cleaned up her manure." "Ha, ha, ha," they both laughed.

"Did you churn yourself much butter over Lent?"

"Not much! Those cows of mine aren't any good. They gave milk the first year when they were milked in the winter, but the feed is poor, they don't give much anymore."

"Just like mine, maybe I got a couple of quarts out of them, that's all. I got to talking and my stove is cooling off. Thanks for the yeast, goodbye!"

Once the mud had dried somewhat in the Vingises's little yard, the path to the granary and up to the threshold was completely dusted with yellow sand. The baskets were still sandy and the yoke for carrying buckets of water thrown down and left by the fence.

The Daughter-in-Law

The sod cottage roof was heavily overgrown with stalks of grass here and there that showed green in the summer, poking up through the gaps, and clumps of lichen puffed up like loaves of bread. The entire surface of the roof looked like a moss-covered mound in a clearing. The log holding up the roof was bent deeply in the middle like a mare's back. Into the middle of it a wooden board shaped like a chimney was thrust. It used to release smoke, except that now it was leaning completely to one side. The cottage seemed to be shaking its head in awe at seeing the yard sanded for the first time. The walls were sloped and sinking, unable to straighten from under the weight of the roof's chimneys. The garret corner leaned over the inner granary, almost kissing the ground; it seemed to be holding up the end of the cottage to keep the windows from sinking into the earth. The doorjamb gaped loosely, preventing the door from ever closing. The front entrance had a high ceiling of narrow planks covered with soot; two hooks hung underneath; the ashes had been swept into a small pile in the fireplace, where a small flame had been stoked. The dishes were placed in rows in the corners; the dirt floor had been dried slightly. The cottage had also been straightened a bit: the bed had been made, the windows had recently been washed, the glass still wet. The broken glass had been patched with twigs and decorated with several bunches of rue; the dry floor had been sprinkled with sand; the ruins of the fireplace and its opening had been swept. The cottage was warm, as though the stove had been heated, but there were no lingering fumes.

Flustered, barefoot, and in shirtsleeves, Kotrė sat ironing clothes. Furious, her face reddening, she looked a little wind-blown, but this stemmed more from frustration than anger. Her black eyes shone; sparks flew as she flung the rollers of the mangle iron around violently.

The father sat on the dirt floor, the mother by the fireplace. Jonas lay on his stomach on a small bench next to the stove. The bench was too short for him, he was forced to extend his legs up the wall, while his head jutted out past the bench at the other end. His chin raised slightly, he was still puffing on a pipe.

With a quavering but strident voice, Kotrė, obviously half-crying, scolded: "I'm not asking for anything fancy! I'm just not used to living like a pig and I won't! At my father's even the dogs and pigs eat better. Here the sour cream is full of worms, but you still keep it tightly under control! Who could eat your whipped butter? The meat is like leather. And not a piece of white bread to break the Lenten fast with! Aren't you ashamed of yourselves? If you could, you'd turn on any friend of yours and devour him! Beggars fix themselves a better Easter than you."

The mother had finally run out of words; flailing her arms, she was shrieking the same thing over and over:

"You little schemer, what an idler! Lazy do-nothing!"

The father roared again in a wheezing voice: "Shut up! You're going to get it in the chops! It's going to be the way I say."

Spitting, Jonas retorted angrily: "Yeah, yeah, that's for sure! Go ahead and waste your breath. Who's afraid of you here?"

Hurrying to finish the ironing, Kotrė hit the table so violently that even the window glass rattled, and without stopping, she kept shouting: "You'd think you brought me home from a pigsty! Did I offer myself to you? I'm not afraid of work and even less of your tongues. It's up to me whether I work or not. I paid off your homestead with my money, but now because of your miserliness I don't have a bite to eat. I'm ashamed to tell anyone about it. I worked by myself like a slave through the whole winter. I looked after all the animals, and all you know how to do is pick on me. May your homestead go to rack and ruin!"

Scolding and shouting, Kotrė slammed the rollers down so hard that even the table shook; that's why the parents backed off from her, though they were still making a fuss. The father roared so loudly that his throat became sore, but he couldn't shout louder than Kotrė, who boldly kept throwing the truth in their faces, driving them into a frenzy. Flying into a rage, the father clenched his teeth and ran outside, slamming the door so hard that even the wall shook. The mother went after him, screeching: "Go to the orchard and bring the men home! You see nothing's going to come of this. We have to hand her over to the inspector, teach her highness a lesson!"

"Go on yammering like a fool! What do I need those men for? I can handle her myself. Even now I would have caught her from behind by the nape if it hadn't been for the rollers in her hands. I restrained myself just this once. You know yourself, I've stayed away from her, such a shrew. Lord God protect me, she can split your forehead in two! If it happens again, I'll show her! It's going to be the way I say," the father muttered as he went off clenching his fists, waving them in the air.

Kotrė's arms and legs trembled, her heart beating furiously, her forehead burned with fever. After the parents departed, she bent over the table and remained leaning on it. She dried her eyes and forehead on her apron and sighed heavily. Turning, she glanced at her husband and once again her eyes filled with tears. Jonas was fast asleep, his pipe had slipped from his mouth and his drool was dangling.

"Here's the husband I dreamed of, chosen by my father. This was the love my heart desired," Kotrė pondered, pressing more lightly each time. "This is how Daddy's words have come to pass: 'He's still young, he'll love you and learn to listen to you.' It's not hard to tell now which one is more worthy of my love–that creature or the stove? Mama, dear Mama, what arms did you send me into? Daddy, my darling, how did I wrong you to make you deliver me into such misery? It would have been better had you not raised me, better you had killed me off somewhere when I was little! You got my dowry ready, you took care of my needs, and for what end? This life pierces my heart like a knife; every day I drink the dregs of a wretched wife. My heart is breaking, my head splitting in two! Who is there to comfort me or to hold me tight?" lamented Kotrė as tears the size of beans rolled down her cheeks. "My heart aches; it aches so badly. I had a premonition, but I just couldn't imagine what horrors I'd have to listen to, how much I'd have to bear! Mother, my dearest, you dutifully taught me to respect his parents, to obey them, and not do anything to offend them, and to love my husband. I promised but look what's happened to me! Oh my dear God, I can't do it; I can't go on. I have no more patience! What have I turned into? The people of Užkulniškiai would be horrified to see me now. It's not my fault, not mine! They themselves brought me to this. What should I do now, how will I stand it? It's only been half a year, but it seems like forever!"

"Why aren't you getting up! Are you crazy to be lying abed so long?" yelled the father as he crossed the yard, but he was mistaken. Kotrė had finished making breakfast and had already done the other chores. True, Jonas was still sprawled out in the granary. The mother was waiting patiently in the cottage, curled up in

The Daughter-in-Law

bed. The father came in and scolded: "I spent all night tending the horses and I'm home, while you lie abed until breakfast! Why don't you get Jonas up? That slut is up and wandering around, but he's probably still lying there!"

"Seems it's hard for her to get him up," reproached the mother. "My head aches so bad. She got herself up, but she didn't wake Jonas on purpose, wanting it to look like she's the only one working here. She's so quick, maybe she hasn't even fixed breakfast? If Jonas hasn't eaten, he can't go anywhere."

"When I start whipping all of you, one after the other, you'll go flying out of here! All of them's up and working, only Jonas, you see, can't go anywhere without eating."

"Lord have mercy, stop that shouting! Can't you see what's going on here? Our boy here shone like a lantern before and now look at him! He didn't get a wife after his own heart, so he doesn't want to do any work. Truth be told, all the chores fall on him alone, why even his health can't take it."

"You just have to get going, that's all. Look here, everybody's been mowing their fields since dawn already, but nobody's been taking care of ours."

"Yeah, yeah, that's for sure!" Jonas burst out, coming into the cottage.

The father fell silent, as Jonas, rubbing his sleep-filled eyes, complained: "All you know is how to rant and rave, but I have to do the chores by myself. Yesterday I went out mowing toward evening until I broke the scythe, now I have to go to market to buy a new one."

"We'll both go!" Brightening, the father piped up. "We'll buy the scythe, and we might even find some mower for hire. Of course, you're not going to be able to do it by yourself."

While the men were making plans, Kotrė brought in the washbowl. Hearing the men's talk, she couldn't stop herself from interjecting: "You mean to tell me there isn't another scythe in this whole place? Pa can manage everything by himself once he gets to the market, so why not let Jonas mow, while I pull the hay out of the water; it's all soaked from the rain. Don't forget that we'll still have the meadows to do on top of all the other work. Isn't it enough that you sleep in all week, but even worse you also have to waste a weekday? When everyone else is working at top speed, you're wandering around the market!"

"It's none of your damn business. It's going to be the way I say."

"Yeah, yeah, sure! No use wasting your breath here."

"You think you're such a great worker. All you do is wag your tongue."

All three of them threw insults at Kotrė. She was relieved to escape out the door.

After breakfast, the men put on their shoes, harnessed the horses, and hitched up the wagon. Hobbling around, the mother declared: "I'd best go along: I've got a chunk of butter and a dozen eggs that need selling."

"What the blazes? That's all we need!" the father scolded. "You know how it is with me: the women are to sit by the stove instead of dragging around after the men like a pair of old slippers. If you've got something worth selling, we know how to do it without your help. Hand it over, I'll pack it up in the wagon, all ready."

The mother glanced around, she didn't want to give up her sale, but without missing a beat, the father grabbed the cup of butter and the basket of eggs from the granary.

Noticing this, Kotrė had to plead again: "You mean to say you've decided to sell the last bite that's left! What are we going to eat Saturdays during the haying?"

"All you care about is eating everything up," the father shot back, "and where are you going to get a kopeck from? Just be glad you've got bread, never mind the butter!"

"All she cares about is the luxuries," reinforced the mother.

Jonas said nothing because he, too, would rather polish off some food instead of selling it.

Approaching her husband, Kotrė asked: "Jonas, at least buy me a pound of soap, please. I have to do the laundry for the haying."

Again it was like she'd jabbed each of them with a thorn. The father spat: "To the devil, that's the only thing missing from my life!"

"Phooey to such a fancy pants!" the mother snapped. "I've lived my whole life without any soap, and that's the reason why I've food to eat."

"Yeah, yeah, sure! A bunch of fancy stuff, that's all we need."

They drove off. The mother's head started aching again, so she rolled back into bed. Kotrė laundered the clothes, boiled them, and carried them to the laundry in baskets hung on a yoke.

The Kutvailiškiai meadows followed the Venta River on a long, flat plain. From the orchard side lie hills and fallow land with stumps. In front, on the opposite side, pine trees flourished. At its widest the Venta turned in all directions, then divided into branches that curled around the bend and ran together again. It rose to flow only during floods, while in summer it lay in the same spot, turning muddy with silt and muck. Because of this the meadows were wet and squishy and dried out only when a sunny summer came along. Often, during the haying, the water flooded and swirled over the grasses, and if a heavier rainfall came down, then the Venta rose as you watched and flowed more widely, feeding water to its branches and gathering them together into one stream. Then they carried off the swaths, hillocks, and haystacks, and the straight grass, flooded up to its top and bent by the swiftness of the waters, lay down right to the ground. This made quite a bit of trouble for the mowers. That was why in spring when the floods had abated and good weather was coming, while St. John's was still far away, the country folk hurried to sing mowing songs.

In the morning, the sun, having lit up the tops of the pine trees with its first rays, scattered the shining bubbles of dew on the soil and awakened the birds to sing. Standing in a small group, the men shouted "hurrah!" The song's echo resounded in the pine forest, and the pleasing sound spread to the orchard on the other side as well. The group there hadn't finished their refrain when the revelry started up again in another area. Elsewhere they rang the scythes and hammered them. The sound of this kind of merriment rose from the earth together with the white mist, dispersed through the air and mixed with the song of the skylark. It reverberated and resounded far, far away in the skies.

The spotted cuckoo by the pines echoed happily and began her trill. In the deep main stream of the Venta, a pike smacked its tail. The girls arrived, bringing breakfast, ready to work. The owners made their way to the meadows with horses and wagons. They brought long branches to fill the holes where they couldn't wade in and put down boards from home and even used doors to make bridges and ramps. They set these out over the ditches and made paths to drag out the hay.

The mowers, hot and sweaty in their shirtsleeves and rolled-up pants, grabbed their scythes and bent far over, wading step by step along the edge of the plot, plunging into both dry patches and swamps. Like fierce soldiers or murderers, they struck with the blades of their scythes, laying the grass down into swaths, turning it to the side like a sash. Then they continued to the one next to it, cutting a wide path. In every plot of land there were two or three men in a row, who kept rising and falling, one after the other in succession. When one got tired and stopped, standing his scythe up, he rang and clanged across the blade with his whetstone. Pushing back his cap, he wiped the sweat away, pulled at the belt on his belly, and embraced the scythe again, and then once more he rose and fell.

The grass still stood stiff and lonely in the swath, tousled, as if unaware it had been separated from its clump and not the least bit sad.

Behind the men, the girls toiled like little bees in the wild roses; they weren't allowing the grass to wither but instead hurried to the swamp, skipping on the boards that had been laid down or plunging in wherever they happened to find themselves. They waded barefoot like ducks with their skirts held high, showing their red legs, getting spattered with mud. Paying no heed to anything, they pushed the swath along the ground as they raked it together, and then placed the dripping hay onto the stretchers by the armful. Pressing the hay down with their rakes, they then threw a rope onto their shoulders, and while holding the ends of their poles, they pushed and waded, slipped and fell to their knees in the muck until they arrived at the laid-out paths. Reaching the bridges, they sped up; they rushed along, almost at a run, like ants, dragging a cart of hay larger than themselves. They pulled their carts onto a hill and dumped the contents out to dry. The girls got hot and tired with toiling. Even though each one was dumping only the hay from her own plot, each girl was envying the others' raking, each trying greedily to grab more for herself.

The men were rising and falling, moving slowly to one side. The women were dragging hay to the other side while crawling in the opposite direction. Billowing like ears of rye, rocked by the wind, men and women intertwined so that the green spaces along the Venta shimmered as if taken over by white geese. They splashed in the water, plunged into the mud, scampered around, looking like a herd of cattle buzzing around madly. All the while the sun burned relentlessly without even the slightest breeze.

Lunch couldn't be far off, because the women started making their way from the farms through the pines toward the banks of the Venta with their lunch pails, their baskets dangling on their rods. Once seated in the shade, an earlier group waited for the workers to come out while they chatted among themselves: "Oh, look at what a heap Kotrė's dragging," one of them pointed. "Sister, she's no slacker! After all, there's no one forcing her here, but she's working like crazy. No doubt about it."

"What else is she going to do if she doesn't work? Because her husband's a lazybones, she has to do all the work. It's always that way."

"God help her, what a barrel of salty brine that girl fell into! Wonder how her parents' hearts can bear it. They laid down such a dowry, sister! Just sticking their child into that kind of hardship. Such misfortune!"

"Of course, the mother feels sorry for her ruined daughter. I saw Kotrė crying in the churchyard, complaining to her parents.

The Daughter-in-Law

The mother was bawling alongside her, but I heard the father saying, 'Stick it out, my daughter. After the parents drop dead, you'll win out: the soil is good!'"

"Stick it out! Stick it out… for sure!" another one laughed. "By the time the sun rises, the dew will eat your eyes out. The parents are still strong as horses. It's the daughter-in-law who could kick the bucket first, working her tail off by herself with all those chores. His mother used to be a hard worker, but once she got herself a daughter-in-law, now she's putting her feet up, doesn't even bring the lunch. When Kotrė goes out to rake, she has to bring it along."

Far off, the sound of splashing grew fierce; the workers weren't coming to eat yet.

"Lord God save us, see how the Venta's flooded this year! Last year the fields were so much drier."

"They're going to have to drag all the hay out themselves; the men won't be able to bring the horses in. Dull work, that. If only God makes the good weather last, then the hay they bring in won't rot."

The mowers started casting glances at their shadows.

"Wonder what time it could be?" asked one of the group.

"The devil, who needs to know the time!" another one laughed. "The stomach tells time the best. There are the girls, bringing our lunches."

They clanged their scythes, wiping the sweat off their brows, then a few at time slowly started off toward the hill. One of the men, wading straight ahead, slipped into the water up to his waist, got completely muddy, and barely made it out. Another one walked along the barrier and got tangled in a branch, causing jokes and ripples of merriment all around. The younger ones started splashing the hired girls with clods of turf, but the latter didn't give in, throwing them right back. Then, laughing and shoving, the youngsters grabbed the women's baskets or held them by the hand, pulling them out of the swamp, creating a lot of ruckus.

Searching for shade, everyone gathered into small groups; each of the girls bringing the lunch spread it out for her family. Then sitting in a circle with their lunch baskets in the middle, the workers ate and joked, while the girls who had brought the food waited on one side.

In the middle of the meal, suddenly the thunder crashed, apparently right overhead. As soon as the lightning flashed all around, they scuttled over one another like ants in a blocked anthill and glanced at the clouds in fright. They even forgot their lunch: some had eaten, others had not. Seizing their rakes, some threw the dry hay into piles or managed to load it into their wagons. Others ran off to bring the horses. No one paid any heed to the mowing anymore; they only rushed around to save the dry hay.

The Vingises also hurried. Carrying the horse bit, the father crept in and out among the alders. Kotrė dumped as much hay as she could into a pile, while Jonas, lying on his stomach, finished slurping the milk from the lunch pail. The wagon stood piled high already.

"Hurry up, Jonas!" Kotrė urged him on. "We have to rake up the hay and secure it to the wagon. It won't take Papa long to get the horses."

"Yeah, yeah, sure, always counting on me. Why don't you climb up on the wagon yourself?"

Kotrė stuck a pole in next to the wagon and, hanging onto it, jumped up on the wheel, then onto the sideboard and rolled on top of the hay. Standing up, she shouted:

"Why are you standing there gawking? Rake up the hay, hand me the pole, hurry, the clouds are almost here already!"

"Yeah, yeah, what are you wasting your breath for!"

Putting his mind to it, Jonas worked away. On top of the wagon Kotrė burned with impatience.

"What's the matter with you? Get busy, look over there, Papa's coming. Throw me the rope–faster," she urged her husband, ready to burst out of her skin.

Jonas started to pull the rope tight. While pulling the rope, he tore it, and it broke with a pop! He tied it, started to pull on it and again–pop! Then he fumbled around until he tied it together. Kotrė was in such a panic, she could barely stand it. The wind had risen and started to roar. It swirled around the haystacks, raising bits of hay from the ground, tearing the ones that were drier, scattering the tufts high. The lightning streaked, each time the thunder rumbled more loudly.

"You devil, you lazybones!" she screamed at Jonas. "Wrap the rope around the pole, for heaven's sake! I'll hold it. Now pull!"

And again the rope ripped apart.

Riding up, the father shouted: "Haven't you lashed it down yet? The rain's almost pounding on our heads. The others are driving off already."

"Yeah, yeah, but the rope keeps breaking!"

The father rushed over, tied the reins on, fastening them together with the rope.

"Push down, lie down on the pole, you worthless thing!" he growled at Kotrė. "And you, you mutton-head, press here."

They were both pulling with all their might when the pole groaned loudly and broke in half, flinging Kotrė from the wagon into the air, her legs flying. Luckily, she landed on the raked hay.

The first large raindrops had already started to splash. The Vingises saw that nothing was going to come of the haying. Hurriedly they harnessed the horses, fell any which way onto the loose hay that had not been secured to the wagon, and without a backward glance, took off for home. Getting up, Kotrė looked around, no one had noticed her fall, because everyone was hurrying, looking out for themselves, not watching out for others much. She tried to make her way home, but her head was swimming, her legs trembling, so she crept into a haystack, because indeed it had started to rain hard.

Falling onto the hay, Kotrė sighed painfully:

"Nobody's waiting for me at home. Is this the kind of love my heart desires? If at least he'd come to me, or at least glance at me. I could have killed myself–it's all the same to him, maybe he'd even rejoice! What kind of reward is that for all my toil and hardship? I'd rather have been a frog jumping around than ending up in the hands of such heartless people. I'm going to crawl back to my parents, I'll hug their legs, maybe they'll take me in, maybe they'll take pity on me. But will that help me any? I'll only cause a commotion. Already my dear brothers are chomping at the bit to beat Jonas up. And how will that help anything? It won't give him a heart! A leopard can't change its spots. If being sweet didn't help, being mean will do even less. Oh, Lord, dear Lord. How can I be so cursed? And there's not the slightest hope in sight."

Kotrė's hot tears rolled down her cheeks. The clouds passed, the rain let up; the thunder rumbled ever farther away.

"Brr-rr, how I despise lazy people! It could all be so wonderful if only he loved me, or if he'd at least stick up for me with a single word. If only sometime a better day would dawn!"

Slowly, slowly the pain in Kotrė's heart calmed, her hot tears cooled, her exhausted eyes closed, and the grim images became more soothing. A sweet warmth enveloped her as she began to daydream about lovingly embracing an infant. At last, everything slipped into a dream.

Rushing home with the wagon, the men headed straight for the hay barn. While waiting for Kotrė's return, Jonas fell asleep. Unharnessing the horses, the father took them to the shelter, then dashed into the cottage. Laughing out loud, he told the mother how the daughter-in-law had crashed from the wagon.

"The Dark Angel isn't going to snatch that Kotrikė. But our sonny-boy could have gotten scared," the mother wrinkled her brows in concern.

"He isn't as stupid as all that, don't you worry!" chortled the father. "He didn't give her a second glance. Left her lying on the grass."

"Don't you know it; she'll just go to sleep, as long as she stays there! At first she was such an eager beaver, tidying up all the time. But just look at her now; she's turned into a good-for-nothin'. It's not enough she can't load a wagon anymore, but she's turned slack as a slipper at home. That lazybones doesn't clean or make anything shine. She just scampers nose first through the sweepings and muck like a hopeless slob!"

"Darn right, and now she isn't dragging herself home either. There isn't anyone to unload the wagon."

Whoever was late with sowing their rye that fall lost their crop because heavy fogs and frequent rains soaked the ground, and it was hard to wade through it. It wasn't unusual for the Vingises to be late with all their chores, so they sowed their rye in water as expected, scattering it into the wet and slushy soil.

Out in the yard the father was getting ready to plow some sheepfolds. Leading the horses home, Jonas got cold and crept into the threshing barn. Kotrė was busy winnowing grain there.

"Hey you, hand me the horse collars from the threshing barn," the father shouted.

"Jonas, take the collars to Papa!" Kotrė called to him.

"What do you know, the dog calls the dog, the dog calls the dog, and the dog's tail goes thump. That's how it's around here! She'll still call someone else to get it, can't you do it yourself?"

"How do you think I'm going to wade through the grain? Get the blasted things yourselves!"

"Don't stand there wasting your breath, just get moving and dig those furrows. That's enough time wasted hanging around the barn."

"So then you carry in the grain, because the pigs are getting in through the foundation, you can't leave it here."

"Order us around some more, why don't you, as if we don't know it ourselves! It's going to be the way I say," burst out the father. "The other one will just lie around, hiding away somewhere."

Jonas showed up too.

"Take the grain into the granary, get out there, and plow right away!"

"Yeah, yeah, sure! I'm gonna wade through this muck! Try carrying it in yourself, if it's so damn easy."

Shaking his head, the father looked at the grain and agreed:

"It's true, you'd be straining to pull it on your own. It would be better to drive it over in the evening."

"You call that heavy," Kotrė chimed in, "A couple of trips on foot! It's more trouble harnessing the horses than carrying it over yourself."

"Yeah, yeah, sure! Carry it over yourself, if you want."

"I'm just telling you, go on, get outside!" screamed the father. "Don't worry about the grain, do what you've been told to do."

In the evening, wet through and through, Kotrė came home frozen. She crept into the threshing barn to warm up. Here she suddenly felt ill. Her head burned with fever while she felt cold. Tremors, aches, and pains went through her body without relief. Realizing that she wouldn't be able to call anyone from the barn, she somehow dragged herself back to the cottage.

Seeing her from afar, the mother opened her big mouth: "You grabbed enough sleep in the barn, so I'm stuck with all the chores on my own. Now you're ready for dinner; must be nice to find a good-tasting meal all ready for you."

Bending down, Kotrė headed straight for the granary, but she couldn't rest; she tossed and turned in the bed and crawled around on the floor. Hearing her moaning, Jonas took himself off to sleep in the straw.

It was already late morning before the mother remembered to see why the daughter-in-law wasn't getting up. Finding her squirming, she immediately understood the nature of her illness. She waved Kotrė back inside the house and summoned an old woman who knew how to handle these things. She offered her some food, but Kotrė couldn't eat anything; she just cried out in anguish:

"Oh, Jesus Mary! I can't bear it, take pity on me, let my Mama know!"

"Don't yell, hold still!" the women tried to calm her, "Don't be scared, everything's going to be all right."

Coming out of the room, the mother ordered Jonas to fetch Kotrė's parents.

"Yeah, yeah, sure! You think I'm going to ride over to those hooligans! The other night, in the tavern, Cipras clipped me on the ear! So if I go over there, they could kill me. Why didn't she go there when she was still well?"

"Father, you go then, if that's what she's got into her head."

"The hell with it! I'm afraid of those Užkulniškises, I don't want to go anywhere near them. Besides, it's raining cats and dogs, how the devil can I get there?"

"There's no need, no need at all," the old woman interrupted the conversation. "Driežienė will just talk nonsense when she comes. She'll say we need the doctor and the midwife, everything, but we don't need anyone here. We can take care of it ourselves, she'll just have to wait it out. Boil some herbs with whiskey."

"Jonas, for the love of God," pleaded Kotrė, "Go fetch my mother."

Pulling his cap over his head, Jonas made it out the door.

"Drink a shot of whiskey," the mother offered Kotrė, "you'll feel stronger."

"Drink, drink," the old woman chimed in with her opinion, "You have to drink it down like medicine."

"Let's have a shot, cheers!" the other one said, and the two of them downed it.

"I'm not going to drink any whiskey, no!" whispered the sick woman, pushing it away, "I feel ill just watching you. It would help, if you boiled me some herbs. There's some sugar at the end of my bed."

"What a fancy pants!" muttered the mother, putting the kettle on to boil. "She needs all of those fine things! I never needed any sugar or teas, or anything, and all her sensitivity, God help us from the likes of her!"

"True, true," agreed the old lady, "this one doesn't have an ounce of patience. It's not like every woman doesn't have to suffer. She's shouting for her mother. Her mother! What can she do here—she'll just boss us around. Good thing you're not going, Father."

"Nobody's going to rush to do her bidding. Cheers!"

The parents and the old woman guzzled the warmed-up whiskey. Back in the barn, Jonas snored away. Kotrė struggled, sobbed alone, cried out for her mother, but no one took pity on her. Toward evening more women showed up–they were know-it-alls and do-gooders. All of them sipped whiskey and waited for the final moment to arrive. Kotrė kept going downhill. The cocks were already crowing, and the women became discouraged. The father intended to send word to the parents when it dawned–if it didn't rain. Toward morning all the women went on their way.

Getting word from others that her daughter was ill, Kotrė's mother rushed over–her horses in a lather. Bursting into the cottage, she took fright. Her sweet daughter was unrecognizable, by now she was turning blue, swollen and stiff–a real corpse. The mother started to scream, scolded the parents and her son-in-law for waiting so long to fetch the doctor and for not sending her word. She turned her horses around to go to the doctor's, told her own son to go as fast as they could.

Kotrė recognized her mama and rejoiced. Hugging her and sobbing, she whispered, scarcely getting her last words out: "For-give–me!"

Kotrė's brother was about halfway to the doctor's when her soul departed this earth. She left behind a big dowry, a homestead, fertile soil, her good parents, and the evil ones, too.

Afterword

Once in a while the world brings forth a truly remarkable person whose strength of character creates an impact. My great-grandmother, Julija Beniuševičiūtė-Žymantienė, commonly known as Žemaitė, was such a force.

My mother, Rožė Jarytė-Račienė, had never spoken to me about her famous grandmother. I now understand that it was too painful for her to talk about her war-torn country, her lost home, her family's desperate escape by horse and cart, fleeing war, Siberia, or death.

Discovering my great-grandmother became a lifelong process. I was to find out later that it was Žemaitė's son, Antanas Žymantas, who sponsored our family's emigration to Canada to live on his small Ontario grain farm in 1949. The first information I had about Žemaitė herself was when her collected works arrived anonymously at our southwestern Ontario tobacco farm doorstep while I was a teenager. It was decades later that I set foot on Lithuanian soil for the first time, visiting the beloved homeland my parents would never see again. My cousin, Nijole Arbačiauskienė, took me to Žemaitė's homestead and museums, revealing how important she was to the national heritage. At that time a desire to translate her works came into my mind. Many years later, when I met Professor Violeta Kelertas, who had been chosen by the Bernice Kellogg Fund at the University of Washington in Seattle to translate Žemaitė's works, I was very pleased to participate in this project.

Translating my esteemed relative's work was a great privilege, but it was also a weighty responsibility to bring out the beauty of her writing. And so began years on the laborious, yet satisfying, task of translating concepts from an earlier era and elusive lyrical passages. Work on the dialect included experimentation with a southern Ontario tobacco migrant worker's language to imitate the oral qualities of her writing for the coarse flavor in "The Daughter-in-Law." However, in the end, as in the rest of the translation, we adhered to the original text as much as possible. Our complementary expertise and talents sustained us both, and we never wavered in our dedication to this daunting project.

Poring over the text, I came in contact with not only an original thinker but a large personality as well. Žemaitė wrote as she spoke, and her ideas were original. She was stalwart, never afraid to say what she thought, especially if it might help someone in distress. In this respect, she was bold and fearless, ahead of her time. She would deeply examine social problems and offer solutions, as witnessed in the speeches she gave in 1907 at the first Lithuanian Women's Congress. In translating her works, I became enamored of her charming personality and strength of character.

What did Žemaitė leave to the world? First of all, her compassion and quest for individual and social justice were exemplary. She adhered wholeheartedly to her convictions, determined to carry out what she saw as the right thing to do in spite of extreme hardship, as in her marriage choice. She even faced danger while writing in the Lithuanian language at a time when it was forbidden by the tsar. Her persistence in showing the inequities of the dowry system may have contributed to the gradual weakening of this social custom in Lithuania.

Maryte Racys
Seattle, Washington, 2019

Acknowledgments

By Violeta Kelertas

This book never might have come to fruition had it not been for the support of Bernice Kellogg of San Mateo, California, who greatly admired Žemaitė. Her bequest to the Baltic Studies Program at the University of Washington made the Bernice Kellogg Fund possible. Ms. Kellogg's wish was to see a book of the famed Lithuanian author available for readers of English, which coincided with my own scholarly intentions. In fact, I devoted a chapter to Žemaitė in my dissertation, analyzing her oral language and translating one of her stories, "The Devil Captured." While writing that chapter, I studied her manuscripts in the archives of the Vilnius University Library and the Institute of Lithuanian Literature and Language. It was at the latter in the late 1970s that I encountered several linguists, especially Aleksandras Šešelgis, who pointed me in the right direction regarding Žemaitė's textological questions. For my understanding of her place in Lithuanian literary history and the force of her narrative techniques, I am grateful to the eminent literary scholar, Professor Albertas Zalatorius. I am also grateful to the late Professor Juozas Girdzijauskas for his help from Vilnius by way of the Internet in translating the *žemaičių*, or Lowland dialect in which Žemaitė's stories were originally written. To Virginijus

Gasiliūnas go thanks for providing the photos from the archives of the Lithuanian Literature and Folklore Institute in Vilnius.

Over the years of rendering selected works by Žemaitė into English, I have been fortunate in being able to draw on the community of scholars and writers who knew her work; others I have consulted with questions about getting published in the United States. Among them special thanks go to Solveiga Daugirdaitė, Daiva Markelis, Elizabeth Novickas, Rūta Mėlynė, Juris Jurjevics, and Melinda Barnhardt. For sharing his expert historical knowledge of the nineteenth century, I thank Saulius Sužiedelis. For reading or listening to various versions and commenting on them, I am grateful to Leszek and Bozena Chudzinski (they also rendered any Polish in the stories), to Donna Mikšys for her unflagging interest and encouragement, and to photographer Rimas Mikšys, who helped bring the ancient photos of Žemaitė up to date. Much appreciation goes to Birutė Putrius, who was a helpful early reader before any of us dreamed that her Birchwood Press would become the book's publisher. I am especially grateful to our copy editor, Jeanette Norris, who put in many voluntary hours correcting inconsistencies as well as punctuation and grammatical mistakes. Her questions about some of the more obscure elements of nineteenth-century Lithuanian life gave me insight into how an American reader would respond to the work.

I don't know what forces of fate brought me to Seattle to eventually cooperate with Žemaitė's great-granddaughter, Marytė Racys, who through our mutual dedication, laughter, and tears helped to shape the book. She proved to be adept at helping to render her ancestor's magnificent nature descriptions and dialogues. Together we made the book what it is today.

My greatest thanks go to Professor Guntis Šmidchens, director of the University of Washington Baltic Studies Program. His patience with the process, his kind and perceptive encouragement at all points of stress and distress, and his optimism that the book would come together in the end are all qualities of his wise and considerate nature.

All in all, some kind of synchronicity was certainly at work to bring this difficult, yet important, work into English, a work that many readers and even scholars have labeled an impossible task.

Maryte Racys, Žemaitė's great-granddaughter, at the statue
of her ancestor in Vilnius, summer 2018.

Acknowledgments

by Maryte Racys

There are many people to thank on this personal passion-filled journey of translating and publishing my great-grandmother's writing.

First, I thank the hands that sent the unexpected arrival of six Soviet volumes of Žemaitė's writing to my mother so long ago, for it sparked me to begin this quest to discover my great-grandmother's life and work.

Numerous relatives and friends in Lithuania gently lit the way, including my cousins Nijolė Arbačiauskienė, Audronė Račiūnienė, Vaida Čepkienė, and Rita Čemnolonskienė, who shared personal memories of those I never met. Family members took me to Žemaitė's home, showed me where she wrote, and brought me to museums in Lithuania that were dedicated to her. They, and my sister Gražina Janušas, allowed me a deeper glimpse into my ancestor's character. I thank Lithuanian journalist Jadvyga Mackevičienė, who led me to Žemaitė's imposing statue in a Vilnius square and encouraged me to translate her work.

Special thanks to Lithuanian TV journalist Zita Kelmickaitė for her generous promotion with Lithuanian National Radio and Television (LRT) programs.

It was deeply rewarding to work with Professor Kelertas on this translation. I thank Professor Guntis Šmidchens, director of the University of Washington Baltic Studies Program, for his unending support and advice. I thank Milda Tautvydaitė for the photographic assistance she provided us, and Jeanette Norris for her expert editing of this book. Last but not least, I thank Birute Putrius, who admired Žemaitė's writing and graciously took on its publication.

I am grateful to close friends Bozena and Leszek Chudzinski, Rajpaul Dhiman, Marina Dunaravich, Jonah Racys Fluxgold, Grace Hunter, Stasys Janusas, Saulius Matas, Danutė Musteikytė-Rankienė, Gintas Nalis, Sandy Sabersky, and Dr. Žilvinas Zakarevičius, including others, who held my hand at every turn.

For my part, I dedicate this book to my beloved Mother, my daughter Rūta Fluxgold, and my granddaughters, Nava, Liat and Meirav Wolfish, female descendants of Žemaitė.

Photo by Rimas Mikšys

Violeta Kelertas is a literary critic, translator, and editor who analyzes the literary scene in Soviet and post-Soviet Lithuania. Formerly the PLB Endowed Chair of Lithuanian Studies at the University of Illinois at Chicago, she is now an affiliated professor at the University of Washington. Her translations from the Lithuanian range from the poet Vytautas Mačernis's "Visions" to the anthology of short stories, 'Come into My Time': Lithuania in Prose Fiction 1970-1990 to a Valdas Papievis story, "Echo, or the Sieve of Time," recently published in the July-Aug. 2019 issue of the Kenyon Review. Currently she is translating an early Papievis novel, Brydė, dealing with the partisan war after the war in Lithuania.

Photo by Doug Olmstead

Maryte Racys is a librarian at the Seattle Public Library. She studied English Literature at Victoria University Toronto, and completed graduate studies in Library Sciences at the University of Toronto. She has been a professional librarian in two countries for forty-five years. She completed training at the Academy of Theater Arts in Toronto, Canada and has had a lifelong interest in Eastern philosophy.

CPSIA information can be obtained
at www.ICGtesting.com
Printed in the USA
LVHW111506090220
646329LV00001B/113